The Vertical File
and Its Satellites

LIBRARY SCIENCE TEXT SERIES

The Vertical File and Its Satellites

A Handbook of Acquisition, Processing and Organization

SHIRLEY MILLER

LIBRARIES UNLIMITED, INC., LITTLETON, COLO.

LIBRARIES UNLIMITED, INC
P.O. Box 263
Littleton, Colorado 80120

CONTENTS

7

ACKNOWLEDGMENTS

I am indebted to the following individuals who shared their know-how with me in the best tradition of the library, archival, and audio-visual professions: Lodisca Alway, Regina Berneis, Kenneth Bonine, Flora Champion, Margean Gladysz, Jule Fosbender, Richard Hathaway, Wayne Mann and his staff, Calvin Noell, Alexis Praus, Grace Scott, Bertha Stauffenberg, David Titus, Donald Toepfer, Grant Wilcox and his crew, and the staff of the Title III Regional Enrichment Center.

I am indebted to my mother for her unwavering encouragement and support.

INTRODUCTION

PURPOSE AND CONTENT

Because of the deep-seated reverence which librarians have for books, they sometimes underestimate the contribution which less standardized sources of information can make.

This volume will attempt to show how supplementary materials can add variety and depth to a library's holdings just as salads and relishes enhance the meat. As well as demonstrating the merits of the various types of auxiliary materials, this book will concentrate on how to acquire them. It will also deal with the organization, processing, housing, and circulation of these resources.

The title of this book, **The Vertical File and Its Satellites,** was carefully chosen to reflect its wide range of coverage. The "vertical file" is a familiar term which is in the working vocabulary of most librarians. Traditionally, it has denoted a collection made up primarily of pamphlets and clippings which are housed vertically in filing cases or similar containers. The potentials and problems of vertical file materials are thoroughly treated in this book. As important as the vertical file is, however, it represents only one aspect of the resources covered. The "satellite" collections which reinforce the traditional vertical file also receive detailed examination in the chapters which follow. Typical of such "satellites" are picture collections and map collections.

The structure of this book has also been shaped by the variety of materials it includes. A roll call of these supplementary aids would reveal pamphlets, flyers, clippings, catalogs, annual reports, bulletins, sample magazines, charts, posters, pictures, postcards, photographs, maps, photocopies, special indexes, and sometimes even manuscripts and archives. This rich mixture of materials means that many new dimensions can be added to library service. But it also means that the processes of selection, organization, and physical management must be flexible enough to take this diversity into account. In developing this book, consideration was given both to the common elements and the diverse attributes of these resources.

The first two chapters are devoted to an overall view. Chapter 1 is a broad introduction to techniques and tools for locating supplementary materials. Chapter 2 is concerned with technical and mechanical routines which are widely applicable. The remainder of the book offers an intensive survey of special types of supplementary resources. Individual chapters focus on the unique features of pamphlets, clippings, vocational material, local history collections, maps, and pictorial material, as well as indexes and files developed to fill special informational needs.

PREVIOUS COVERAGE

Librarians looking for other comprehensive guides to the principles and practices of supplementary collections will find scanty pickings. Most of the old standbys are out-of-print and out-of-date.

In 1968 Geraldine N. Gould and Ithmer C. Wolfe collaborated on a volume entitled **How to Organize and Maintain the Library Picture/Pamphlet File**. The authors directed most of their attention to pictorial resources, with pamphlets and clippings receiving secondary consideration. The book clearly reflects the fact that it is based on experiences in an elementary school library. While the authors have attempted to broaden their outlook to include secondary schools, the needs of public libraries are given only cursory treatment.

1968 also marked the publication of **Readings in Nonbook Librarianship** by the Scarecrow Press, Inc. The collection was edited by Jean Spealman Kujoth. Some of the articles deal with pamphlets, clippings, maps, and pictorial materials. However, they are often directed to very specialized library situations. Furthermore, **Readings in Nonbook Librarianship**—like all anthologies—offers a sampling of ideas rather than an overall, unified approach. There is enough here to whet your appetite, but no more.

Although **The Pamphlet File in School, College, and Public Libraries** by Norma O. Ireland is still available from the F.W. Faxon Co., Inc., its 1954 copyright date should be fair warning that the passing years have diminished the usefulness of its contents.

Lester Condit's **A Pamphlet About Pamphlets**, which was originally published in 1939 by the University of Chicago Press, is now being reprinted on demand by University Microfilms. However, it is of interest as a historical landmark rather than as a current handbook.

Hopefully, **The Vertical File and Its Satellites** will help to fill the gaps which still remain in the coverage of supplementary sources of information.

THE REWARD

Before you commit yourself to reading the remainder of this book, you may properly ask, "What do these supplementary sources of information offer in return for my effort, time, and money?"

The answer is "Plenty!" In the first place, they will nourish the good will and the confidence of your users by increasing the percentage of times you can send them away satisfied. In the second place, these materials will save staff time by making the search for information easier and quicker. Many of these items are bargains to boot. Furthermore, they will help you cope with the inescapable fact that many requests are not book oriented. Nor are some patrons.

These supportive resources are valuable allies in all types of libraries. In school libraries they will make excellent instructional devices for teachers and prime research tools for students. A large chart showing ecological relationships may be just what a science teacher needs to dramatize a lesson presentation. Brochures or clippings that deal with the problem of drinking and driving will be eagerly welcomed by pupils taking driver education. A high school senior who wants to compare the programs in oceanography at various universities will be grateful for a collection of college catalogs.

Supplementary sources of information are just as important to the broad clientele served by the public library. A pamphlet on making hairpin lace will delight a senior citizen who wants to revive this art remembered from her childhood. A handy map will help you direct patrons to the bird sanctuary in a neighboring county. An old postcard may settle an argument about the height of a building that once stood on Main Street.

GROUND RULES

One of the minor but aggravating problems in writing about supplementary sources of information is the lack of a descriptor that is both appropriate and generally accepted. It's misleading to lump all of these varied resources under the heading of "vertical file materials." The traditional definition does not make allowance for some of these informational tools. In addition, some of these resources may be housed in horizontal cases, pamphlet boxes, flat folders, or index drawers rather than in vertical files.

Nor is it accurate to refer to these materials as "ephemeral" or "fugitive." An instructive pamphlet on taxidermy is not really "ephemeral." It will be hoarded longer than many books. Well-organized brochures and clippings are not "fugitive" at all. They are waiting at your fingertips.

Because of this confusion, it was necessary to decide on a substitute expression that would more adequately delineate the variety and nature of the resources covered in this book. The term chosen was "supplementary sources." It is relatively short and reasonably descriptive. Whenever you encounter the words "supplementary sources" in this volume, they will be used to indicate the complex assortment of materials which can be found in the vertical file and its satellites.

In the pages that follow, you will find prices quoted and many individual items mentioned as typical examples. This has been done in the full knowledge that many of these specifics will have changed by the time this book reaches the reader. Nevertheless, the prices will give a relative indication of cost and the examples will add flesh to otherwise nebulous concepts.

Instead of placing a bibliography and a roster of suppliers and sources at the end of individual chapters, a composite list of references will be found at the back of the book. Referral numbers will lead you from the text to the proper entries in the master list.

In the course of this book you will encounter such expressions as "In our library. . ." or "We have found. . ." These comments refer to the Kalamazoo (Michigan) Library System where your author is currently employed in the Reference Department.

November, 1970   S.M.

CHAPTER 1

LOCATING SUPPLEMENTARY SOURCES

THE SEEKING MIND

Money and professional tools are handy aids in building a collection of supplementary sources, but they aren't nearly so important as the proper state of mind. To succeed in this field, the librarian must be an eager and talented scrounger. First, he must be enthusiastic about the value of supplementary sources. He must display alertness, ingenuity, and perseverance in searching out choice items. Above all, he must have a seeking mind that will recognize riches wherever they occur, even in his own backyard.

To demonstrate how productive a "backyard" can be, I toured my hometown to see what I could discover without consulting a single list or sending a single postcard. Here is my itinerary and my crop of acquisitions.

Chamber of Commerce
    Local bus schedule
    Guide for new residents in our community
    Calendar of local events
    Local church directory
    Travel material on all parts of our state
    Travel material on Canada and Mexico

Branch office of the Michigan Secretary of State
    State snowmobile regulations
    State boat laws
    Booklet on financing state highways
    Leaflets on state motor vehicle accident claims fund

Physician's office
    Series of booklets from pharmaceutical house on problems
    connected with raising children

City-county health department
    Over 100 different publications from the state department
    of health, the federal government, various health associa-
    tions, and public-spirited business firms. Cover all aspects of
    health from calorie counting to drug abuse and first aid.

Republican Party headquarters
    Selection of publications from the U.S. Dept. of Agriculture
    on homemaking and gardening
    Booklet on county taxes
    Biographies of candidates for election to county board of
    supervisors
    Study of state expenditures

Garden store
Lawn and flower booklet from garden chemical manufacturer containing potential clippings on geraniums, installing a sprinkler system, etc.

Police department
Protection techniques for businessmen
Self-protection for women
Police cadet program
Description of a policeman's work

Savings and loan associations
Customer "magazines" from two local associations. Worth clipping for such articles as making bas relief plaques and preserving wedding gowns

Gas station
Maps of this state and all nearby states

Paint store
Illustrated brochures that can be clipped for color schemes and decorating ideas

Bank
Map of the city

Social Security office
Wide range of leaflets on Social Security benefits and regulations

Oculist
Brochures on the Michigan Eye Collection Center, including instructions for donating one's eyes

Sheriff's department
Coast Guard regulations for pleasure craft
State regulations for pleasure craft
Sheriff's safety guide giving safety regulations for traffic, waterways, and firearms

Credit union
Credit union quarterly, **Everybody's Money,** with consumer information on such subjects as franchising, home swimming pools, and lawn food
Consumer Facts—a series of brochures on such subjects as wills and insurance needs

Civil Defense headquarters
Large selection of materials on tornado safety, fallout shelters, radiation protection, and fire protection

Holiday Inn
Holiday Inn Magazine for Travelers, to be clipped for travel articles

Cooperative extension service
> Shelf after shelf of materials on farming, gardening, home-
> making, building, health, pets, and hobbies. Everything
> from how to make braided rugs to basic beekeeping.

In my tour of the city I exhausted my available time long before I exhausted the sources of information.

Seeking out materials is like a game that can be played wherever you are. The most unlikely places and occasions can result in happy discoveries. This explains why a good searcher is always on the alert. One of my finds was a paper place mat from a local Oriental restaurant which explains the history and use of chopsticks. My intention was simply to get a good meal, but I ended up with an addition to my files as well.

Your friends, your family, and your patrons can become happy middle-men in your search for materials. If you are enthusiastic, they will be infected with the virus, too. My fellow workers keep my blotter well-covered with spoils from their trips or meetings they have attended.

Of course, you can't rely solely on footpower, friendship, and seren-dipity. Fortunately, there are more conventional devices for locating supple-mentary sources which you can use in the comfort of your own library.

One inescapable truth must be kept in mind, however. No matter what guides you use in acquiring supplementary sources, you will never be able to fold your arms and say, "Well, that's done!" A collection of supplementary sources is a dead file unless it is constantly being replenished. Nourishing such a collection is an eternal undertaking.

KEEPING CURRENT: SERIAL INDEXES AND BIBLIOGRAPHIES

Because currency is one of the strong points of heavily used supple-mentary source collections, there must be ways to ferret out new publications as quickly as possible after their release. Even annually revised compilations represent a time lag.

Since 1932 the **Vertical File Index (192)** has been offering one solution to the problem. The H.W. Wilson Company publishes this list monthly except in August. It presents a rich variety of materials arranged by subject and cross-filed in a separate title index. The coverage is most suitable for public and secondary school libraries. Annotations are included for some titles. Number of pages is indicated.

The publishers claim that the **Vertical File Index** is a selected list of "pamphlet material," but many of the so-called "pamphlets" are very large in size and price. For example, a recent issue listed a handbook about recrea-tional vehicles which had 224 pages and cost $4.50. Since there is great con-troversy over what constitutes a pamphlet, I suppose the H.W. Wilson Company can be forgiven for this liberal interpretation. From a broad view-point, the listing of paperback books might be considered a disguised blessing, since the index can be used as a selection tool for both the vertical files and the book collection.

Items for sale far outweigh free materials in the **Vertical File Index**. Even pamphlets of modest size sometimes carry big price tags.

Despite these drawbacks, the **Vertical File Index** is an important tool which should be purchased by any library attempting to maintain a thriving pamphlet collection. The price is currently $8.00 per year.

Other bibliographic indexes include leads to supplementary sources, but with much less emphasis.

At irregular intervals the American Library Association's **Booklist (22)** features a section entitled "Pamphlets and paperbacks." The column appeared only three times in 1969. The number of entries is small and pamphlets vie for space with paperbacks.

Larger libraries which subscribe to the **Public Affairs Information Service Bulletin (151)** sometimes use it as a guide to selecting pamphlets. Because this index also includes periodical articles and books, it's a real challenge to dig out the few references to pamphlets. PAIS is much too expensive to buy only as a pamphlet source, but it can serve as an additional checklist in libraries which order it as a reference tool.

Libraries attempting to strengthen their service to businessmen will want to consider the **Marketing Information Guide (112)** which is an annotated bibliography of current governmental and nongovernmental materials including pamphlets. It is published monthly by the Business and Defense Services Administration of the U.S. Department of Commerce. The **Guide** may be ordered from the Superintendent of Documents for $4.50 a year.

Another tool for locating business materials is **What's New in Advertising and Marketing (196)** which is prepared by the Advertising and Marketing Division of the Special Libraries Association. This listing of books and pamphlets is published ten times a year for an annual subscription of $5.00.

FOR SALE: COMPILED GUIDES TO SUPPLEMENTARY SOURCES

For the brand-new library seeking to start a supplementary source collection or for the library hoping to fill gaps in its holdings, there are compilations for sale which will serve as helpful checklists. Most of them were designed for use by teachers but they can also be employed successfully by both public and school librarians. Some of these lists are like shooting stars—they make one appearance and then fade from view. Others have established themselves so firmly that they are revised and reissued at set intervals. The following paragraphs single out compilations which are either very new or which have demonstrated their usefulness through several editions.

In deciding how much of your budget to invest in these lists, remember that they serve a double purpose. They can be of direct value to patrons as well as librarians. Students writing for free materials for school assignments find them a boon. These lists also have a two-edged usefulness in locating materials. They not only list individual items but also include offers of bibliographies, catalogs, and publishers' lists which will expand your horizons still further.

Where funds are very limited, a group of neighboring libraries can band together to buy these lists and then rotate them among participating agencies.

General Compilations for Sale

The "granddaddy" of the general compilations is **Free and Inexpensive Learning Materials (72)** published biennially by the Division of Surveys and Field Services at George Peabody College for Teachers. The fifteenth edition published in 1970 contains more than 3,700 instructional aids including maps, posters, pictures, charts, and pamphlets. They are grouped under 120 subject headings related to units taught in elementary and secondary schools. Size of items is usually indicated. Grade levels are often noted. Brief descriptions accompany most entries. Cross references are provided. There is an index but it is a classified index rather than a dictionary index. The prospective buyer should be aware that the list includes a good many paperback books, some of which are in the neighborhood of 300 pages. Many entries are for items that cost a dollar or more. Despite these qualifications, the Peabody list is a very helpful guide. The price of the fifteenth edition is $3.00.

Ruth H. Aubrey's **Selected Free Materials for Classroom Teachers (14)** is in its third edition. It has been revised every two years. In the 1969 edition over 600 sources of free classroom materials are listed. The aids available from these producers include booklets, leaflets, maps, posters, charts, pictures, and films. The sources are alphabetically arranged under broad curricular areas, some of which are subdivided. An extensive index is provided which not only includes subjects but the names of all sources in the book as well. Grade levels are given. Some descriptive notes are included about individual items or the general publishing policies of the source. The 1969 edition sells for only $2.00. It is a good buy.

A new edition of Gordon Salisbury's **Catalog of Free Teaching Materials (158)** was released in 1970. Over 8,500 resources such as posters, charts, pictures, maps, pamphlets, and filmstrips are listed. Some of the subject headings are very specific but others are quite broad. Access to entries under broad headings is facilitated by subdivisions and many cross references. Size and reading level are indicated. Brief descriptions are included. Names and addresses of suppliers are listed only at the back of the book in a numerical rather than an alphabetical arrangement. The number assigned to each source is repeated whenever one of its publications is listed anywhere in the book. This arrangement is a little awkward to manipulate, but the list is a useful one. The price of the new edition is $2.68.

Dover Publications, Inc. is planning to publish a fourth edition of Thomas J. Pepe's **Free and Inexpensive Educational Aids (144)** late in 1970. The third edition, 1966, contains references to over 1,700 pamphlets, folders, charts, posters, maps, pictures, and films. The publisher claims that 88% are free and 9% cost less than 25 cents. There are 19 broad headings and 60 subdivisions under which individual entries are alphabetically arranged. A more specific approach is made possible by an alphabetical index. Descriptive notes are included for all entries. Size and age level are indicated. A separate alphabetical listing of contributing companies with their addresses is a valuable feature. The 1966 edition is priced at $1.75. Wait for the new revision.

The Publications Co. **Directory of Free Teaching Aids, 1968-69 (153)** includes pamphlets, folders, charts, maps, and filmed material. The entries are arranged under 19 broad categories and 49 subdivisions. There is no index. Because of the small number of subject headings and the lack of an index, it is difficult to locate material on smaller topics. Some booklets are almost lost under the generalized headings. Descriptive notes are included for most entries. Size and grade level are sometimes indicated. A good portion of the book is devoted to filmed resources. While this list contains some interesting leads to supplementary sources, it is an expensive buy at $5.00 unless it is utilized as a film guide as well.

Educators Progress Service is a name well-known to teachers for the many guides to curricular resources which it issues. Among its publications is the **Elementary Teachers Guide to Free Curriculum Materials (54)**. Like all the Educators Progress productions, it is revised annually. The 1969 edition records 1,739 items from 616 sources. The entries are arranged under broad curricular areas which are subdivided. There are separate title and subject indexes as well as a source index. The annotations are thorough and often quite chatty. The coverage includes all types of printed materials. Some entries are for the teacher's reference or professional use. The price of the 1969 edition is $9.75. This compilation is of interest primarily to elementary school librarians and children's librarians who want a highly screened list of resources.

Educators Progress Service also publishes the **Educators Index of Free Materials (54)** which is a card file devoted to printed free materials at the secondary school level. The index costs $25.00 a year. Schools are the principal purchasers of this index.

Bruce Miller has been active for many years in publishing guides to vertical file materials and pictorial resources for the beginner. The 1968 edition of his **Sources of Free and Inexpensive Teaching Aids (117)** is only 30 pages long. However, many of the entries suggest lists or catalogs describing extensive offerings. The headings are fairly specific. There is no index. Grade level is indicated for some listed materials, but not all. This guide would be useful only to the very small library. It costs 60 cents. The pictorial reference lists offered by Bruce Miller Publications are discussed in a later chapter.

Esther Dever is planning a fourth edition of **Sources of Free and Inexpensive Educational Materials (50)** but no publication date has been set. The third edition which appeared in mimeographed form in 1965 is, of course, outdated although it is still offered for sale. It covers sources for charts, posters, pictures, pamphlets, maps, filmed materials and tapes. Headings are sometimes very broad, sometimes very specific. Access to topics grouped under general headings is impeded by lack of an index. Sources are *not* alphabetized under the subject headings. This random arrangement is frustrating. While attention is given to filmed materials, tapes, and even fund-raising projects, the third edition does offer wide coverage of pamphlets, maps, and resources for the picture files. Descriptive notes are included for many items. Some grade levels are noted. The price of the 1965 edition is $5.30. Hopefully, the planned revision will be reorganized to enhance its usefulness.

Because laymen as well as librarians are delighted to get something for nothing, the publishers of paperback books have attempted to cash in on this interest from time to time by bringing out lists of free "things" which include not only samples and services but printed materials as well. These give-away guides are fun to read and they offer some intriguing leads if you use discrimination in selection. While they won't take the place of the more conventional lists, they are like frosting on the cake. Watch your paperback outlets for new compilations since these lists come and go.

Specialized Subject Guides for Sale

In addition to general bibliographies of supplementary sources, there are lists for sale which concentrate on special subject areas. The following titles are representative.

In 1969 Teachers College Press released its third edition of **Free and Inexpensive Materials on World Affairs (101)**. The compilers are Leonard S. Kenworthy and Richard A. Birdie. As the title indicates, the list concentrates on the peoples and countries of the world in relation to culture, education, geography, economy, and international relations. A special section is devoted to the United Nations. The compilers point out that they've tried to represent different points of view. As a result, they warn that some of the materials included are highly "slanted." All items listed are either free or obtainable for 85 cents or less. Few descriptive notes are included. Age level is rarely indicated, usually only when a resource was especially prepared for younger students. Number of pages is noted with few exceptions. In using this list, be extremely cautious about copyright dates! A surprising number of publications from the 1950's and early 1960's are included. The price of the list is $1.95.

Sources of Medical Information (2) by Raphael Alexander suffers from an attempt to be all things to all men. While most entries are usable by laymen, there is also a liberal inclusion of extremely technical articles from medical journals as well as some studies written expressly for physicians. Although there is no index, the major headings and subdivisions are detailed and specific. Cross references are also provided. Use is hampered because subdivisions are not arranged alphabetically under the main headings. There is need for a guide that pinpoints topics and sources in the complex fields of physical and mental health. **Sources of Medical Information** does attempt to spell out specific areas and indicate the organizations and materials that deal with them. The public and school librarian will have to decide whether to buy the list in spite of its handicaps and its $4.50 price tag.

Educators Progress Service publishes four lists, revised yearly, devoted to specialized subject areas. These school-centered compilations are:

Educators Guide to Free Guidance Materials (54)
Educators Guide to Free Health, Physical Education and Recreation Materials (54)
Educators Guide to Free Science Materials (54)
Educators Guide to Free Social Studies Materials (54)

In all four of these books printed materials are slighted in favor of filmed resources. Furthermore, the lists are expensive. They do not justify purchase if they are to be used only for the limited inclusions of pamphlets, charts, and posters which they offer. Since **Educators Guides** are often represented in curriculum libraries, school or public librarians may consult them there.

Representative of the useful compilations sponsored by the federal government is **Consumer Education: Bibliography (149)**, a timely list which was completed in 1969. It was prepared for the President's Committee on Consumer Interests by the Yonkers Public Library. This bibliography which sells for only 65 cents incorporates over 2,000 resources in the field of consumer interests and education. While there is wide coverage of books, filmed materials, and even magazine articles, many entries for pamphlets and leaflets are also included. Helpful annotations are provided. Age level is indicated. Since most public and secondary school libraries will want this bibliography for the reference collection, its value as a guide to supplementary sources comes as an added bonus.

Another useful federal publication is the **Aerospace Bibliography (121)**, compiled for the National Aeronautics and Space Administration by the National Aerospace Education Council. This graded and annotated list includes many supplementary sources on space flight and space science. The fifth edition which was released in 1970 costs $1.00.

When investing in lists, it's wise to remember that the words, "sources" and "resources," can refer to a wide variety of materials. For example, Bruce Miller Publications sells a booklet which is called **Let's Celebrate a Holiday! Sources of Free Materials on Holidays, Festivals and Special Occasions**. Examination reveals that all entries are references to features which have appeared in magazines.

FREE FOR THE ASKING: COMPILED GUIDES TO SUPPLEMENTARY SOURCES

From time to time some public-spirited group or agency will issue a free guide to supplementary materials, usually on a special topic. Since there is no set formula as to the bodies or subjects involved, a librarian must exercise real alertness to keep up with these publications.

A sampling of recent lists will give the reader an inkling of what to expect.

The Insurance Institute for Highway Safety distributes a free guide called **Highway Safety Pamphlets: What's Available—and Where (98)**. This is a list of sources of "handout" material on such topics as teenage drivers, bicycle safety, motor-driven cycles, and drinking and driving.

The Pharmaceutical Manufacturers Association will send you a free copy of **The Story of Health (146)** which describes over 200 publications and motion pictures produced by manufacturers of prescription drugs. There is no charge for the printed material covered in the list.

From the Health Insurance Institute you can obtain a free copy of **Health Education Materials and the Organizations Which Offer Them (89).** This booklet indicates the national organizations which distribute free or inexpensive literature in the field of health.

Each fall Dow Jones & Company, Inc. issues a new edition of its **List of Free Materials Available to Secondary School Instructors (52).** This list is sent without charge to secondary school libraries, but it is *not* available to public libraries.

Don't forget that many organizations with extensive publishing programs offer free catalogs of their own publications. It's well worth establishing a collection of these lists both for your own ordering needs and for use by your public. Here are just a few of the many groups that will supply you with lists of their materials.

American Dental Association
American Medical Association
American Trucking Associations
League of Women Voters of the United States
National Association for Retarded Children
National Dairy Council
National Wildlife Federation

GUIDES TO UNITED STATES GOVERNMENT PUBLICATIONS

Since the United States Government Printing Office is the world's largest publisher, it is both a golden opportunity and a real challenge to keep up with the many publications that pour out of the federal presses.

Fortunately, there are practical selection tools available which will help you cope with this avalanche of materials.

Every library should be on the mailing list to receive free copies of **Selected United States Government Publications (164).** This annotated list which is distributed biweekly is devoted to "newly issued or still-popular" publications for sale by the Government Printing Office. It acts as a quick survey of government documents likely to be of interest to general libraries. To receive this bibliography, relay your request to the Superintendent of Documents.

While you're corresponding with the Superintendent of Documents, ask him to provide your library with a free set of **Price Lists (150).** At this moment there are 47 of these subject bibliographies in print. The topics range from consumer information to American history. The entries represent items for sale by the Government Printing Office and, according to the Superintendent, the **Price Lists** are revised "approximately once a year." In reality, the revision span may stretch out for a longer period.

It is important to note that neither the **Price Lists** nor **Selected United States Government Publications** include free materials which are distributed by the individual agencies themselves.

The most comprehensive listing of newly released federal documents is the **Monthly Catalog of United States Government Publications (119).** As well as recording publications for sale by the Superintendent of Documents, it also lists those which are available from the issuing offices and those published for official use only. The **Monthly Catalog** is a cumbersome tool to use for selecting and ordering supplementary sources and careful study of each monthly issue for possible acquisitions is a process usually limited to the larger library. But even in small libraries, the **Monthly Catalog** will prove useful from time to time in running down ordering information on documents that are desired for the collection. However much or little it is used as an ordering device, the **Monthly Catalog** should be available as a reference and referral tool in libraries serving adults or advanced-level students. The yearly subscription is $7.00.

Individual departments and agencies of the federal government independently issue bibliographies of their publications that are handy references.

One of the more ambitious publicity devices involves the U.S. Department of Commerce which produces a weekly guide to its publications under the title, **Business Service Checklist (30).** The annual subscription fee is $2.50. The U.S. Department of Labor announces its fresh output in a free monthly circular entitled **New Publications (134).**

A host of other agencies issue compiled lists from time to time, some of them free, some technically for sale. We have found that we can obtain most publications lists without charge by writing directly to the issuing office. To give an indication of the wealth of lists available, here are just a few of the federal bodies which have bibliographies for distribution.

Business and Defense Services Administration
Children's Bureau
Copyright Office
Federal Trade Commission
National Aeronautics and Space Administration
Office of Juvenile Delinquency and Youth Development
Public Health Service
Small Business Administration
United States Commission on Civil Rights
U.S. Department of Agriculture

Not all guides to federal documents are published by the government itself. A sampling of recent United States government publications is scheduled to appear six times a year in alternate months in the American Library Association's **Booklist (22).** This is a highly selective annotated list. **Wilson Library Bulletin** includes a sprightly monthly column by Dr. Frederic J. O'Hara which is called "Selected Government Publications." Dr. O'Hara's comments often resemble a capsule documents course rather than a check-list of brand-new publications, but they offer good insights into the publications programs of the federal government.

Dr. O'Hara is also the compiler of a paperback book devoted to federal documents. Published by the New American Library, this Signet Reference Book is called **Over 2,000 Free Publications: Yours for the Asking (138)**. It is for sale for 95 cents.

In Michigan we are fortunate enough to receive a biweekly service from our state library which is labeled **The Best in Documents**. It picks out the most important current publications of the federal government. Check with your state library agency to see if it carries on a similar screening program for libraries in your state.

While it is designed as a guide to agencies rather than publications, the **United States Government Organization Manual (186)** can be a valuable partner in your search for pertinent federal documents. By studying the guide you can determine which agencies are likely to be active in producing the material you need. Addresses are provided. The manual is revised annually.

Extensive studies of documents have been published by scholars in the field. They may be consulted for basic information, but with federal programs and policies changing so rapidly these days, they quickly become dated as ordering lists. One of the best surveys is **Government Publications and Their Use (159)** by Laurence F. Schmeckebier and Roy B. Eastin. The third revised edition was released in 1969.

GUIDES TO STATE GOVERNMENT PUBLICATIONS

Access to state documents may call for a greater degree of detective work on the part of the librarian.

The major selection aid in this field is the **Monthly Checklist of State Publications (120)** which is compiled by the Library of Congress. It is arranged alphabetically, first by the geographical entity and then by the issuing agency. Frankly, some of the inclusions for university publications are esoteric enough to tickle even a tired librarian's funnybone. However, the **Checklist** also incorporates such practical items as state road maps, cooperative extension service bulletins, publicity brochures, and hunting, fishing, and trapping regulations.

As well as introducing you to useful publications from other states, the **Checklist** will also help you to fulfill your special obligation to collect documents of your own state.

As valuable as the **Checklist** is, it does have limitations. Since it is a record of state documents submitted to the Library of Congress, the cooperation of state agencies is essential. If a state neglects to send certain publications or is tardy in sending them, these oversights are reflected in the **Checklist**.

The **Checklist** is for sale by the Superintendent of Documents for $8.00 per year.

Within each state there are sources of information which a librarian can tap in his search for documents. In Minnesota the Documents Section of the Department of Administration issues a comprehensive free bibliography of state publications for sale. In Michigan our state library publishes a cumulative monthly list of Michigan documents which it has received.

Individual state agencies often produce separate lists of their own publications. Among the best-known examples are the cooperative extension services affiliated with the land-grant universities.

PERIODICALS AS GUIDES TO SUPPLEMENTARY SOURCES

Magazines can be invaluable allies in your efforts to keep up with the changing world of supplementary sources. Some boast of formal lists; others offer more incidental references. However they're presented, all of these clues are worth considering.

The popular magazines are surprisingly rich in leads.

Each month in its special section, "The Better Way," **Good Housekeeping** sets aside a portion of one page for a listing of booklets which it recommends. Descriptive notes are provided. This column of free and inexpensive supplementary sources is called "Booklets Worth Writing For."

In alternate months **Changing Times: The Kiplinger Magazine** includes a full-page feature, "Things to Write For." It offers a selection of useful pamphlets, reports, and circulars which are available gratis or for a small fee. Thorough annotations are included for all entries.

Today's Health has scattered box inserts headed "Worth Writing For," indicating pamphlets and leaflets that might be added to a library's files.

Family Handyman features a column called "Booklets You Should Know About" which describes in some detail materials of interest to the homeowner or do-it-yourselfer. Orders are placed through the magazine.

House & Garden distributes items noted in a monthly column, "Best in Booklets." A postage and handling charge is made.

It would be a mistake to end your surveillance with these patterned listings. Additional hints can occur almost anywhere in a periodical. Feature articles often mention helpful pamphlets which the reader can acquire or sources to which he can write for literature. **Harvest Years** and **Changing Times** stress such references.

The regular departments or columns that appear in each issue of a magazine deserve particular attention. A pet column, or etiquette page, or monthly feature on household hints may contain good leads to significant materials. Question-and-answer columns to which readers appeal for information are particularly good hunting grounds.

Even the ads that appear in magazines are worth scanning since they sometimes include offers of interesting material. We've managed to glean some unusual handicraft booklets from the manufacturers of various household products by using this approach.

Alongside the publicity for vitamin tablets and vacations, you may discover ads for reprints, plans, catalogs, pictures, and booklets which the periodical itself publishes and offers for sale. **Better Homes and Gardens,** **Woman's Day,** and **Good Housekeeping** are examples of popular magazines with active publishing programs which advertise their wares in their own pages. Since **Today's Health** is published by the American Medical Association, it carries advertisements for the prints and health booklets which that organization produces.

Professional, trade, or business periodicals follow the pattern of the popular magazines in furnishing suggestions. They, too, can be searched for lists, incidental references, advertisements, and offers of reprints.

Among library periodicals a productive source is the **Library Journal** which has a regular column called "Checklist" that is devoted to free and relatively inexpensive materials. While some of the entries are of professional interest only, there are many titles which are excellent additions to school and public library collections. Great emphasis is placed on helpful bibliographies. Annotations are included for all items.

Periodicals associated with the teaching profession may be of assistance, too. Columns which contain leads appear in **Science and Children** and in the **Secondary Teachers' Supplement** which is issued nine times a year as an adjunct to **Scholastic Teacher.** The advertisements in **What's New in Home Economics** often feature interesting possibilities.

In the industrial arena **Modern Manufacturing** is a good example of supplementary source coverage. Not only does it carry on an extensive reprint service, but its many columns include hints about helpful booklets, surveys, catalogs, and charts.

In employing magazine references, a neat gimmick for padding bald spots in your collection is to establish a watch over periodicals specializing in the subject. By screening announcements and ads you may be able to discover materials that do not make their way into general lists. For example, a need for materials on recreational boating might send you to **Motor Boating** which along with many ads has a monthly column of literature called "Worth Writing For," as well as a regular report on new Coast and Geodetic survey charts.

NEWSPAPERS AS GUIDES TO SUPPLEMENTARY SOURCES

The newspaper you scan while you drink your morning coffee or relax in your armchair after dinner can report supplementary sources as well as current events.

The Sunday edition of the **Chicago Sun-Times** regularly prints a list of free materials for which the reader can send.

The prospects for lucky finds are particularly high in the columns and sections of a newspaper which are devoted to special interests. The garden column may list booklets on African violets or poinsettias by the garden editor. The daily health feature often includes offers of authoritative leaflets by the physician who conducts the column. The women's page is a rich mine of possibilities. Homemaking columns frequently include pamphlet suggestions or offers of handicraft plans. Even the advice-to-the-lovelorn column has on occasion produced some useful recommendations. The outdoor page often alerts sportsmen to such helpful items as newly printed fishing and hunting regulations. Sections devoted to the interests of youth produce leads to literature in such fields as careers and college attendance. Financial columnists may suggest guides to investments or income taxes. Travel pages offer a variety of sources for the vacationer.

Currently, there is a great proliferation of direct action columns in newspapers which offer the know-how and influence of the press in answering calls for help from readers. These services carry such names as "Action Line," "Beeline," "Help Wanted," "Action Express," or "Contact 10." In replying to requests for information, these columns sometimes suggest such sources as pamphlets or maps.

From time to time newspapers may produce special printings of features on red-hot interests such as drugs or space exploration which they then offer for sale to their readers.

CHAPTER 2

TECHNICAL AND MECHANICAL PROCESSES: GENERAL ASPECTS

Since the broad term, supplementary sources, incorporates a variety of specialized collections and materials, only the technical and mechanical procedures which are widely applicable will be discussed in this chapter. Techniques which are structured to fit a particular resource such as maps or pictures will be covered in separate chapters.

ORDERING

Postcards serve very well for most routine requests for free materials. Form postcards can be invaluable time-savers. Below is a sample of one form for soliciting free material.

GENTLEMEN:

We would appreciate receiving _____ free copy/copies of the following:

May we be placed on your permanent mailing list to receive this publication regularly as it is issued?

Thank you very much.

REFERENCE DEPARTMENT
KALAMAZOO LIBRARY SYSTEM
315 SOUTH ROSE STREET
KALAMAZOO, MICHIGAN 49006

Form letters offer little advantage over form postcards. I have yet to see a form letter that wasn't easily pegged as a form letter even when "disguised" with typed headings and handwritten signatures.

Let's face facts. Most requests for free materials are handled by clerks far down in the ranks who are going to treat form letters with the same degree of nonchalance that they reserve for postcards. Form letters do nothing to call forth any warm, personal response since they are so obviously mass productions. Sometimes they only annoy the recipient because he has to wade through paragraphs which could have been succinctly summarized on a postcard.

There are occasions when a letter should be substituted for a postcard, in spite of the extra expense involved.

1. If special explanations are necessary or personalized attention is being requested, a letter is more appropriate.
2. When the source is an unusual one—unaccustomed to handling requests for materials—a letter will help to smooth the way.
3. If the supply of an item is limited, a letter may have a better chance of receiving first attention.
4. If there is any doubt about addresses, a letter is more likely to be forwarded.

When letters are sent, they should be on the institution's letterhead.

Money and effort can be saved by asking to be placed on mailing lists for free materials.

Take advantage, too, of the readers' service postcards which some magazines include for the convenience of their readers.

If you anticipate heavy usage or the need to provide access under more than one subject heading, it would be logical to ask for two copies at the time of the original request or order.

In ordering materials marked with restrictions such as "For teachers only," your library imprint will usually erase all barriers. As a safeguard you may include a statement to the effect that your library serves the group in question.

Should free material be requested by title? Or is it better to place subject requests? Asking for a specific title is appropriate if you are soliciting a newly published item; a particularly significant or unique publication; or a title mentioned in a recognized list of free materials.

It must be pointed out, however, that there are hazards in requesting specific titles, especially older materials. If the item you are seeking is out-of-print, you may get nothing at all in response to your communication. If the title you request is still available, a clerk may send it to you while ignoring newer and better materials filed alongside.

Subject requests can sometimes be more productive than title requests. When making them, be careful to precisely define the topics that interest you. If you are serving a particular type of clientele, indicate that also. Avoid vague requests such as "Send all your publications." If you're unsure about the output of a particular source, ask for a list of their publications. You can then order more intelligently and profitably.

When you order a new edition of a publication, retain the old edition in your files until the replacement arrives. But pencil a note on the outside indicating that a revision has been requested. The date of the request should also be recorded. If a reply is received indicating that no new edition is available, you may decide to keep the old edition in the collection. In this case, make a note on the face of the item indicating that no new edition is obtainable.

Since there is more than one person in our department, we are careful to add our names to even form postcard requests. This saves time in routing mail.

If you are choosing supplementary sources from a list of free and inexpensive materials, it is useful to mark the entries which you have decided to order. This will give you a quick picture of the status quo if you consult the same list again. It is also important to keep notes of contacts made for free publications destined for local history files. Here a follow-up is necessary if the needed items are not promptly received. But other than these exceptions, there is no need to maintain records of free materials requested unless you want to keep tabs on a very special production.

Not all librarians agree with this stand. In their book, **How to Organize and Maintain the Library Picture/Pamphlet File (83)**, Geraldine Gould and Ithmer Wolfe recommend a system of controlling requests for free publications which involves a three-section card file. The first section is devoted to a list of sources which have been approached for free material and from which replies have not yet been received. The date of the request is noted. When a response is received, the record card is transferred to the second section of the file after a description and evaluation of the incoming material is added. The subject heading chosen for the material is also indicated on the card. Notations are made of items which are judged inappropriate for the collection. In the third section of the file are subject cards on which are listed all sources from which free material has been received on a given topic.

Records are also kept for "dead" sources.

The authors maintain that in actual operation this is a simple system which saves staff time.

Despite their sincere endorsement, I continue to believe that the time used in detailed record keeping might be better spent in canvassing more sources for more free materials. You may infrequently find that you have sent two requests to the same agency. However, this occasional lapse consumes far less time than typing and leafing through lengthy packs of records. If the librarian occasionally suspects that an item has already been received, it's an easy matter to check holdings and circulation records—much easier than maintaining an inventory of every single item requested. The charm of free material is that it does not sap the library's finances. Part of this economy can be dissipated by keeping involved order records.

Attempting to use such records as an evaluative checklist of sources or as a list of contacts on given subjects has its limitations, too. In a rapidly changing world, such a list loses its currency almost at the moment of creation. Company and organization policies are altered frequently. New publications programs are started, others abandoned. Yesterday's "dead" source might be tomorrow's darling.

If you feel the need for checklists on given subjects, turn to the many compilations of free and inexpensive materials which are published periodically. It's much cheaper and just as productive to use them. If you want an alphabetical list of addresses, at least two of these bibliographies will provide that, too. Thomas J. Pepe's **Free and Inexpensive Educational**

Aids (144) incorporates a separate alphabetical listing of suppliers. In Ruth H. Aubrey's **Selected Free Materials for Classroom Teachers (14)** the index provides an alphabetical list of all sources with page references indicated for complete addresses.

When supplementary materials must be purchased, the picture changes. Because of the need to account for expenditures and to avoid unplanned duplications, a record should be kept of outstanding orders. The pattern this record takes will depend upon the order routine practiced in your institution. Whatever the system, there should be an order card or carbon copy on file for every item ordered.

Do not throw these order records away when the material arrives. With the addition of a sequential number and a notation of the subject heading chosen for the item, you have the makings of a simple circulation system. More will be said about this later.

Special techniques are sometimes required in buying federal documents. If you are ordering publications from the Superintendent of Documents, you may elect one of these methods of payment:

1. Check or money order
2. Coupons sold in sets of 20 for $1.00
3. Deposits of $25 or more against which orders are placed.

You will find full instructions in the **Monthly Catalog (119)** and in most of the **Price Lists** issued by the Superintendent of Documents. If you do not have these guides, write to the Government Printing Office for a free descriptive folder about ordering documents.

As well as its headquarters in Washington, D.C., the Government Printing Office maintains Branch Bookstores in Chicago, San Francisco, and Kansas City, Missouri.

Some federal bodies outside the Government Printing Office have been designated as official sales agents of the Superintendent of Documents. This is true of the Department of Commerce. Its Field Offices across the nation sell Department of Commerce publications as well as certain other government documents relating to business. In addition to such joint sales arrangements, there are some government publications which are for sale *only* by the issuing agency. This practice will be discussed more fully in the chapter on acquisition of maps.

When unusual provisions are made about the sale of federal documents, you can expect to find them described in the publications lists or announcements of the agency involved.

Bargain Hunting

It's a delightful and heady experience for a financially pressed librarian to discover that materials which have a price indicated can often be obtained free. Many organizations will generously contribute complimentary copies of their publications to libraries. Just make sure that the word, "library," is prominently displayed on your request.

Changes in economic conditions affect this philanthropy, of course. The British Information Services which had sent us free copies of their pamphlets for many years curtailed that practice when Great Britain faced financial difficulties.

Despite such defections, libraries can still bolster their resources with complimentary copies of many publications.

In acquiring federal documents money can be saved by using the right approach. Federal agencies will often provide single free copies of publications which are offered for sale by the Superintendent of Documents. For example, the Women's Bureau of the U.S. Department of Labor issues a series of career booklets for women which nominally cost from 5 to 10 cents each. But a set can be obtained free by writing directly to the Bureau. The Public Health Service will provide single copies of its health information leaflets and pamphlets without charge. The State Department distributes free single copies of certain publications to persons engaged in the dissemination of information—such as librarians. This points up once again the importance of indicating your library affiliation when contacting sources.

Congressmen can be invaluable agents in your search for federal documents. They are usually very cooperative about filling any reasonable request for free copies of federal publications. Election years are particularly opportune times to encourage this relationship.

Pamphlet Jobbers

In an effort to centralize the acquisition of pamphlets, some libraries turn to firms which are variously known as pamphlet jobbers, pamphlet services, or pamphlet agents. The arguments for ordering materials through these middlemen rather than directly are these:

1. It simplifies bookkeeping.
2. It cuts postage costs.
3. It facilitates follow-ups on unfilled orders.

As an added attraction, some pamphlet services publish selected bibliographies which may contain descriptive notes.

The reaction to these jobbers among librarians is mixed.

Many small libraries with staffs that are limited in number or lacking in training welcome these services eagerly. Librarians from such communities have told me that they find the annotated lists issued by some jobbers very helpful in making their selections.

On the other hand, I have heard complaints about the length of time it takes for orders to be filled. One jobber openly admits in his publicity that it takes longer to get pamphlets from his service than from the individual publishers! Other complaints have dealt with incomplete orders which dragged on for months and unrequested duplicates which had to be mailed back.

A major drawback is that some agencies will not accept orders for free materials.

The lists which are issued by some jobbers are helpful but they do not give comprehensive coverage and they are heavily weighted with paperback books which are too large and too costly for wholesale inclusion in pamphlet files.

Among the established pamphlet jobbers are the following:

1. Bacon Pamphlet Service, Inc. **(16)**
   Will accept orders for any pamphlet or paperbound book published in the U.S. or Canada unless it is free. This includes documents from U.S. Government Printing Office. Issues free lists of pamphlets and paperbacks with some brief descriptive notes. Service charge on orders under $5.00. No postage charge if remittance is sent with order.

2. VF Materials **(191)**
   Publishes **VF Materials**, a selective and annotated list of pamphlets and paperbacks which is issued 8 times a year. Subscription fee is $1.70. Will also handle orders for pamphlets not listed in **VF Materials**, including federal documents. But will not accept orders for free material. Subscription to **VF Materials** is not required to use purchasing services. Usual charge for first copy of any title is 4 cents. Charge of 2 cents for each added copy. No postage charge.

3. William-Frederick Press **(197)**
   Will accept orders for free materials as well as for pamphlets and paperbacks that are for sale. Service charge of 15 cents per title (not per copy), plus postage.

My preference is for placing orders directly with publishers or sponsoring organizations because of the quick, uncomplicated contact this establishes. Pamphlets may go out-of-stock if too much time is consumed in working through an intermediary. Speedy acquisition is particularly important when pamphlets deal with topics of intense and immediate interest. In addition, direct responses from publishers or organizations will frequently furnish leads to other publications.

Still I recognize that in some libraries the use of a pamphlet jobber may spell the difference between having a viable pamphlet file or having one that is moribund.

If you are interested, the pamphlet services will provide you with descriptive literature. It is also helpful to talk with librarians who have used these agencies.

INITIAL PROCESSING: SOURCING, DATING, PRICING

When all of your solicitations and orders begin to bear fruit, you must have an efficient routine established to cope with these riches.

As you open envelopes or wrappers, do not discard them until you make sure that the name and address of the issuing agency is repeated on the item. In an unhappily large number of cases, identification is incomplete or entirely lacking on the pamphlet, poster, or map. Such omissions must be corrected by adding the information by hand. Why? The origin must be indicated to orient the staff and public to the purpose and authority of the publisher or distributor. Identification of the supplier is also essential when new editions are needed or when patrons desire to obtain personal copies.

Every supplementary source should be stamped immediately with the date of receipt. Obviously this is crucial when the item itself bears no indication of date, since the usefulness of most supplementary sources is directly related to their timeliness. While the date the librarian applies does not necessarily equate with the date of publication, at least it gives an indication of the period when the item was being actively distributed.

Do not skip this step even when the item itself carries an indication of its publication date. When your request for the latest edition of a statistical publication produces one that was released two years ago, your date stamp will indicate that this was the newest compilation available at the date of receipt.

Dating a pamphlet or leaflet in a prominent place will also be useful to the inexperienced patron who is not skillful at hunting for the publisher's indication which is often fairly well-concealed or disguised with a code.

Dating can be expedited by the use of a band dater stamp on which the month, day, and year can be changed. These daters which come in various sizes can be purchased in dime stores, office supply stores, or from library supply houses. Band daters, made to order, are available with the library's name incorporated into the stamp.

The new material should also be marked with an indication of its cost or free status. This can be useful information to the librarian deciding on replacements or to the patron who wants to obtain a copy for himself. It's desirable to place this information in the same spot each time to facilitate location. In dealing with pamphlets, we place this information at the top inner corner of the first inside page. We also add a small check to indicate that the order card has been pulled, if there was one.

This is the strategic time for a rough sorting of incoming supplementary sources according to their eventual disposition—maps, general pamphlets, vocational monographs, pictorial material, local history items, etc. Once this division has been accomplished, the materials are ready for incorporation into the library's files.

ORGANIZATION

The usefulness of supplementary sources is determined to a large extent by the way they are organized. The scheme of organization must be simple to use and provide quick and thorough access to the material. The choicest pamphlets, pictures, and maps lose their value if you must depend on flashes of memory, blind intuition, or sheer chance to locate them.

Unfortunately, supplementary sources are so diversified in format and use that it is impossible to wrap them all up in one neat little organizational package. Pictures present different organizational problems than pamphlets. Vocational monographs offer some organizational complications that are not associated with college catalogs. Because these variations are inescapable, the organization of the different types of materials will have to be considered individually in later chapters.

LABELING

Speed in finding and filing supplementary sources is directly related to the manner in which they are marked.

Once again the varied nature of supplementary sources may call for a variety of approaches. This is true of pictures and maps. Their special labeling problems will be discussed in the chapters devoted to these materials.

As you establish your labeling procedures, beware of certain common traps. The first consists of merely underlining words in the cover titles of pamphlets or in the headlines of clippings to serve as guides to placement. The few seconds gained by omitting proper labeling will be lost many times over in the filing process. Headings which are instantly recognizable and uniformly placed do much to reduce filing time.

A second pitfall to avoid is penciled headings. The theory behind this practice is that supplementary source headings are subject to change and, therefore, should be in pencil to permit easy alteration. The need for occasional heading revisions does not justify penciling. Penciled headings are not bold enough to begin with. To compound the problem, they quickly become blurred and smeared. Not only are they difficult to read, but they are messy looking as well. It is not hard to effect a heading change even when the original is inked or typed. A gummed label or pressure sensitive label can be applied in no more time than it takes to erase old lettering.

Is it better to hand print headings or make labels on the typewriter? Many librarians prefer typewritten labels because they are always uniform in appearance while printing ability varies from staff member to staff member. The usual procedure is to type the headings on labels which are then applied to the supplementary sources. Thin leaflets or flyers, however, can be inserted directly into the typewriter. Some libraries use special typewriters which have extra-large type in an effort to increase legibility.

I would cast my vote for handprinted headings. It's a rare staff that cannot produce at least one clerk or student assistant who can letter neatly and legibly. Handprinted headings are much more forceful than typed headings, thereby facilitating quick identification. They usually can be applied directly to the material or folder, saving the cost of adhesive labels as well as the time needed to adhere them.

Choosing a favorite brand of marking pens is a highly individual process, much like selecting shoes. There are many makes of fine-line marking pens available in a variety of colors. You will want a pen that has a bold line but that is fine enough to form clear letters in the space available. Try out prospective choices on difficult letters such as "e."

From time to time there will be pamphlet covers which are so dark that direct handprinting is impossible. Some libraries cut out a section of the cover and print on the page below. An easier and better solution is to apply an adhesive label and print on that. Adhesive labels will also solve the problem of high gloss covers to which ink will not adhere.

A variety of adhesive labels are available. Gummed labels come in perforated sheets, in pads, in rolls, and in fan folds. Pressure sensitive labels can be purchased on separate backing sheets or in rolls. Folder labels are offered which fold over the top of the folder tabs. Some libraries use these folding labels for other purposes as well, such as labeling pictures. Adhesive labels can be bought in a wide range of colors or with color bands.

Most librarians are willing to settle for paper labels. But the energetic director of one small but highly successful library used a tape embosser to make plastic self-adhesive labels for the folders in her files. She admits that the project consumed a good deal of time but she claims that it has made replacing the folders "a breeze." Tapes of different colors were used to distinguish the various collections of supplementary sources in the library— i.e., general vertical files, vocations, maps, and local history. Individual items were headed by hand in matching colors.

This experiment points up the key role which color can play in facilitating access to material and preventing mistakes in filing. Color coded labels and inks provide a quick and effective way of separating resources.

Stamps offer another easy means of differentiating groups of supplementary sources. For example, the word, "Travel," stamped just above or ahead of the subject heading is a quick and effective way of indicating that certain leaflets belong in a special collection of travel brochures.

Stamps can also be used to relay instructions. Items meant for reference purposes only can be stamped "Not for circulation" or "For use in library only."

In addition, stamps offer a fast method of marking supplementary sources with an indication of library ownership.

When stamps are applied to glossy surfaces, an application of clear plastic spray will keep the letters from smearing.

Stamps made to individual specifications can be obtained from local firms for a surprisingly modest fee.

There are rubber stamp kits available from which you can construct stamps as the need arises. But the time spent in picking out the letters and inserting them in the holder cancels out any monetary savings.

The location of subject headings on supplementary sources is important in achieving effective use of these materials. A uniform spot should be selected for the placement of the headings. On pamphlets, leaflets, mounted pictures, and mounted clippings headings should be at the upper left-hand corner as the item will stand in the file or box. Maps, unmounted pictures, and unmounted clippings may call for adjustments which will be covered in later chapters.

The upper left-hand corner is a logical place for subject headings because this is the starting point to which we have been oriented in our reading.

Since smaller items can stand erect in either boxes or file drawers, the heading will always be at the true top of the material. But bigger items may have to be turned to fit into vertical files. Large pamphlets should be turned so that the "spine" or closed edge is at the top. The heading should be applied along the closed edge.

There are two good reasons for electing to keep the closed edge uppermost in the file drawers. First, when cut edges are turned upward, it's very easy for small items to be carelessly slipped between the pages. Second, it is hard to distinguish where one pamphlet ends and the next one begins.

HOUSING

Don't expect sympathy if your excuse for failing to supply supplementary sources is a lack of elegant equipment. Improvise! Sturdy cardboard boxes will serve as filing cases. So will wooden crates if you're lucky enough to find any. Large laundry soap containers can be cut down to serve as pamphlet boxes. These makeshifts can be painted or covered with wallpaper or contact paper to disguise their humble origins. Roomy mailing envelopes can be sealed at the flap and slit open along the side to substitute for file folders.

Filing Cases

Metal filing cases are the most popular devices for housing supplementary sources. Critical judgment is needed in their selection. They should be made of heavy gauge steel. A full suspension system is essential to allow easy access to the last folder in the drawer. Drawers should glide effortlessly on roller bearings. Following blocks or compressors should be provided to keep file folders erect. These supports should be easy to operate. Thumb latch controls are helpful in keeping drawers safely closed when not in use.

Choice of case size will depend on the projected location, the nature of the materials to be housed, and the available budget. The two most popular sizes in vertical files are letter size and legal size. Dimensions vary slightly among the various manufacturers. Legal files are more expensive than letter files.

Many libraries prefer legal size cases because the extra width will accommodate larger items and also because many pamphlets will stand two to a row. Legal size drawers are certainly the logical choice for housing pictures since these resources are likely to be outsized and it is undesirable to fold them. However, for a collection consisting of pamphlets and clippings, the extra floor space and money consumed by legal files may not be justified. Theoretically, legal files should result in great savings in space because materials can be spread out horizontally. However, I conducted an actual test run, transferring pamphlets and clippings from a letter size file with letter size folders to a legal size file with legal size folders. The saving in space averaged only one-half inch for every eight inches of closely compressed material. This saving is offset by the extra floor space required by the wider files. The discrepancy between theory and practice is that the contents of folders in real life are a mixed bag. They do not consist of neatly matched pamphlets that will stand two by two in perfect order. Some are fat, some are lean. Some are wide, some are narrow. Many folders contain uneven numbers of pamphlets so that perfect pairing is impossible.

Because of the special needs presented by pictures, some libraries go one step beyond legal files and invest in oversize files which will house these large-scale resources more comfortably. The housing of pictures is discussed more fully in a later chapter.

As well as drawer size, the choice of filing cases involves a decision as to height. Four-drawer vertical files are less expensive than lower cases in terms of the amount of material which can be stored. They also require less floor space per cubic foot of enclosed material. However, strong arguments can be advanced in favor of three-drawer units. They provide an ideal counter-height top on which to examine material. They will not impede vision. As a result, they offer more flexibility in placement than four-drawer units.

Filing cases differ in type as well as size. Many libraries choose horizontal filing cases for their map collections or for storing charts and posters. The use of horizontal cases in map storage is examined in detail in Chapter 8.

Lateral files represent still another variety of storage. These cases are approached from the "side" rather than from the "front." Their potential importance lies in their adaptability to areas where conventional files are impractical. They can, for example, nestle against the wall in narrow quarters where a standard file would project too far.

Lateral files also present a pleasant appearance since they do not jut sharply into the room. This has tempted some librarians to buy lateral files for aesthetic rather than practical reasons.

Caution should be exercised in buying lateral cases. The shelves or drawers which house materials at right angles to the user are difficult to consult. Even when they pull out, it is difficult to work entirely from the front of the unit. As a result, locating and refiling materials involves a great deal of neck twisting. Much more practical for library supplementary sources are lateral cases with partitioned drawers which allow materials to be arranged facing the user. Several manufacturers offer this alternative in their lateral files.

Internal Filing Devices

The accessories used within file drawers can be as important as the files themselves. Good quality manila folders are the mainstays of pamphlet files. While envelopes are useful for storing unmounted pictures and unmounted clippings, folders are much more appropriate for filing pamphlets.

Folders must, of course, be selected to match the dimensions of file drawers. Reinforced tabs are a desirable feature to watch for in choosing folders.

To make it easy to spot folder headings in the files, it is advisable to use staggered tabs. Although some libraries use fifth-cut folders, I prefer third-cut because of the added tab space available for labeling.

In the pamphlet files in our reference department, we have provided a folder for every subject heading. While this procedure sounds expensive, the initial cost is balanced by time saved in locating material and in refiling it. Furthermore, it eliminates the bugaboo of having lighter materials slip to the bottom of the drawer where they are overlooked or crushed by heavier items.

In using manila folders, take advantage of the scoring at the fold which permits bending the bottom into box form to cope with increased contents.

When materials overflow the original folder, a second folder can be added. Be sure to label the folders "1" and "2" so that users will be alerted to the existence of two containers. An even better solution for handling swollen resources is to use expanding file pockets. These durable devices will absorb quantities of material without sagging. While expanding wallets are available with flaps that fold over the top, the best choice for library files is the file pocket with its open top and closed sides. The closed sides keep materials from sliding out while the open top allows for easy accessibility.

Choose your brand and style of expanding file pockets with care. There is a great variation in the amount of expansion possible. The best pocket I have discovered is manufactured by the Alvah Bushnell Company (29).

File guides are used in many libraries to indicate letter divisions, major subject headings or cross references. They can be improvised from old manila folders. Pressboard guides are available from library and office supply houses. They may be purchased with regular tabs or with metal tabs into which labels can be inserted. Metal tabs are stronger and facilitate the changing of headings, but they do add to the price of the guides.

We have dispensed with file guides in the cases which hold our pamphlets and clippings since we have a labeled folder for each item in the files and since we record SEE ALSO references on these folders. Nor do we see any need for inserting guides with SEE references since we assume that users will consult our card index when the subject is obscure.

If funds are obtainable, hanging file folders are a splendid addition to any vertical or lateral file. Frames are available which can be inserted in any standard file drawer. Rugged folders are suspended from the frame. They slide freely back and forth on the rails. You can transfer your manila folders and their contents to the hanging folders or you can file items directly into the hanging folders. Because they do not rest on the bottom of the drawer, hanging folders can accommodate large amounts of material without bulging or sagging. It is easy to remove or replace material because folders are so maneuverable. **Pendaflex** is the best-known name in the field of suspension files. **Pendaflex** frames and hanging folders are manufactured by the Oxford Filing Supply Co., Inc. (140).

Specialized filing devices for maps, pictures, and clippings are discussed in the chapters devoted to these supplementary sources.

File Boxes

Material stored in pamphlet boxes on book stacks consumes less floor space than if it were housed in filing cases. Furthermore, extra space must be allowed in planning library quarters for the opening of file drawers.

Despite these facts, most librarians would be reluctant to part with their floor files. They are convenient. They allow for maximum organization and control. They offer protection from dust and light.

Still, the file box has an important role to play in housing supplementary sources. There is no "either or" ultimatum in managing these resources. It's perfectly proper to house part of your holdings in filing cases and part in file boxes. In our library we employ many metal filing cabinets. Yet our extensive collection of travel brochures is stored in pamphlet boxes on shelves.

File boxes are also excellent devices for storing back runs of annual reports or statistical series which might otherwise clog file drawers. These boxes can be tucked away in back rooms or basements until the material is needed.

When material is withdrawn from the file drawers for housing elsewhere there should, of course, be a notice in the file that this shift has been made. This applies not only to back runs of continuations, but also to oversized material that is stored away from the filing cases.

Boxes should be selected to fit their station in life. If they are to be used for long-term storage in secluded areas, inexpensive closed boxes are suitable. Hinged pamphlet files also provide good protection from dust and light, but they cost considerably more than regular storage boxes.

When boxes are to be used on open shelves in the public service areas, sturdy construction is essential. Visibility, accessibility, and security become major considerations, too.

In using ordinary pamphlet boxes which are closed except for the back, it is difficult to examine or pull out individual items without removing the entire contents of the containers. Back openings are always hazardous, too, since it is very easy for stored materials to fall out. This danger applies to Princeton files as well as to ordinary pamphlet boxes.

Open top, cut-corner boxes are a vast improvement. Since they are enclosed on four sides, they prevent spillage. Yet the diagonal cut of the boxes allows easy access to materials.

We have improvised another solution which we find very satisfactory. Ordinary open-back pamphlet boxes are turned so that the front panel rests on the shelf. This provides a four-sided container open at the top.

Serial Shelving

In an all-out effort to conserve space, a few libraries place pamphlets on shelves in the order in which they are received. A serial number or a combination letter and number is assigned to each pamphlet. Access to individual pamphlets or to subjects covered is achieved through a card catalog.

WEEDING

Subtraction is as crucial a process as addition in maintaining a healthy collection of supplementary sources. Some librarians obtain a deep-seated comfort from seeing file folders jammed full of material even if it is dated and inappropriate. In reality, they are doing themselves and their patrons a disservice. They mislead their public with these bloated folders by promising something they can't really deliver. They risk misinforming their patrons through the presence of invalid material. They waste the time required to leaf through useless items. They squander space that might be put to more profitable use.

Weeding should not be a "sometime" thing. There is little justification for postponing action until the situation gets desperate and then indulging in a crash project. Weeding of supplementary sources must be done regularly, consistently, and constantly.

In a well-controlled collection, the processes of adding and discarding materials are inseparable. For weeding properly begins when the librarian leafs through the daily pile of mail or examines a stack of leaflets presented by a patron. Hopefully, he will avoid thinking, "Oh, well, I might as well keep this since it's free." If he employs critical standards of currency, authority, age level, and format at this point, he will have less deadwood to deal with later on.

In our reference department the conjunction between acquisition and weeding is carried even further. As new materials such as maps or pamphlets are prepared for addition to the collection, we actually check them against the holdings we already have. This gives us an opportunity to assess the older material against the potential contribution of the new. We watch for such factors as these:

1. Will the new addition supersede older publications on the same subject? Or do the older materials contain historical or background information which is omitted in recent works?

2. Does the new item add a different dimension or merely restate what is found in other materials on the subject? If it does not offer a fresh approach, do we need it anyway because of the popularity of the topic?

3. If a new item is found to be the duplicate of a supplementary source already in the collection, is there enough demand to justify keeping both copies? If the answer is "Yes," the original copy must be pulled to allow for adding a distinguishing copy number.

4. If the new item is an annual report, statistical compilation, or serial bulletin, should only the latest edition be kept? If a backfile is considered desirable, how long should it be? In

the case of statistical publications, the decision may hinge on whether statistics for past years are repeated or summarized in the newer issues.

As we conduct this process of checking new resources against the old, we simultaneously go through the traditional steps of the weeding process. We watch for:

1. Material that has outlived its usefulness or its authority.
2. Material that needs repair or replacement because of physical condition.
3. Continuations such as annual reports or catalogs for which newer editions need to be ordered.
4. Subject headings which need modernizing or which should be split into finer groupings.
5. Overcrowded folders, boxes, or drawers.

Another type of spot weeding used in some libraries consists of checking the contents of folders which are awaiting refiling after being used. To indicate that a group of materials has been evaluated, an inconspicuous date notation may be penciled on the folder.

While the forms of spot weeding just described are helpful, they provide a random approach at best. There must also be opportunity for an orderly, overall assessment of the collection—from the first drawer to the last. This progressive weeding should be carried out on a steady, continuing basis. It will enable you to review *all* subject areas. It will help you discover interest fields which are dormant because they need an infusion of fresh, new material. It will alert you to headings which are no longer needed and which may be profitably eliminated. (But remember to pull the index cards when you delete those headings!)

In an attempt to expedite weeding and to shift part of the burden to clerks and student helpers, some libraries have experimented with symbols which predict the prospective life span of supplementary sources. For example, subject headings written in red might indicate items of permanent value while those in green signify ephemeral materials. A "P" stamped on a supplementary source might represent a permanent addition while a "T" stands for "temporary." Some libraries have even stamped supplementary sources with a weeding date indicating the probable length of time they would be of value.

When a weeding date is supplied, pages can pull any "expired" items as they refile materials. When color or letter coding is used, clerks or pages can withdraw "temporary" materials from drawers or shelves when weeding time rolls around. Both of these schemes call for the librarian to review the material that has been pulled.

I do not recommend either of these plans. A librarian would have to be equipped with a crystal ball to make the required predictions. Furthermore, these schemes discourage the librarian from assessing all the material under a given heading as he weeds.

In libraries where statistics are critical in the fight for funds, it may be desirable to keep a tally of the number of supplementary sources discarded as well as those added so that some estimate can be made of the total holdings.

Local history materials call for an entirely different concept of weeding since long-term preservation is the goal. The treatment of local history resources will be discussed later in this book.

CIRCULATION

Should supplementary sources be restricted to use in the library since they have a high potential reference value? Or should they be allowed to circulate so that the public can use them at home, at work, or in the classroom?

In trying to reconcile these opposite pulls, one major library established two comprehensive collections of supplementary sources, one for reference use and the second for circulation. This approach is too demanding of time and space for most libraries.

If there are certain choice statistical items in your files which you find invaluable for reference use, try to get an extra copy so that you can circulate one and still have a backup copy in the library. The second copy can be marked "Not for circulation" or "For use in library only" or "Reference copy." If you are unable to obtain a duplicate of the latest in a series of statistical publications, restrict only the newest edition and allow the remainder to circulate.

Because of their diverse nature, the circulation of supplementary sources is a complex process. It has the potential for more misunderstandings and conflicts than the circulation of more standardized materials.

Circulation control of supplementary sources ranges from one extreme to the other. There are libraries in which a card and pocket is affixed to every pamphlet. There are others where circulation control is so minimal that pamphlets and clippings are recorded only as miscellaneous materials, no overdue notices are sent, and no follow-up is ever made on unreturned items.

The libraries which use cards and pockets argue that these pamphlets represent an important information resource, accumulated with effort and sometimes with a respectable expenditure of money. They also claim that the time and money spent in providing cards and pockets is balanced by the time saved when pamphlets are circulated.

This system is most workable in a library with a very limited collection of pamphlets or in a library which can take advantage of volunteer labor to cut production costs. Some school libraries resort to cards and pockets because they want to unitize all resources by assigning Dewey numbers to pamphlets and shelving them with books on the same subject.

Libraries which exercise only a token jurisdiction over the circulation of pamphlets and clippings operate on the theory that these items are entirely expendable. The suspicion arises that libraries which subscribe to this philosophy either have very poor collections which do not justify greater control or else they are blind to the value of these resources to staff and public alike.

Are supplementary sources really expendable? Yes, if being expendable means that they should be used freely and fully until they wear out or outlive their usefulness. No, if being expendable means that they should be treated as giveaways.

It was a painful moment when we learned that a student had lost the materials on adoption which we had laboriously accumulated over a period of time. It was painful not only for the library staff but also for other students who had hoped to use the information. We find it hard to lightly write off such resources as being "expendable."

Most libraries try to steer a precarious middle road between the two extremes of circulation control. The most common circulation record maintained is a very simple designation of type of material, subject, and number of items borrowed. The patron's identification and the due date complete the record.

In public libraries a separate card or slip is normally used for each transaction. Libraries which have charging machines may imprint the borrower's card number and the due date on a regular book card and then fill in the descriptive information by hand. Some libraries make do with old scratch cards on which they pencil a record of the loan. Others have special forms printed.

In designing a special charge form, the grouping of items depends on what is considered prime information for filing the records. If the charging devices are to be sorted by subject, that piece of information should have top location.

Some libraries prefer to use the name of the borrower as a filing guide since a patron may borrow material on several subjects at the same time. In this case, the borrower's name should be given a prominent location. Under this setup the patron's name must be repeated on the circulation envelope.

If cards are used for the circulation of supplementary sources which in any way resemble those used for books, confusion may be avoided by choosing a different color of card or by selecting a card of a different size.

Instead of individual transaction slips or cards, school libraries may turn to large master cards or notebooks with one transaction being listed below another. When a loan packet is returned, the transaction is crossed off. A refinement of this system is to maintain an individual card for each subject represented in the library's files. The cards are kept in a separate arrangement. All loans involving a particular topic are entered line after line on the appropriate subject card. One argument for employing this system is that it measures the relative demand for each subject area.

Another technique which school libraries have developed to facilitate circulation is the subject envelope. For example, a group of clippings and pamphlets on milk will be housed in an envelope which carries a card and pocket. The card and pocket bear a record of the subject and the number of items in the envelope. The envelope is circulated as a unit. In theory this sounds like an excellent idea, but it has its drawbacks in actual practice. In the first place, the tally on the card and pocket must be changed each time an item is added to or subtracted from the packet. In the second place, treating the envelope as a unit makes it very difficult to borrow only a few items at a time.

The weakness of all circulation systems which limit description of the loaned material to type, subject, and number is that they provide no identification of individual items.

Does it really matter? It does if you want to make sure that you aren't sending overdue notices for material that has already been returned. It does if a patron can find only part of his loan and asks, "Exactly what is it that's still missing?" A little more effort spent on circulation records might pay off in better public relations. Conflicts and uncertainties arising from vagueness over circulation records do nothing to convince our borrowers that we are sharp, well-organized entrepreneurs.

One way of aiding the identification of circulated items is to jot down a few words from the pamphlet title or from the headline of a clipping. A clipping might also be pegged by jotting down the initials or abbreviated form of the newspaper's name and a numerical notation of the date.

Another method of pinpointing materials and speeding the circulation process is to use accession numbers which can be recorded on the transaction slip. Libraries may maintain an accession notebook in which they place a simple record of each pamphlet added to their files. The accession number is duplicated on the pamphlet itself. Since numbers are not repeated, they constitute a foolproof device for charging out material and checking on its return.

As indicated earlier, order cards may be converted into accession cards with the addition of a sequential number and a subject heading. If you want to extend this control to free pamphlets, a "bare-bones" accession card may be typed for each of these items. Good sense should be the guide. It's wasteful to type accession cards for serials, catalogs, or annual reports since it's so easy to describe these publications. "Red Cross 1967 Annual Report" is almost as easy to write as "Red Cross 67397." Clippings do not need accession cards. As pointed out in a previous paragraph, they can be readily identified by a notation such as "Chic Trib 1-9-70."

A variant use of accessioning is to stamp or print a sequential number on each item without maintaining a notebook or file to indicate the assignment of numbers. Since no records are kept, it is impossible under this system to determine the title of an individual pamphlet from its number. However, the scheme does simplify the charging out of material and the checking of files for returned items.

A numbering machine may be used to speed up the mechanics of accessioning. These machines usually number from 1 to 999,999. However, a new machine (168) is on the market which features a year band as well as consecutive numbers, e.g., 70-3691. At the beginning of the new year, the year band is reset and the accession number returns to one. This type of accessioning immediately reveals the age of a pamphlet.

If separate accession numbers are not provided in the case of duplicated titles, the copy number becomes an important part of the charging record.

Libraries which utilize photographic charging have attempted to adapt this form of circulation to supplementary sources. One large library preserves its order slips for all pamphlets that have been purchased. The slips remain clipped to the pamphlets while they are in the file. When a patron desires to borrow a pamphlet, the order card is used to make a photographic record of the loan. When no order card is available, the circulation clerk tries to take a picture of something on the cover that will identify the pamphlet.

Pamphlets and clippings are usually circulated in large paper envelopes. These containers serve to isolate each loan group, protect the materials, and offer a place for recording pertinent circulation information.

Old mailing envelopes can be utilized for circulation. Envelopes constructed especially for the purpose are sold by library supply houses. They are made of sturdy kraft paper with reinforced edges. Office supply firms offer envelopes with string ties for added security.

When old mailing envelopes are used, circulation data can be placed directly on the surface of the envelopes since they are readily discarded. Libraries which purchase special envelopes usually apply a date due slip or printed form to the front of the envelope.

The date on which the material is due is the most crucial bit of information to add to the outside of the envelope. In addition, a notation of the number of items taken will assist the borrower to collate his material and it will enable the librarian to make a quick check when the envelope is returned. Besides this information, some libraries indicate the type of material taken and the subject heading. A full notation of this sort would look like this:

Dec. 17, 1971   Conservation — 3 pamphlets
4 clippings

The name of the borrower is not essential on the envelope unless the charge slip is filed alphabetically by this information.

Instead of writing circulation information on the envelope, one library provides the patron with a carbon copy of the charge slip. This duplicate is returned with the envelope.

In libraries which choose to circulate pamphlets without benefit of an envelope, the due date is frequently stamped on the back cover or on the inside of the back cover. Librarians following this pattern point out that the accumulation of dates indicates the demand for a pamphlet which is useful knowledge in weeding or reordering.

School libraries which loan large groups of supplementary sources to classrooms may find it practical to circulate these subject collections in pamphlet boxes. Use the type of box which is closed on four sides and open at the top, or tip a standard box up so that the opening is at the top. This will prevent spillage and will allow headroom for tall items. A card and pocket may be affixed to the front of each box. The cards and pockets should carry numbers to differentiate the various boxes. When a box is sent to a classroom, the card should be marked with the subject and number of items taken as well as an indication of the teacher borrowing the material. The card is filed in the circulation records.

Since many libraries treat picture resources as a separate collection, the circulation of these supplementary sources is discussed in detail in a later chapter.

CHAPTER 3

PAMPHLETS AND CLIPPINGS:
THEIR VALUE AND THEIR ORGANIZATION

Pamphlets and clippings under most circumstances are organized jointly, housed jointly, and used jointly. The mixture of these two resources is what most librarians mean when they refer to "vertical files."

Despite this marriage of convenience, clippings and pamphlets spring from different origins and demand separate processing.

Any study of these supplementary sources must reflect this blending of similarities and differences. In the pages that follow, the elements which are common to both clippings and pamphlets will be discussed together. Considerations that are peculiar to one or the other will be treated separately.

THEIR VALUE

Why bother with clippings and pamphlets? You're busy enough coping with the ordering and cataloging of books. Why take on another chore?

The answer is simple. For your investment of time and money you will get a return great enough to turn a Wall Street speculator green with envy.

The unique contributions of these supplementary sources are many.

1.   COMPACTNESS AND ACCESSIBILITY

Many people prefer the compact, readily accessible nature of information in the vertical file. Patrons who back away from thick books may feel perfectly comfortable with pamphlets and clippings.

When time is limited, the vertical file becomes all the more important because of the concise nature of the material it contains and the quick approach it offers to specific subjects. Students discovered this virtue years ago. They are enthusiastic fans of the vertical file. Many of them turn hopefully to the vertical file for any and all subjects before consulting other resources. I remember the boy who wistfully inquired about pamphlets on the Peloponnesian War.

2.   MULTIPLICATION OF SOURCES

No library, however large, has the book resources to satisfactorily cope with mass demands. What do you do when several classes are assigned to study air pollution? How do you handle the heavy seasonal demands that occur at Mother's Day or Christmas? Clippings and pamphlets offer a way to bolster your book collection with a variety of supplementary offerings on popular topics. Because they are free or relatively inexpensive, you can enjoy the luxury of adding them lavishly without serious budgetary implications.

3. CURRENCY

Despite technological advances and crash publishing projects, there still is a time lapse in the production of books. Vertical file publications can help you to fill this gap. Because these supplementary materials are quick and inexpensive to produce, new ideas and the latest statistics often appear in this form long before they laboriously work their way into book format. Because of these very same virtues, vertical file materials are frequently revised. They are such good bargains that you can afford to keep up-to-date.

Typical of this flow of current information is the annual statistical report on recreational boating distributed free by the Boating Industry Association (21).

A dramatic demonstration of the up-to-the-minute quality of vertical file materials occurred when the State of Michigan announced restrictions on the sale of DDT. Cooperative extension service bulletins on household, garden, and agricultural insects were quickly revised to substitute alternate methods of control. Our book collection could not duplicate this rapid and complete realignment.

4. UNIQUENESS

Veterans of the reference corps know that many times the answer to a trying question is available only in pamphlets and clippings. When the craze for making jewelry from "fried" marbles hit our community, the only instructions we could offer were newspaper clippings from our vertical files. When local stores started to sell kiwi berries, book material was of no help with the questions we received. Luckily, we were able to obtain informative flyers on kiwi berries from two firms involved in distributing this exotic fruit.

Even when some coverage is available in book form on certain difficult subjects, it may be very sparse. Here again the vertical file may help to fill the gaps with unique material. In our library we know that the fine points of flag etiquette are better represented in our vertical files than in any book we own. We have laboriously collected clippings, pamphlets, and even letters of response from national authorities which go far beyond any book coverage.

5. AUTHORITY

Vertical file materials often possess an authority which matches or even surpasses that of books. The publications distributed by the federal government usually wear this cloak of reliability. Nothing inspires more confidence than a pamphlet like **Subterranean Termites: Their Prevention and Control in Buildings** which bears the imprint of the U.S. Department of Agriculture. The series of five booklets on child care and development which are issued by the Children's Bureau have been the trusted allies of many parents over the years. Authority is also the outstanding feature of the folders in the **Health Information Series** from the Public Health Service which summarize current knowledge about various diseases.

6. EXTENSION

The vertical file offers an opportunity to provide information in areas where there is occasional or sporadic demand. When budgets are limited, each book must be weighed for the contribution it makes to the library week after week. Since vertical file material does not involve the same financial drain, it is possible to be much more liberal in selection. While you may not feel justified in buying an expensive book on paperweights, pamphlets and clippings on the subject will enable you to satisfy a patron.

7. REFERRAL

Librarians in small institutions often shudder at the word, "bibliography," but we eagerly add bibliographies to our vertical files. Naturally, we don't own all the resources described, but these lists do open broad horizons to our patrons. We often can arrange interlibrary loans or obtain photocopies of items suggested in these bibliographies. Representative of these publications is **A List of Worthwhile Life & Health Insurance Books (96)** which is revised annually and published jointly by the Institute of Life Insurance and the Health Insurance Institute. Many other institutes and associations issue bibliographies relating to their areas of special interest. Government agencies are also active in compiling lists of informational sources. A growing number of libraries now offer their bibliographies for distribution on a national scale. We have recently acquired helpful bibliographies from other libraries on such critical subjects as Mexican-Americans, poverty, and drug abuse.

The vertical file can also point to resources beyond the walls of your library through the use of ordering lists. Many associations and publishers offer intriguing selections of plans for handicraft projects. The American Plywood Association, the Western Wood Products Association, and **Popular Mechanics** are among the sources that will send free lists of the project plans they have available. **Better Homes and Gardens** has an extensive catalog for sale. Our library even solicited a catalog from a syndicate which furnishes home pattern features for newspapers. You may not be able to buy widely among the plans included in these lists, but the lists themselves will serve as guides for your patrons so that they can order personal copies of the projects that answer their needs.

THEIR ORGANIZATION

Dewey or Dictionary?

It should come as no surprise that some librarians propose classifying pamphlets and even clippings by the Dewey Decimal Classification System. After all, Dewey is the glue that holds most public and school libraries together. In theory, using Dewey for all library resources would simplify and correlate their use.

This is not a new concept. It appears in the early literature of the profession when the few pamphlets permitted inside a library were given legitimacy by being classified and placed on the shelves with their more respectable cousins. Sometimes single pamphlets were allowed this distinction.

Oftentimes related pamphlets were bound together into what were called pamphlet volumes. Or groups of associated pamphlets might stand in boxes alongside their book counterparts.

The classification of pamphlets is still an active practice today. Some librarians shelve their pamphlets with related books in the traditional manner. Others have set aside small rooms or corners where boxes of pamphlets stand in class order. Classified pamphlets and clippings have even been housed in vertical files. While a few stabs have been made at constructing special classification codes, by far the most widely used classification scheme for pamphlet material is Dewey.

The arguments marshalled for using Dewey classification sound like this:

1.   It is easier to organize pamphlets and clippings if a ready-made scheme like Dewey is used.

2.   It is logical to apply the same finding code to all library resources on the same subject. By following the numerical guide, 636.7, you should be able to locate everything the library owns on dogs—whether it be books, pamphlets, or clippings. The concept of unifying all library resources is particularly appealing to school librarians. They are eager to be able to present a quick overview of all library holdings on a given subject to teachers and pupils.

3.   It is helpful to have related subjects standing in close physical proximity. The patron who is interested. in sports will find it useful to have all sports pamphlets within easy eye range at once rather than having them dispersed alphabetically under such widely separated headings as "Baseball," "Volleyball," and "Golf." Physical closeness also makes it more convenient to work one's way back to broader classes if the answer can't be found under a specific topic. If 637.3 (Cheese) doesn't produce the needed items, there are pamphlets nearby under the general number, 637 (Dairy and related industries), which may help.

4.   It is easy to survey the library's holdings in the basic areas of knowledge because of the classified arrangement. Strengths and weaknesses in relation to the collection as a whole are readily apparent.

Unhappily, Dewey classification of pamphlets and clippings is neither as simple nor as appropriate in actual practice as it seems in theory. One of the special characteristics of pamphlets and clippings is that they can concentrate on small areas of emphasis. The Dewey Decimal Classification (a book classification) simply is not constructed to cope with that approach. How do you apply Dewey to bring out the exact nature of a pamphlet on toy banks or a leaflet on scavenger hunts? The potential choices in dealing with a highly specialized subject are to create a Dewey number so long and complex that it looks like a takeoff on the national budget or to bury the item under a general class number that will not reflect its precise content.

Shelving pamphlets with related books only serves to guarantee that the fineness of identification possible in an alphabetical subject arrangement will be lost. The tendency will be to simplify shelving by assigning the generalized Dewey numbers used for books. To compound the problem, it will be physically and economically impossible in most libraries to provide for dispersal of pamphlets and clippings in exact position among the books. If you own just two pamphlets on a particular subject, are you going to put them in binders or provide a separate pamphlet box so that they can stand in precise order on the shelves? The answer is usually "No" with the pamphlets being lumped in a box at the end of a major classification group. Generalized classification and generalized shelving blur the emphasis on specifics which is the prime contribution of so many pamphlets and clippings. Perhaps this is not such a grim prospect in a very small library where resources are so limited that they can be quickly screened. But the larger the collection, the more frustrating a generalized approach becomes because of the sheer number of items that must be handled to find a specific fact.

Currency is another problem in applying Dewey. Since new ideas or developments often are represented in clippings and pamphlets long before any book appears on the subject, what is the librarian to do until catalogers get around to making a pontifical judgment about the proper Dewey designation? If you guess, you may find yourself completely out of line when the "official" decision is finally made. If you put the materials aside to wait until the book publishers catch up with the subject, you will have lost an opportunity to be of immediate help to your patrons.

Nor is Dewey the most flexible of arrangements. A major breakthrough in science that might be easily handled in an alphabetical arrangement can cause a real crisis in a numerical system where one division is balanced precariously on another.

There is good reason for challenging the benefits that supposedly derive from placing pamphlets and clippings in schematic order so that related subjects rub shoulders. These claims simply do not jibe with the usage that is most commonly made of pamphlets and clippings. Laymen and librarians alike usually have a very precisely defined subject in mind when they approach these resources. The patron who wants to get rid of the bats in his attic couldn't care less that the pamphlets on bats, 599.4, stand in neighborly order with the pamphlets on whales, 599.5. He's not interested in whales.

It's true that in school libraries teachers may request blanket loans of materials in terms of broad units such as transportation or energy. But the students preparing reports for those same units will approach the library for information on such isolated topics as ground effect vehicles or solar batteries.

Rather than simplifying access to pamphlets, Dewey classification creates an extra barrier. An artificial symbol stands between the user and the material. Instead of turning directly to the files for a pamphlet on fences, it becomes necessary to determine what numerical code has been assigned to pamphlets on that subject.

Because of these many drawbacks, Dewey classification is a poor choice for dealing with pamphlets and clippings.

These supplementary sources should be organized instead by an alphabetical arrangement of subject headings. This approach which is sometimes called a dictionary arrangement has much to recommend it.

1. It is direct. There is no need to translate verbal ideas into an artificial number code.

2. It is simple. Alphabetical arrangement is easy to understand and manipulate. In libraries where patrons are encouraged to help themselves, this simplicity will be particularly appreciated by the young, the inexperienced, and the undereducated.

3. It is detailed. A dictionary approach allows for the use of individualized and definitive terms which speed access to materials and enable them to make their fullest contribution.

4. It is adjustable. New subjects are easily added to a dictionary arrangement. Refinements of old subjects are also easy to incorporate.

All in all, alphabetical arrangement is the most efficient, economical, and productive scheme currently available for coping with pamphlets and clippings.

Full Cataloging or the Subject Approach?

Even the strongest advocate of the alphabetical arrangement will admit that there are a few important pamphlets which should not only be classified, but fully cataloged as well so that they can take their places as mini-books on the shelves. Governmental publications of a statistical nature may qualify for this treatment. Pamphlets depicting facets of local history are sometimes candidates for such special handling.

Aside from such exceptions, there is really no need in the average school or public library to catalog individual pamphlets. An author or title approach is rarely required. Pamphlets are requested almost entirely by subject.

In a university or research library there may be pressure for more ambitious treatment of pamphlets, but it is not justified in a public, elementary school, or secondary school library.

If you find it difficult to settle for a subject approach alone, remember that **Public Affairs Information Service Bulletin** and **Business Periodicals Index** are subject indexes exclusively. Even the **Readers' Guide to Periodical Literature** omits title entries and **Vertical File Index** makes no provision for author indexing. The subject approach is the one feature which all these tools consider essential.

Librarians are sometimes tempted to single out well-known series such as the **Public Affairs Pamphlets** for full cataloging. A pamphlet series is usually housed as a unit after this processing. The need for this cataloged information simply is not great enough to justify the expense. A more practical plan would be to file the pamphlets by subject while retaining a series list indicating where each pamphlet is filed. It would be worthwhile to contact the publisher for a catalog of the pamphlets since this could be converted into an easy referral chart. Managing pamphlet series in this fashion will save the cost of full cataloging and still provide a variety of leads to the pamphlets.

Since the successful use of pamphlets and clippings depends on the rightness of subject headings assigned to them, this job takes on a sobering importance. Choosing headings for supplementary sources is an even more exacting job than classifying and cataloging a book. It's true that a single classification number must be selected for a book, but many alternate approaches can be arranged through subject entries in the card catalog. On the other hand, the subject heading that is chosen for a pamphlet or clipping provides the only access to that item.

Where does a librarian turn for help in carrying out this important task? Through eight editions that spanned 39 years many librarians relied on **Subject Headings for the Information File (17)**, a list that was based on headings used in the Public Library of Newark, New Jersey. Unfortunately, this old standby is out-of-print and there are no plans at this time to revive it.

In 1964 the Toronto Public Library **(176)** issued a list of the subject headings used in its vertical files. The list is currently being revised for reprinting. It is heavily weighted with entries that are purely Canadian in application. As a result, its value to libraries outside Canada would be as a sample of a working system, rather than as a precise guide to follow.

While it is still being sold, Ireland's **The Pamphlet File in School, College, and Public Libraries** (F.W. Faxon Co., 1954) is outdated. To my knowledge, there are no other comprehensive lists of subject headings on the market.

Some librarians turn to the **Sears List of Subject Headings (163)** for guidance. This is most likely to be true of school librarians who want to correlate all their book and nonbook holdings. By using Sears for all resources, they can record their vertical file headings in the card catalog on a par with the subject entries for books. This sounds like a tidy idea. Unfortunately, it's not as flawless as it sounds. Sears was designed for use with books just as the Dewey Decimal Classification was. Like Dewey, it is much too generalized for pamphlets and clippings. Using Sears' headings for vertical file materials is like giving directions for finding Philadelphia by saying only that it's in the State of Pennsylvania. Sears does have one contribution to make toward the establishment of a vertical file. It can be studied for leads to cross references and for techniques in manipulating them.

There is no need to forgo referrals from the card catalog to pamphlets and clippings simply because headings differ from book entries. Alternate methods will be discussed later in this chapter.

The objections which apply to use of Sears for subject headings also hold true for the use of headings in the **Standard Catalog Series** of the H.W. Wilson Co. These excellent lists are organized around books, not supplementary sources.

The **Vertical File Index** (192) can be more profitably consulted for leads to subject headings for supplementary sources. When you order from this buying guide, mark your order record with the subject heading under which the pamphlet is entered. The notation will be a handy check when you are deciding on terminology. The **Vertical File Index** is also useful in supplying suggestions for cross references.

But don't expect the impossible of the **Vertical File Index**. It will not solve all your heading problems. In the first place, it incorporates a fairly small list of subject headings. Furthermore, the range of subject headings is spotty since it reflects only the pamphlets which happen to be selected for each issue. With the discontinuance of the annual compilations, it is harder to use the **Vertical File Index** as a heading tool: it is now necessary to browse through separate monthly issues in an effort to find appropriate suggestions.

Most headings in the **Vertical File Index** are specific and contemporary but, occasionally, subject choices are included which are either very general or very traditional in tone.

This means that selectivity should be your motto in using subject designations from **Vertical File Index**. A heading such as "Charitable uses, trusts and foundations" has an impressive ring, but it's hardly what I would recommend for a vertical file.

The staunchest friend of a librarian in search of vertical file headings is the **Readers' Guide to Periodical Literature.** Its coverage is broad and current. Because it deals with magazine articles, it must provide for detailed subject entries.

Until recently the **Readers' Guide** was burdened with a good many awkward and outmoded headings. Fortunately, there has been a crash program within the last few years to update these antiquities. For example, "Children, Backward" has disappeared, to be replaced by "Slow learning children." However, **Readers' Guide** still contains some unnecessarily oblique or faded terms. As of this moment it is still using:

"Mental hygiene" for mental health

"International correspondence" for pen pals

"Group relations training" for sensitivity training

"Treasure troves" for treasure hunting

Nor are all the subject headings used in **Readers' Guide** clearly delineated in meaning or consistent in form. If you look up material on hiking, you'll find it buried under "Walking." Ask any enthusiastic hiker if he considers these terms synonymous. It's also hard to understand why the inverted form, "Children, Handicapped," is retained when **Readers' Guide** employs regular word order for "Mentally handicapped children."

The wisest use of the **Readers' Guide** in selecting subject headings is as a guide and not as a commitment. It is a mistake to adopt any or all **Readers' Guide** headings without adjusting them to your concepts of clarity and to the peculiar needs of your resources and clients. Unfortunately, there are many libraries which rely so heavily on **Readers' Guide** that they don't even bother to create a subject heading index of their own. They simply use a duplicate volume of **Readers' Guide** as an index, checking the headings which they have activated. Headings chosen from later issues of **Readers' Guide** are penciled in this master book. One large library I have visited doesn't attempt to maintain even this type of record. Since all of its subject headings are copied from **Readers' Guide**, it assumes that staff and patrons can consult any issue for leads to its vertical files. The fact that many headings in the **Readers' Guide** have changed drastically doesn't seem to have struck home.

In creating subject headings for specialized subjects, it may be necessary to turn to specialized sources to establish valid terms. For example, the **Business Periodicals Index** is a good introduction to the vocabulary which is employed in commerce and industry. A few of the other specialized indexes which may be helpful are:

Applied Science & Technology Index
Art Index
Education Index
Public Affairs Information Service Bulletin

In coping with specialized topics, don't forget the basic reference books in these areas. Encyclopedias, handbooks, and dictionaries can often supply the background information or authoritative terminology you need to make a proper decision.

Despite all the professional aids you can muster, in the end you will be thrown on your own good judgment and ingenuity in choosing subject headings. There will be many times when you will have to deal with pamphlets and clippings long before the **Readers' Guide** gets around to admitting that such subjects even exist. Some of your choicest finds may be on minor topics which are beneath the notice of the standard indexing tools. In addition, there will always be the need to personalize subject headings to fit the contents of your files, the personality of your community, and even the phrasing of the requests you receive.

Assigning Subject Headings

A few easy principles and procedures can help you win this challenging game of wits.

The first rule is that one person should be in charge of assigning subject headings. This is not a job which can be parceled out to several staff members. To achieve a coordinated system, it is necessary to concentrate control with one individual who can work toward an overall view of the scheme and provide for the intermeshing of its many parts.

At a certification workshop sponsored by the Michigan State Library, I asked one group of participants to organize a local history file. In their report to the full workshop they took pains to stress their discovery that a committee is not a good medium for assigning subject headings.

While subject heading selection is a one-man job, this does not mean that the advice of other staff members should be ignored. They can often suggest pertinent cross references for which a need was demonstrated as they actually worked with the collection. They can also be good sounding boards when you encounter pamphlets that are difficult to categorize. I frequently poll the librarians in our department to see how they react to possible headings for stubborn materials. I do this because I hope to provide avenues of approach to these items that will be natural and logical to the people who will use them. A recent survey revealed that my co-workers would never think to look under "Products, New" which is the **Readers' Guide** heading. They unanimously declared that they would turn to "New products" instead. The latter heading is now in our files.

Good subject headings are always specific. This quality reflects the nature of the calls for help which we receive. The woman who wants to raise water lilies in a backyard pond is not interested in general flower growing. She has a very precise need in mind.

This natural emphasis on the specific has been magnified by the increasing sophistication and complexity of the world in which we live. While students five years ago were asking for material on drug addiction, today they have narrowed their requests to LSD, marijuana or amphetamine.

Specific headings are also more comfortable for patrons and inexperienced staff members who use the files. They can't always make the mental jump between the information they seek and generalized subject headings. Not everyone will think to look for bookcase plans under "Storage."

What about the embryonic collection of pamphlets and clippings that is just getting under way? What about the vertical files in a very small library? Aren't broad headings more logical in these circumstances? Broad headings do save time in assigning subjects and preparing index cards. They save supply money because fewer folders are used. When resources are skimpy, it's easy to leaf through general folders to find what is needed.

But a collection that is a living collection is also a growing collection. Sooner than you think, the time will arrive when your folders are literally bursting with riches. To make them manageable you will have to divide the contents. Wouldn't it be better to avoid as much of this disruption as possible by assigning specific headings in the beginning?

Good subject headings should always be simple and direct. Don't try to be elegant or scholarly. You'll just create intellectual smog. If you have a pamphlet on stump removal, it belongs under that stark, simple heading rather than an artificial euphemism.

In our files we've wiped out that cherished library phrase, "Architecture, Domestic." Instead we use the heading, "House plans," because this is the term in common usage. We have substituted "Pen pals" for "International correspondence" because every request we receive is phrased that way. Colloquialisms are a legitimate choice for subject headings if they help to provide easier access to the facts in your files.

While we're in the process of stamping out artificiality in subject headings, are you brave enough to go one step further? In our files we have eliminated the use of lowercase letters for names that laymen always capitalize. You won't find "Mother's day" in our collection of pamphlets and clippings. Our heading is "Mother's Day." Similarly, the FBI is proudly labeled "Federal Bureau of Investigation."

In the interest of simplicity and clarity, inverted subject headings should always be judged critically before they are employed. They were originally intended to emphasize key words and to bring affiliated subjects together but they often hinder more than they help. Awkward inversions such as "Mothers, Unmarried" and "Education, Higher" are prime examples. My pet peeve is "Buildings, Prefabricated." The artificiality of this inverted form is demonstrated by the fact that most people refer to these structures as "prefabs."

Also to be shunned is extreme reliance on subdivisions. There are many instances where subdivisions are necessary devices. For example, they provide a way of neatly separating the materials that accumulate on each country. But where subdivisions can be gracefully and sensibly changed to independent entries, this should be done. Why pyramid "Pets" into "Pets—Cats" and "Pets—Dogs" when these animals could be placed under direct headings? Now and then you may find it necessary to turn to a general pamphlet about pets to find the answer to a question on cats or dogs, but this is a pretty fragile excuse for building a hierarchy of headings under "Pets."

Subdivisions tend to become lengthy and convoluted. Let's suppose that your material on dogs is so extensive that it needs to be separated. If you use the generic approach, you may now find yourself with such overgrown headings as "Pets—Dogs—Care and training."

It is necessary to maintain currency in subject headings. As new nations emerge, or government agencies are renamed, or scientific terminology changes, or women like Jacqueline Kennedy remarry, your subject headings should reflect these shifts. The homemaker who wails that woman's work is never done has a counterpart in the librarian supervising files of pamphlets and clippings.

Subject headings should honestly reflect the contents of pamphlets and clippings. This means that the librarian must venture beyond the title or headline to determine what the text really covers. A little investigation before assigning a heading not only insures access to information but may save you embarrassment as well.

Inevitably you will find yourself faced with the problem of deciding what to do with a pamphlet that covers two subjects—both of which constitute important areas in your files. You can, of course, arbitrarily decide on one heading and ignore the other. Or you might toss the pamphlet into a very general heading where there is a good likelihood that it will be overlooked completely. A happier solution is to obtain a second copy and cover both approaches. Or you might photocopy portions to provide for placement under the second heading. Isn't this an expensive solution? No more costly than using staff time to agonize over the dilemma.

One word of caution, however! If you duplicate material under two headings, be sure to note on each item the location of the other copy.

When you chance upon one of these supplementary sources at some distant date, you won't have to wonder if you assigned the right heading to convey its dual nature. You will immediately be reminded that you covered all possibilities. The simple notation becomes a great time-saver.

When a new edition of these bifurcated pamphlets is issued, you can make do with a single copy. Place the latest edition under the more popular heading. Leave the older issue under the alternate subject but add a note referring the user to the new edition.

A great deal of time and mental anguish can be saved by an "authority file" which records decisions and directions about subject headings that are troublesome or confusing. Memories are short. Staffs change. An authority file can serve both as a quick refresher for an established librarian and a helpful orientation for a newcomer.

With the help of this file you can define once and for always what will go under "Food" and what will go under "Nutrition" in your collection.

Ideally, the authority file and the index to your holdings should be combined. It's possible to give hints on the index cards themselves about policy decisions. For example, the index card for "Motels" might carry this note: "For material covering both motels and hotels SEE Hotels." However, authority explanations are often too lengthy to squeeze on index cards. For this reason, it would be much better to record your policy decisions and directions on cards of a different color which would stand directly behind the corresponding index entries.

For the novice setting up a brand-new file or reorganizing a tired old file the best procedure is to start with the easy and obvious subject headings. As you gather confidence and experience, you will be able to venture into more precarious areas.

Novice and veteran alike must avoid becoming so possessed by a subject heading system that it turns into a master and not a servant. Don't be afraid to make changes and violate patterns if these deviations will better represent your resources.

Indexes

An index to the subject headings employed in pamphlet and clipping files is essential. Some librarians who are hunting for shortcuts insist that an alphabetical file is self-indexing and needs no separate record. They point out that even cross references can be self-contained by recording them on the file folders or on separate guide cards. This is the sort of shortcut that turns out to be the long way home. An alphabetical file is self-indexing only so long as no one is allowed to remove items from it. The moment you pull a folder the file loses its authority as an index. Using the file itself for an index also causes excessive wear and tear on the librarian. In assigning subject designations to pamphlets or clippings, you would find yourself trotting back and forth to the files to refresh your recollection of headings. The wear and tear on file drawers is greater, too, when users must trace down the correct heading by opening and closing file cases rather than consulting a separate index.

A card index is preferable to a book index. It is admittedly easy to flick one's eyes down a page of headings to get a clear view of subdivisions or associated headings. But book indexes are not capable of absorbing quantities of new subject headings. Notes are soon penciled in every odd bit of free space and using the book index becomes equivalent to working one's way through a maze. The alternative is to retype the book index frequently which is a very costly process.

A card index is an open-ended structure. It can be added to indefinitely. Corrections are easy to make, too.

Normally, each subject heading is represented by a separate card. The one exception which is often made is in the area of political entities. A great expenditure of time and space is involved when separate cards are typed for each subject entry under each country in the world. Since these subheadings are uniform, librarians often substitute a series of master cards on which they indicate all the countries for which a heading has been activated. A similar pattern can be followed for subdivisions under the states. These master cards should not be interfiled, but placed in a special section at the end of the index. Card stock of a special color may be used to distinguish them.

```
Education

    Brazil
    Canada
    France
    Great Britain
```

Cross references employing the common directions, "SEE" and "SEE ALSO," should be a prominent feature of your card index. If a topic calls for several cross references, they are placed on a single card. Typical cross reference cards are shown on page 62.

```
Footwear    SEE    Shoes
```

```
First aid
    SEE ALSO    Artificial respiration
                Snakes
```

As you can see, these samples do not follow the indentations or spacing traditionally used on cross reference cards. This revised format was adopted for our indexes because of its clarity. We type "SEE" and "SEE ALSO" in **red** capital letters for added impact.

To prevent blind leads when headings are eliminated, tracings should be recorded on the back of each subject card, indicating the references from other headings to this particular entry.

Don't be stingy in your inclusion of cross references. People's minds are as varied as their fingerprints. What seems perfectly obvious to you may be obscure to your co-worker. Try to provide for all possible roads that others might travel in getting to the heading you've selected. This may even mean stretching logic a bit. For example, I have a reference in my index which reads "Fish SEE ALSO Shellfish" even though I know that technically this is a faulty referral. But in common parlance the difference between fish and shellfish becomes blurred.

Good sense must be used in recording cross references. They may sometimes be entirely too numerous to list. In this event, use a blanket referral.

```
Diseases
     SEE ALSO    Names of individual diseases
```

Some librarians suggest making cross references based on the contents of individual pamphlets or clippings rather than on the logical relationship between subject headings. We have a booklet on awnings which contains an unexpected but useful section on cabanas. These librarians would make a cross reference from "Cabanas" to "Awnings" on the basis of these few pages in a single pamphlet. This is a dangerous practice. If you use cross references to lead to isolated pamphlets or clippings rather than to normally allied subjects, you are destroying the integrity of the subject headings. When the items you've singled out for special treatment are lost or discarded, the artificial references become meaningless gibberish because they have no intrinsic validity. Cross references must be based on a natural relationship between subjects and not on temporary expediency.

Our solution in the example noted was to photocopy the section on cabanas and place it directly under that heading. Instead we might have placed a note inside the folder on "Cabanas" suggesting that the awning booklet be consulted. Either of these procedures would allow the subject headings to retain their long-term reliability.

Cross references can legitimately be used to lead beyond the confines of the vertical files. For example, our index card for "Pen pals" indicates that the material in the files can be supplemented by consulting the magazine, **Pack-O-Fun**, which has a column listing pen pals.

If it is at all possible, "SEE ALSO" references should be added to the fronts of the folders in your files. This will eliminate trips back to the index to check on supplementary headings. If desired, "SEE" references can also be inserted on separate guide cards.

To round out the picture of library resources offered by the card catalog, some libraries insert cards calling attention to subject headings for which there is vertical file material. Usually these catalog cards are provided in addition to the special index to pamphlets and clippings. Occasionally they replace the separate index entirely.

In most libraries, the referral entries in the card catalog are interfiled alphabetically with the book cards.

This common alphabetizing calls for some way of distinguishing between the resources and their locations. The subject entries for supplementary sources may be typed on colored cards or cards which are color-banded at the top. The words, "Vertical file" or "Information file." may be typed or stamped at the top left side of the card. On the other hand, the referral card might read like this:

Greenhouses

For additional information on this subject, consult the vertical files.

The differences in the headings chosen for books and supplementary sources do not present insurmountable difficulties. There are ways of compensating for these discrepancies if you want to use the card catalog to publicize your vertical files. One solution would be to house the vertical file references in a separate tray in the card catalog. Or you can adjust the wording of the referral cards to make up for the differences. If books on resumes are entered under "Applications for positions" and you are using the direct heading in your vertical files, the referral card might look like this:

Applications for positions

    For more material on this subject, SEE the folder on "Resumes" in the vertical files.

Another solution might be to evade any mention of the vertical file headings and use this general instruction instead:

Applications for positions

    For pamphlets and clippings on this subject, SEE the reference librarian.

The inclusion of supplementary source headings in the general catalog is a favorite technique of school librarians who want to create a "unit" catalog which melds all media. It is also useful in public libraries where the card catalog is in a separate room from that housing pamphlet resources.

However, serious questions can be raised about the need for such entries in a small public library where the vertical files are very obvious and where the same librarian services both books and supplementary sources. Under such circumstances, some librarians suggest that a large placard or poster calling attention to the vertical files is a more economical approach.

CHAPTER 4

PAMPHLETS: THE BROAD VIEW

What is a pamphlet? It's anything you want to think of as a pamphlet. There is no agreement even among authorities as to the definition. **The Random House Dictionary of the English Language** describes a pamphlet as "a complete, unbound publication of generally less than 80 pages stitched or stapled together." On the other hand UNESCO says, "A pamphlet is a non-periodical printed publication of at least 5 but not more than 48 pages, exclusive of the cover pages..." **Webster's Third New International Dictionary** carefully straddles the issue by defining a pamphlet as "an unbound publication other than a periodical having fewer than a fixed number (as 50, 80, 100) of pages..."

In practical terms, treatment seems to count more than format. If you treat a publication like a pamphlet, it becomes a pamphlet to all intents and purposes. And the decision as to treatment should be based on what type of handling will make the publication most useful.

Despite emphasis on number of pages as a distinguishing feature, this criterion is ignored in most libraries. A one-page flyer may get pamphlet treatment. At the other extreme, our vertical files contain several husky paperback books that deal with elusive subjects.

It's equally important to be flexible in determining the classes of materials that can be described as "pamphlets." In actual operation, a "pamphlet" collection may encompass such oddities as trade catalogs, government documents, annual reports, travel brochures, school catalogs, sample magazines, and bulletins. To demonstrate how broad this interpretation can be, we incorporate announcements from national lecture bureaus in our "pamphlet" holdings. Once again, potential usefulness is the test.

The guides to supplementary sources discussed in Chapter 1 will be of great comfort in locating conventional pamphlets as well as the more unusual items that masquerade as pamphlets. But even more essential than good guides is a keeper of the files who is prepared to search out and welcome useful material, no matter how or where it makes its appearance.

The paragraphs that follow will delineate some of the special resources that can be treated as pamphlets.

GOVERNMENT DOCUMENTS

Government documents represent a mother lode of informational gold. If your mind is conditioned to thinking of government documents as indigestible studies or obscure reports, take a second look.

The federal government provides authoritative pamphlets on everything from raising guinea pigs to obtaining a small business loan. Not only are they authoritative, but they're excellent bargains as well. The number of topics covered by federal publications is astronomical. A beautiful booklet on harpsichords and clavichords from the Smithsonian shares the rank of government document with a no-nonsense pamphlet on septic tanks. Statistical reports are a specialty of the federal agencies. Many times they present figures that are unobtainable elsewhere. Good examples are the statistical summaries on Indian education and health published by the Bureau of Indian Affairs.

State governments are also active in publishing a wide range of documents. As well as those which give you insight into your own state's present and past, state documents can be concerned with such everyday practicalities as building picnic tables, recognizing edible wild mushrooms, coping with childhood diseases, or raising a good crop of strawberries.

A touch of imagination pays off in acquiring government publications. For example, copies of hotly debated laws make star additions to a "pamphlet" collection. The recent federal gun control act is typical. Individual printings can be obtained long before bound volumes of the laws are available. Furthermore, they can be circulated to interested patrons.

Don't forget that documents from foreign governments can add depth and richness to your pamphlet holdings. The Canadian Department of External Affairs (31) has even compiled a bibliography of English-language publications which are available for sale or free distribution to persons and organizations outside Canada.

TRADE CATALOGS

Trade catalogs are an appropriate embellishment of a supplementary source service.

In our library we have a sizable collection of garden catalogs from leading nurseries and seed firms. We attempt to include choice items such as catalogs of wild flowers, rock plants, and water lilies. We make a point of trying to represent firms headquartered in our part of the country. This collection serves a twofold purpose. It keeps our green-thumb set happy and it functions as a reference tool for the library staff in identifying trees, shrubs, and flowers. Most of these catalogs can be obtained free although a few special publications such as Wayside Gardens' famous catalog require a fee.

Mail-order catalogs of the "wishbook" variety form another island of interest in our library. Not only do we watch for such obvious favorites as the Miles Kimball catalog, but we also seek out publicity from folkcraft sources. For example, we have a catalog from Liberty House in Jackson, Mississippi which sells handcrafted products made by poor people from all over the world. We also have the **Fact Sheets (94)** from the U.S. Department of the Interior which list sources of Indian and Eskimo arts and crafts.

Because these collections of garden and mail-order catalogs are quite distinct and quite extensive, we house them in pamphlet boxes. We've found that patrons like to browse through these boxes.

Needless to say, we solicit and save the huge mail-order catalogs such as Sears', but these are processed as books in our library and are housed with other books.

Specialized trade catalogs are sprinkled throughout our vertical files. Many varieties are represented—for example, school supplies, electronics, scientific equipment, and agricultural paraphenalia. Nor are hobby interests ignored. We have catalogs that concentrate on model trains, plastic crafts, jewelry making, and needlework. These catalogs are filed by subject among the other "pamphlets" in the vertical files.

Most libraries, big and small, collect publishers' catalogs. These are usually kept in the department or closed area devoted to book ordering. I would urge, however, that catalogs for skits and plays be housed in a more accessible place since they are in demand by schools, clubs, and amateur theaters. Catalogs for large-print books should also be readily available since they will be consulted by patrons who want to choose gifts for friends or relatives.

Your involvement with trade catalogs can be as modest or as extensive as your needs warrant. Special libraries often scour the field for all available catalogs in their interest areas. Large libraries with business and technology sections sometimes build up collections of thousands of trade catalogs. Where such extensive concentrations of catalogs are involved, they are usually housed separately in files or on shelves. Arrangement can be by manufacturer's name or by subject. Indexes are often developed to cover all angles of approach.

SCHOOL CATALOGS

No public or secondary school library is living up to its obligations if it doesn't have a collection of college and technical school catalogs that is both up-to-date and widely representative.

With enrollments and production costs soaring, institutions of higher learning do not distribute their catalogs to individuals as generously as they once did. This restriction makes the library collection all the more important. Although there are a few exceptions, colleges and universities normally furnish catalogs to libraries free of charge.

Catalogs, bulletins, and announcements from vocational and correspondence schools can be as important to your patrons as those from the most prestigious universities. Locating such schools and discriminating among them is a challenging job. The first and best course of action to follow is to contact your state department of education for a list of trade, technical, business, and correspondence schools approved to operate in the state.

Educational associations in these fields which have been recognized as accrediting agencies by the U.S. Office of Education will provide lists of their approved schools. Among these are the National Association of Trade and Technical Schools (123), the National Home Study Council (129), and the United Business Schools Association (180)

Publishers have released directories of vocational schools from time to time which can be helpful in ordering catalogs. There is a problem in updating these directories frequently enough to keep pace with this ever-changing field. **Lovejoy's Career and Vocational School Guide (108)** is revised only at lengthy intervals. Croner Publications, Inc. issues a loose-leaf list, the **American Trade Schools Directory (10)**, which it does attempt to keep current by an amendment service. Chronicle Guidance Publications is going to enter this market sometime in 1970 with a new guide.

If you are completely stumped in locating training schools for a particular trade, write to a labor union or trade association in the field. Methods of discovering such organizations are discussed in the chapter on vocational materials.

If there are well-known military or boarding schools in your region, you may need to represent these schools, too, among your catalogs.

In collecting information about educational institutions, your first obligation is to achieve blanket coverage in your own area. Next make a concentrated canvass of your state. Finally, spread your nets for important schools across the nation and even in foreign countries. Community interest is the key factor in deciding how thorough your inclusion of distant schools should be.

Because their numbers will be large, school catalogs should be housed separately from other supplementary sources. College catalogs are usually arranged alphabetically. Ignore the generic term, "university," in alphabetizing them. Special types of educational institutions such as military and preparatory schools should be kept together for easy consultation. Trade and technical schools are most usable if grouped by the kind of instruction offered.

A card file that is a combination of source list, shelf list, and index will expedite maintenance and use of the school catalog collection. This device is particularly essential if catalogs are allowed to circulate. Cards are arranged alphabetically by name of the school. Addresses should be indicated to facilitate future orders. Any unusual ordering procedures should be noted. Information essential to proper labeling and housing should be specified. Finally, a record of the catalogs, bulletins, and announcements currently in the collection should be added in concise form.

There is no need to keep older issues of catalogs unless they represent local schools. In this case, you may choose to establish a long run as part of your community history collection.

ANNUAL REPORTS

Annual reports are available from such diverse sources as the American National Red Cross, the FBI, and General Motors. As founts of information about organizations, businesses, and government agencies, annual reports possess a potential for usefulness in two directions. The current report provides a contemporary picture of the body and its activities. On the other hand, a series of reports spanning a period of years reflect the evolution of the body.

How many years you choose to represent should be determined by the character of the requests you receive. In many cases only the latest issue will be required to give sufficient insight into the nature of the issuing body. A one-year limit is especially easy to enforce if the current report summarizes statistics from several previous years. A longer run of annual reports may be desirable if each edition presents important and unique material that is not repeated elsewhere. Certainly, annual reports originating from local sources should be considered for long-term preservation.

While annual reports are useful for the information they furnish about their sponsors, they have another role to play in public libraries which should not be overlooked. They can serve as patterns for institutions, organizations, or firms that want samples to follow in planning their own reports.

Larger libraries often become involved in very extensive collections of annual reports from businesses and industries. The theory behind such collections is that they will be studied by investors and job hunters. A small library should exercise caution before plunging into such a project. It's true that the reports are free, but they do require time to solicit and maintain. Unless you're willing to go all-out in soliciting these reports, your collection will prove more frustrating than helpful. Nine times out of ten, the company you're asked about will be one you don't have represented. Small libraries might well limit themselves to collecting a representative group of annual reports to serve as models for local businesses and industries. It's another matter as far as the reports of firms in your community are concerned. These should be collected intensively.

Secondary school libraries may want to acquire annual reports from some of the corporate giants to assist classes that make mock investments in the stock market as part of their study of economics.

REPRINTS AND TRANSCRIPTS

Reprints can be utilized in two ways.

They may reproduce sections of resources that the library already owns. Reprints of this type may be acquired to help meet the demand for material on popular subjects. Another reason for adding such reprints is to make circulation of the information possible.

On the other hand, reprints may represent resources which the library does *not* own. In this case, reprints permit the library to make a discriminating selection of items from a tool which could not otherwise be easily consulted.

Reprints are available from a variety of periodicals ranging from highly specialized publications like **Chemical Engineering and Modern Manufacturing** to more popular magazines such as **Look, Harvest Years,** and **Nation's Business.**

Techniques for keeping up with reprints must vary with the periodical. A note at the end of the article will indicate when **Nation's Business** can provide reprints of a particular feature. Each issue of **Chemical Engineering** contains a list of available reprints. **Modern Manufacturing** touches on certain reprints each month but will send a complete listing on request. **Look** does not print a catalog of its reprints. Instead, it suggests watching for entries in **Vertical File Index (192)** and in **Free and Inexpensive Learning Materials (72)** from George Peabody College for Teachers. References to the reprints offered by **Harvest Years** are found in the pages of the magazine. You can also write to the publisher for a leaflet about the reprints.

An interesting duplication project is being carried on by **Popular Mechanics** which offers photocopies of the "most exciting and useful" articles that have appeared in the magazine over the past several years. Write to **Popular Mechanics** for a list of available reproductions.

An extensive collection of **Scientific American** offprints are for sale by W.H. Freeman and Company **(73)**. These faithful reproductions are particularly useful in libraries serving science students. Send to W.H. Freeman and Company for a free catalog.

The federal government provides for reprints of articles that have appeared in some of its periodicals. Reprints from **American Education** and the **Department of State Bulletin** are for sale by the Superintendent of Documents, but you are likely to obtain free copies by writing directly to the publishing agencies which are, respectively, the Office of Education and the U.S. Department of State. Reprints of certain key articles in the **Monthly Labor Review** are available free of charge from the Bureau of Labor Statistics of the U. S. Department of Labor.

Encyclopedia publishers are not as generous as they once were about furnishing reprints of articles from their sets. Field Enterprises Educational Corporation still offers an interesting list of reprints from **World Book Encyclopedia** and they are willing to provide single copies free to librarians. A few reprints from **Compton's Encyclopedia** are for sale.

Reprints available in the area of vocations are discussed in the special chapter on that subject.

Transcripts of radio or TV programs have a contribution to make if they are selected judiciously. Be particularly cautious with interview programs such as **Meet the Press (113).** This format with its broken continuity is very disconcerting to some patrons. Center your choice on subjects that are of great interest or that are lacking in adequate coverage.

Some transcripts such as **Yale Reports (201)** and **Meet the Press** are listed in **Vertical File Index.** Others take a bit of exploration to discover.

New developments in the field of science are well-covered by the transcripts from three radio programs. One is **Men and Molecules (114)** sponsored by the American Chemical Society. The transcripts of these broadcasts are available free of charge. The other programs are **The University Explorer** and **Science Editor,** both of which originate at the University of California **(189).** Transcripts from these programs sell for 25 cents each. Subscriptions are also available.

MAGAZINES AND NEWSLETTERS

Yes, there's a place for these alien resources in the vertical files. Under certain circumstances they masquerade nicely as pamphlets.

When a library cannot afford to subscribe to specialized periodicals, sample issues in the vertical files will serve a double purpose. They can be examined by patrons who want to subscribe to magazines in special interest fields. These trial copies also function as reference sources since the ads, feature columns, and terminology represented in even a single issue can be instructive. In our files we have incorporated samples of such specialized magazines as the **Western Horseman**, the **Antique Trader Weekly**, and **Hunting Dog**. Sample magazines are furnished to us free of charge by publishers or contributed by staff and patrons. They are filed by subject.

Newsletters or regularly released bulletins may also be absorbed into the vertical file when a library desires to preserve a few late issues rather than maintain a longer run. When a new release arrives, the oldest copy in the files is discarded. Among the publications which we house in this short-term, revolving fashion are the **National Humane Newsletter** of the American Humane Association, the **American Foundation for the Blind Newsletter, What's New in Co-op Information** from the Cooperative League, and the Chase Manhattan Bank's **Petroleum Situation**. These newsletters and bulletins are arranged by subject in our files.

Similar treatment may be given the newsletters and bulletins which are available for the asking from the information services and chambers of commerce representing various foreign countries. Typical of these publications are **News from Sweden** released by the Swedish Information Service, **Spanish Newsletter** from the Information Department of the Embassy of Spain, **Venezuela Up-to-date** from the Information Service of the Embassy of Venezuela, and **Netherlands-North American Trade** from the Netherlands Chamber of Commerce in the United States.

TRAVEL LEAFLETS

Travel leaflets do more than merely entice the vacationer to distant spots. They can also help to answer reference questions. Every public librarian knows the tourist who was so busy taking slides that he neglected to jot down any identification of the scenes. Travel leaflets may help to solve this dilemma. They can also assist with many other types of information such as ferry schedules, opening dates of tourist attractions, admission fees, and insert maps of parks or recreation areas. My favorite example of travel reference concerns a local family that was hosting a foreign student. They wanted to take her with them on a short trip to Canada but didn't know if she would be allowed to cross the border and return. We found the answer in travel literature which the Canadian Government Travel Bureau had sent to us.

Since travel material will be needed both by the public and the staff, accumulate it generously and update it frequently.

As well as the customary leaflets, try to acquire schedules for the airlines and railroads that serve your area. Collect material on steamship cruises, summer study programs abroad, and student travel arrangements. In addition to covering standard attractions, be alert to special developments such as world's fairs which call for a concerted effort to collect literature. Road maps are a helpful addition to the travel collection. They are discussed in detail in Chapter 8.

Fortunately, there are many groups and agencies which are eager to furnish information on travel attractions.

On the national level the U.S. Department of the Interior deserves praise for the publicity efforts carried on by its National Park Service (130). The numerous descriptive folders which the Service releases on national parks, monuments, recreation areas, historic sites, seashores, riverways, and lakeshores are invaluable. They are concise, authoritative, and specific. Insert maps are featured. While a number of these leaflets carry a price tag and are for sale by the Superintendent of Documents, the National Park Service will place libraries on a free mailing list.

Much more elaborate in nature are the **Historical Handbooks** produced by the National Park Service. While they do include some information about current status, their primary purpose is to furnish background information about the historic sites which the National Park Service administers. Pictures and maps add to their effectiveness. They should be as fascinating to travelers as to history buffs. Write for a list of titles and prices.

Another agency within the Department of the Interior is active in publishing booklets about national wildlife refuges. These publications from the Bureau of Sport Fisheries and Wildlife (28) in the Fish and Wildlife Service not only describe the wildlife and the area, but also indicate recreational opportunities. Maps are included. Although the Government Printing Office stocks many of these titles for sale, libraries will want to approach the Bureau directly for free copies.

The Forest Service (69) of the U.S. Department of Agriculture is responsible for a wealth of material about recreational use of the national forests. While publications of a general nature originate with the national headquarters, the Regional Offices and the individual forest supervisors carry on their own publishing programs as well, turning out excellent maps and descriptive textual material that is distributed free of charge. Forest Service headquarters in Washington, D.C. will provide you with a list of addresses for Forest Service Regional Offices. This list also indicates the cities in which national forests have their headquarters but for exact addresses of forest supervisors you will have to contact the Regional Offices.

State chambers of commerce make good contacts for travel literature. State governmental agencies are also productive sources. Titles and jurisdictions vary from state to state. The responsibility for encouraging travel may rest with such bodies as a tourist council, a state development board, or the state department of commerce. Parks departments or departments of conservation often have excellent material to distribute on park areas, picnic grounds, and campgrounds. Agencies which supervise water resources may have printed information on water access sites or canoe trails. Game and fish commissions will furnish guides to hunting and fishing possibilities and regulations.

As well as statewide groups, there often are regional organizations that can be tapped for literature. For example, in Michigan we have such groups as the West Michigan Tourist Association and the Southeast Michigan Tourist Association.

Travel material about individual cities can be obtained from local chambers of commerce. Convention and visitors bureaus are also promising sources.

A wealth of material about foreign countries is available through their travel offices in the United States. Embassies and consulates may also be approached.

Your patrons and your staff can be cultivated as sources of travel literature, too. The descriptive material they acquire on their journeys can be choice additions to your collection since many booklets or leaflets are distributed or sold only at the site of a tourist attraction.

There are shortcuts and tricks-of-the-trade which will make it easier for the librarian to take advantage of the many agencies distributing travel literature.

Many of the supplementary source guides described in Chapter 1 contain lengthy lists of contacts for travel material.

New publications about the travel areas administered by the National Park Service and the Bureau of Sport Fisheries and Wildlife are likely to be listed in **Selected United States Government Publications (164)**. **Price List 35, National Parks, Historic Sites, National Monuments (150)** surveys documents on these subjects which were available in the Government Printing Office at the time of going to press. A free copy of the price list can be obtained from the Superintendent of Documents. Another price list which contains leads to federally published material about tourist attractions and recreational resources is **Price List 87, States and Territories of the United States and Their Resources (150)**. This list, too, is distributed free by the Superintendent of Documents.

On the state level, leads can be obtained from the **Monthly Checklist of State Publications (120)**. In addition, the Chamber of Commerce of the United States publishes a guide called **Sources of State Information and State Industrial Directories (35)** which is very helpful in pinpointing state contacts. A new edition is due to be published early in 1971. While the old edition carried a charge of 40 cents, our library was able to obtain a free copy.

In collecting material about individual communities, a handy list of addresses is furnished in the **World Wide Chamber of Commerce Directory (200)**. This guide is published annually by the Johnson Publishing Co., Inc. While its most important feature is the access it offers to local chambers of commerce, the directory includes references to state chambers of commerce as well. It also provides coverage of an international nature. The price of the 1970 edition is $4.00.

Another tool which cuts across several levels—national, state, and regional—is **Guides to Outdoor Recreation Areas and Facilities (26)** published in 1968 by the Bureau of Outdoor Recreation of the U.S. Department of the Interior. This 116-page publication will alert you to recreation guides produced by private, state, and federal organizations. You can obtain a free copy from the Bureau.

There are several source lists which concentrate entirely on the international scene. Trans World Airlines, Inc. **(177)** issues a free directory of offices in the United States which represent the various countries of the world. The Office of Public Information of the United Nations distributes without charge a publication titled **Information Services and Embassies in the United States of Members of the United Nations (181)**. The Chamber of Commerce of the United States is releasing a new edition of its **Guide to Foreign Information Sources (35)** in the summer of 1970. Although the earlier edition sold for 25 cents, our library was furnished with a free copy. Still another source to contact for assistance about foreign countries is the **European Travel Commission (60)**.

Of course, any library that owns a copy of the **Congressional Directory (41)** has at hand a full listing of foreign embassies in the United States.

Our neighbor to the north is particularly outstanding among foreign governments for the quantity and quality of its travel publications. To facilitate use, the Canadian Government Travel Bureau has issued a special list called **Publications and Posters (32)** which records the tourist material that it has for distribution.

The ads in travel oriented magazines can provide productive leads to travel literature. Such periodicals as **Holiday, Sunset, Travel**, and **Travel & Camera** are especially rich in possibilities. The travel sections in newspapers also are sprinkled with ads for free materials.

Frequently, travel articles in both magazines and newspapers will specify sources of literature or single out booklets of special merit.

Some libraries with minuscule holdings in the field try to treat "Travel" as just another division in the general files, with a breakdown provided by geographic regions. However, a travel collection of any significance will soon outgrow this arrangement. Separate housing is desirable. In our library we shelve our tremendous travel collection in pamphlet boxes that are open at the top for easy visibility and accessibility. Patrons are quickly attracted to this center.

PRINCIPLES OF SELECTION

Much of the material that we've lumped under the heading of "pamphlets" originates as advertising or publicity. This fact makes some librarians uneasy.

The trick is to guard against the crass sales pitch but to be quick to salvage anything of potential value no matter how "commercial" its origins.

The test that any pamphlet must meet before achieving acceptance is how much it will contribute to the collection.

In our files we have booklets from manufacturers of plumbing fixtures which contain excellent pictorial material on bathroom design. We also have information on planning a luau from nationally known food processors as well as from a firm specializing in Hawaiian decorations. It's true that brand names appear in the recipe ingredients and the Hawaiian decorations are clearly for sale, but the American public has learned to pick the diamonds from among the pebbles when it comes to this type of advertising material. And they are much too sophisticated to conclude that the library is in any way endorsing these products.

I am strengthened in my flexibility by the realization that most printed material contains some element of salesmanship. A booklet issued by a government agency to describe its activities and goals will be carefully edited to present a favorable image. Publications designed to attract new industry to a state are going to concentrate on the more attractive aspects. Pamphlets issued by professional groups to encourage career recruitment among young people are likely to paint a highly complimentary picture.

The apprehension which librarians once felt about pamphlets on "controversial" subjects has diminished. In an era when junior high school students are writing papers on abortion and tenth-graders are studying homosexuality, there is less need for trepidation in most communities.

The one cautionary principle that has survived the years intact is to present a variety of viewpoints on touchy subjects. If you have a good collection in favor of fluoridation, try to obtain some material from those who oppose it. Despite the tired old library cliches, it is literally impossible to represent *all* points of view about every controversial issue. But you can attempt to represent the major ones.

Years ago it was quite common to mark pamphlets with a warning to the patron when they were considered to be "propaganda" for a particular cause. That practice has declined as a result of the American Library Association's strong stand against labeling.

The librarian's best defense against charges of conveying propaganda is the variety of interpretations he includes in his files. I am, however, a complete realist. I know that in some communities this technique will not furnish adequate protection. If labeling must be used, the least harmful method is to apply a note to the folder using words to this effect:

There are differing points of view about this subject. The library has attempted to represent some of them in the material in this folder.

Despite his dedication to the freedom to read, the librarian must never abandon the need to critically assess material on controversial subjects. Is the issuing source clearly identified? Anonymous material of this nature should never be added to the files. The patron has a right to know what individual or group is presenting these opinions. In the body of the pamphlet does the writer identify his stand openly and honestly so that the reader can judge his comments and information sources accordingly? Does the pamphlet attempt an intellectual approach rather than a purely emotional one?

Assessing community needs is important in choosing pamphlets just as it is in choosing books, but it is essential not to interpret these needs too narrowly when building your pamphlet resources. The small expenditure of money and space involved will allow you to venture into areas that are impossible to represent in your book holdings. It is a mistake to devote your entire pamphlet collection to what is immediately and constantly popular. The vertical file offers you a golden opportunity to explore the back roads of information. A pamphlet that tells how to estimate the board foot volume of trees in a woodlot may not be called for every day. But when a patron does ask for this information, his need is real and immediate. He will go away marveling at the crackerjack librarian who was able to produce the necessary facts at a moment's notice.

School librarians are particularly prone to fall into the trap of restricting pamphlet acquisition to narrow limits. Certain school libraries acquire only material that is curriculum related. This rigid delineation may help to cut the time and money invested in the vertical files. Unfortunately, it will also help to convince students that libraries are agencies useful only with school assignments and not with their needs as complete and independent human beings.

As libraries become more aware of groups with special needs within their communities, they will be comforted to know that pamphlet material is being developed both at the federal and state level to help these groups. Simple pamphlets with controlled vocabularies are being distributed by cooperative extension services in several states to assist people with limited reading ability. The federal government is also reacting to the need for easy-to-read material. For example, the Social Security Administration has just released a group of guides which deal in simple terms with such matters as receiving cash tips or working in someone's home.

The special requirements of Spanish-speaking citizens are also being recognized. **Price List 86, Consumer Information (150)** contains an appendix devoted to consumer publications available in Spanish. This price list is distributed without charge by the Superintendent of Documents. State agencies are also active in providing Spanish-language materials. Some cooperative extension services publish homemaking leaflets in Spanish. Driving manuals rewritten in Spanish are distributed by some state agencies in charge of driver licensing.

Before choosing pamphlets, it might be helpful to take a course in fortune-telling or at least market analysis. For the librarian must predict future swells of interest in order to be prepared for them. When the first inklings reached us of the burgeoning interest in decoupage, we began to scour the field for material. Long before environmental control became as popular a topic of discussion as the weather, we were building a hefty collection of pamphlets on the subject.

Librarians must do some fancy divining for another reason. Sadly but understandably, publishers sometimes try to disguise or ignore the advancing age of their releases. The passage of the years does little to affect the value of a pamphlet on the first Thanksgiving, but time erodes the usefulness of materials about changing topics such as industrial development. Watch for evidence of copyright dates.

In selecting materials for the pamphlet files, librarians need to be aware of the regional flavor of much printed information. For example, cooperative extension services issue helpful booklets on flower gardening, but the librarian must remember that rose growing in California is not the same as rose growing in Minnesota. Career booklets published by the employment services of the various states will reflect conditions peculiar to the area. Yet it's a mistake to be too rigidly bound by geographical boundaries. To use Kalamazoo as an example, an unusual number of our residents winter in Florida. Because of the questions they bring home with them, we've eagerly acquired pamphlets on aspects of life in Florida which theoretically are beyond our scope.

Decisions about duplicating pamphlets must be based on the popularity of the subject, the value of the publications, and the type of library involved.

School libraries have the greatest need for multiple copies yet they are often fainthearted about duplicating pamphlets even in areas where crushing demands exist. If mass assignments are regularly given on narcotics, the school library should be prepared with masses of pamphlets to meet the onslaught. If it is impossible to house heavily duplicated items in the vertical files, extra copies can be kept in reserve in storage areas. A note on the file folder will indicate that multiple copies are available.

PAMPHLET SERIES

In library circles the term, "pamphlet series," immediately calls to mind the well-established subscription services such as **Public Affairs Pamphlets** or **Editorial Research Reports**. Actually, these subscription services constitute only a portion of the output. There are many commercial publishers, associations, government agencies, and business interests engaged in producing pamphlets which are homogeneous enough in approach, subject matter, and format to be called pamphlet series. In the field of civic affairs the League of Women Voters publishes its **Facts & Issues** series (105). The National Better Business Bureau, Inc. (125) sponsors a **Consumer Information Series** as well as a series of **Fact Booklets**, all in the area of consumer education. The Chemical Bank New York Trust Company compiles in-depth studies of various countries under the series title, **International Economic Survey (37)**.

To meet school centered demands, the University of Minnesota Press has initiated a series of pamphlets on American writers while Columbia University Press has launched the **Columbia Essays on Modern Writers**. Also curriculum oriented is the new social studies pamphlet series from the Steck-Vaughn Company **(171)** which touches on such issues as McCarthyism and the rise of organized labor.

The federal government is the matrix for numerous pamphlet series including such famous ones as the Small Business Administration's **Small Business Management Series** and the Department of Agriculture's **Home and Garden Bulletins.**

This rapid run-down can do no more than hint at the hundreds of useful series which are available beyond the traditional subscription services.

As far as the subscription services are concerned, most of them need no introduction to librarians. Among the old favorites are:

> **Editorial Research Reports (53).** Published four times a month. $2.00 each. Annual subscription plus semiannual bound volumes containing additional material $108.
>
> > Excellent surveys on timely topics. Especially good for historical and statistical coverage.
>
> **Focus (67).** Published monthly except July and August. 85 cents each. Annual subscription $3.50.
>
> > Authoritative, concise, and thorough studies of countries of the world. Special emphasis on geographical and economic factors. While **Focus** is technically a periodical, each issue is an independent publication, focusing on a single geographic area. Therefore, it should be handled as a "pamphlet series."
>
> **Headline Series (88).** Published five times a year. $1.00 each. Annual subscription $5.00.
>
> > Primarily directed at world problems and relations between nations, but also covers the internal concerns of key countries. Scholarly.
>
> **Public Affairs Pamphlets (152).** About 15 pamphlets a year. 25 cents each. Subscription to 15 issues $3.50.
>
> > A long-established series which attempts to cover a wide range of social and personal concerns. Very readable. Likely to be asked for by series title. A fictionalized approach is sometimes used with imaginary characters and dialogue. This annoys some readers who are looking for cold facts.

Is it better to order pamphlets separately or to subscribe to an entire series? There's a calculated risk in placing a subscription. You may find yourself acquiring items in subject areas where your files are already well-stocked. Topics may be covered that have no pertinency at all for the clientele you serve. Quality may vary from release to release.

On the credit side, it's much cheaper to subscribe to some pamphlet series than to buy the publications separately. In addition, a subscription is a guarantee that you won't overlook important titles and that you will receive them promptly.

However, even the better-known series need to be reassessed carefully and constantly to make sure that they continue to fill your needs.

More attention will be given to specialized pamphlet series in later chapters.

When a library subscribes to a pamphlet series, some means should be provided for checking on their arrival. The schemes used for recording the receipt of magazines can usually be adapted for pamphlets.

As indicated in Chapter 3 there is no special virtue in housing a series of pamphlets together in isolated glory. They should be distributed by subject since most requests for pamphlets are subject requests.

CHAPTER 5

CLIPPINGS

SOURCES OF CLIPPINGS

Armed with no more than a keen eye, a lively imagination, and a sharp pair of scissors, any librarian can garner clippings that will add both breadth and detail to his collection.

Clipping Newspapers

Where does one turn first for clippings? To newspapers, of course. It's obvious that the local newspaper will be fertile ground for clippings about community events and personalities. To stop with local affairs would be a great mistake, for newspapers can be harvested for articles on all categories of knowledge.

A distinguishing aspect of newspaper coverage is that it often provides a degree of elaboration lacking in periodicals and yearbooks. A good example is the painstakingly detailed coverage that precedes a presidential inauguration. Newspapers thrive on the informational oddity that adds delight to a reference librarian's day.

And, of course, newspapers beat magazines to the punch with current news. If a librarian suspects that he will get questions about new developments such as awards or appointments, he would do well to clip the newspaper articles, at least for temporary consultation, since magazine coverage will lag behind and indexing in **Readers' Guide** will be even slower.

Special newspaper sections or columns devoted to sports, finance, homemaking, gardening, travel, and health should receive particular attention since they often produce prize clippings. We treasure the excerpt from a newspaper garden column which tells how to raise fruit on a homegrown pineapple plant. While most special columns will contribute occasional gems, some are regularly productive. One such column is "The Compleat Consumer" in the **National Observer** which offers frank, detailed surveys that supplement the material in the consumer magazines.

The rotogravure sections which are part of many Sunday editions are worth screening, too. It was a rotogravure section which furnished our files with a comprehensive article on cryonic internment, complete with the names of the people who lie frozen in cryonic suspension.

The "action" columns to which readers write for intervention or information are often clipable. They give detailed replies to such questions as these: Is there a service for "sending" cakes by wire just as flowers are sent by wire? Who designs the United States pavilions that are built at world's fairs and expositions?

Odd facts of this sort are hard to come by!

Clipping Unindexed Periodicals

The wealth of information incorporated in unindexed periodicals can be tapped only through a program of regular and generous clipping. Leafing through an issue of **Woman's Day** or **Family Circle** will demonstrate how much helpful material escapes the nets of the **Readers' Guide** and its companion indexes.

Possibilities are everywhere if you are receptive to them. For example, fraternal or club publications such as the **Kiwanis Magazine** and **Elks Magazine** can be used as clipping sources since they frequently include articles on topics of general public interest. Even that old standby, the **TV Guide**, can be clipped for hard-to-find information on entertainment personalities and new TV shows.

"House organs" published by various businesses, industries, and associations offer a rich potential for clipping. If the car owners on your staff don't receive copies of the **Dodge News Magazine** and the **Ford Times**, ask your local dealers to put your library on the mailing list. While the **Ford Times** concentrates primarily on travel and sports, the Dodge publication includes articles on many other topics as well. **Ward's Bulletin (193)** which is distributed by Ward's Natural Science Establishment, Inc. features articles related to biology and geology. The biological wonders of the Amazon basin and the discovery of a new gem stone named tanzanite are indicative of coverage in recent issues. Another area of scientific development is the focal point of the Radio Corporation of America's quarterly, **RCA Electronic Age (154)**.

Don't forget that "house organs" originating with nonprofit organizations are worth surveying, too. The **National Tuberculosis and Respiratory Disease Association Bulletin** and the American Cancer Society's **Cancer News** are representative of these publications.

Fortunately, the usual policy is to distribute house magazines free of charge.

For a descriptive sampling of house organs, consult "Appendix B" in **Magazines for Libraries** by Bill Katz **(100)**. This selection has been bolstered by a supplement which appeared on page 51 of **Library Journal** for January 1, 1970. A broad survey of thousands of the leading house magazines is provided in the **Gebbie House Magazine Directory (79)**. A new edition of this "bible of the house magazine field" is to be published at the beginning of 1971. While it is expensive ($24.95 for the 1968 edition), Gebbie's can function as a reference tool for the free-lance writers and businessmen in your community as well as guiding the library to useful house organs.

Financial institutions can help to enrich your files with periodical publications which are more in the nature of economic surveys than house magazines. **World Business (199)** published by the Chase Manhattan Bank and the **International Economic Review (66)** issued by the First National Bank of Chicago are first-rate sources for clippings on economic conditions around our globe. **Finance Facts (65)** from the National Consumer Finance

Association digests statistical trends in a manner which is easy for the layman to understand. It can be clipped for summaries of new information in such areas as population migration or the economic value of an education. Elementary and junior high school librarians will want to assess the clipping possibilities of periodicals published for these age levels. The **National Geographic School Bulletin (128)** is an example. Issued each week during the school year, this publication is distinguished by full-color illustrations. It concentrates on the same interest areas as the **National Geographic Magazine.**

While unindexed magazines are generally considered fair game for clipping, occasionally librarians will be reluctant to cut up an unindexed magazine which has long-term merit and popularity. Obtaining extra copies for clipping is the ideal solution, but it is not always practical. **Pack-O-Fun** is a good illustration of this dilemma. Patrons like to browse through this publication for craft ideas and it does not lose its appeal with the passing years. The solution to this problem is to construct a simple, homemade index or to photocopy the most pertinent articles for the files.

Clipping Indexed Periodicals

Some librarians will shake their heads at the thought of clipping indexed magazines, but there are good practical reasons for doing so.

Despite the priceless assistance furnished by the **Readers' Guide to Periodical Literature**, it is only fair to point out that there are omissions in our beloved **RG**. Many years ago it stopped indexing poetry. It will not help you keep tabs on those once-in-a-lifetime poems that can be converted into toasts for mother and daughter banquets. If you are lucky enough to find good holiday or program poetry in periodicals, the only way to insure finding it again is to clip duplicate magazines, make photo-reproductions, or create your own index.

Nor does **Readers' Guide** index the contents of the special columns which are an outstanding feature of so many magazines. The little treasures of information which appear in these sections are literally lost unless you can arrange to transfer them to your files.

Now a new menace is threatening the universality of coverage in **Readers' Guide**. In the **ALA Bulletin** for February, 1968, Elin B. Christianson (38) wrote with alarm about the increase in variant magazine editions. The use of diversified material for different parts of the country and, to a lesser extent, for special interest editions means that the particular magazine you hold in your hand may not be the edition chosen for indexing in **Readers' Guide**. Public libraries are more likely to encounter regional deviations. School libraries may also face problems with special school editions.

The variation from one part of the country to another may be so great that each regional edition is almost an entirely new magazine. On the other hand, only a section or filler may be inserted for different parts of the country. You can often detect these inserts by the strange pagination they carry. The features in these special inserts are rarely noted in the table of contents, let alone in **Readers' Guide**.

The implications are clear: Librarians cannot blissfully assume that **Readers' Guide** is going to provide total access to indexed magazines. They are going to have to clip, or photocopy, or do supplementary indexing if they want to make use of information that is bypassed by **Readers' Guide**.

There are occasions when clipping, or at least photocopying, is desirable even for magazine articles that are fully indexed in **Readers' Guide**. When the brown recluse spider first made its appearance in our part of the country, we experienced a rash of calls from frantic parents. Information on the spider was sparse and scattered. We photocopied or clipped duplicate copies of all magazine articles we could find so that they would be immediately available in our files.

The highly touted reducing diets that are featured in magazines like **Ladies' Home Journal** and **McCall's** have been part of our clipping program, too. It's a matter of self-defense. We've discovered that our patrons will request these regimens after a lapse of years when their recollection of the exact name and nature of the diet has dimmed.

In clipping magazines—whether indexed or not—don't be bound by rigid tradition. Ads, for example, are perfectly acceptable additions to library files if they can solve a patron's problem. We regularly watch for advertisements which give instructions for making gaily decorated cakes or centerpieces for holiday celebrations. If General Foods pays for a full-page advertisement featuring an Easter egg cake, I have no qualms about clipping it for my collection.

When libraries face a space squeeze that forces them to discard back runs of magazines, clipping provides one way to salvage some of the more important material for continued use.

Sources of clippings for picture files will be discussed in Chapter 9.

PHYSICAL TREATMENT OF CLIPPINGS

Supplying Copies

If you are going to do a thorough job of clipping magazines and newspapers, you will frequently find yourself faced with the need for multiple copies. This can occur because important articles are printed back to back. Particularly in the case of local history clippings, it can occur when you find it necessary to place an article under more than one subject heading. There are two solutions:

1. Provide extra copies of the newspapers or magazines.

In the case of your local newspaper, staff members can be recruited to donate their back papers. In the case of unindexed magazines such as **Family Circle** or **Woman's Day** which are filled with desirable articles, buy two copies right away or watch for extras among old magazines donated to the library.

2. Arrange for access to a photocopy machine.

This solution is more satisfactory for newspaper clippings than for magazine articles since the machines commonly available to librarians at this time do not reproduce color. In fact, reproducing any kind of pictorial material on these machines is often a gamble.

Marking

While the selection of articles to be clipped should be done by the person in charge of the files, the actual clipping may be carried out by someone else, such as a student assistant or clerical helper.

With a second person involved, the marking of the newspaper or magazine for clipping becomes a pivotal process. It must be done clearly and carefully so that the clipper can proceed quickly and confidently with his job.

In the case of newspapers, slash marks or brackets can be placed with a fine-line marking pen at the top and bottom of the article to be clipped. Red is a good marking color.

If only an occasional article in a newspaper is marked, the page numbers can be listed on the front page to speed the clipper's work. However, in the case of local newspapers most pages carry some article of interest. Under such circumstances it would be wasteful to bother listing page numbers.

When scanning magazines for clipping, I staple a slip of paper to the front cover so that I can record the pages to be saved as well as other necessary instructions.

If subject headings can be jotted down during the marking process, the clipped articles can immediately be sorted to make them accessible for quick reference even before their processing is completed.

Clipping

Good equipment is essential to establishing speed and efficiency in your clipping operation. Invest in a really good pair of scissors. This is one case where false economy can be truly disastrous. Nine-inch editors shears are the best choice for clipping purposes.

There are other clipping devices on the market in addition to scissors. One type is widely distributed through retail stores under the tradename, **Clipit.** It has a piercing point that permits a column to be removed from the center of a page without cutting in from the edge. The manufacturer's claim that it cuts the top sheet only is quite true since the sheet must be raised slightly to operate the gadget. In my experiments with the **Clipit,** I find that it leaves a slightly ragged edge and is more difficult to guide than a pair of nine-inch editors shears.

Razor blades mounted in special holders or knives with razor-sharp tips may also be used in clipping. The **Lewis Safety Knife** is a particularly good tool. It can be used with a steel-edged ruler to insure straight lines.

In working with knives or razor blades, be sure to put a protective mat under the sheet being cut.

When dealing with newspapers, the clipping process can be expedited by slitting the joined pages apart before you begin.

Ragged, uneven edges should be avoided in clipping since they are more likely to catch on other items. Because of this problem some libraries even try to eliminate right angles when doing their newspaper clipping. They use a slanting cut and block out the extraneous matter with pencil marks.

It is important to allow generous margins on newspaper clippings whenever possible, unless they are to be mounted at an early date. These clippings are extremely fragile. The extra margin area will provide some protection from wear and tear.

When a newspaper article involves more than one piece of paper, care is necessary to prevent loss of the separate parts. Sections of an article may be held together with a tiny bit of transparent tape. Choose the non-yellowing variety. If the tape is applied to margin areas, the taped portion can be cut away without harm when the clipping is mounted. I prefer this method to using paper clips. Paper clips can work loose, especially if they have been slightly bent. They add considerable bulk. Over a long period of time, metal clips may discolor clippings.

In clipping magazines I find it profitable to remove the staples which are applied along the spines of some periodicals, making it impossible to open them fully.

Trying to cut or tear pages from a magazine stapled in this manner is hazardous and frustrating. If you are clipping just a small portion of a page, it may be possible to do this satisfactorily without pulling staples. If you are attempting more ambitious clipping, you will find that the project becomes very cumbersome because the magazine will not lie flat. Nor will it open wide enough to allow the cutting of adequate inner margins.

Specially designed staple pullers can be purchased at small cost. You can also use a small screwdriver to straighten the staple ends and act as a lever for removing the staples.

While staples can be a nuisance when clipping magazines, they can be very helpful in dealing with the detached articles. Stapling magazine clippings that extend to two pages or more will prevent accidental separation.

Because magazine articles often are continued for several pages, care must be taken to make sure that all sections of an article have been clipped.

Some librarians scrupulously trim off every bit of advertising from clipped magazine articles. Unfortunately, this operation results in odd-shaped little pieces which are particularly susceptable to wear and tear. It's much better to leave magazine sheets intact unless you plan to mount them. The extraneous material will protect the vital portions and it will not disturb the patron any more than it does when he reads the complete magazine.

Sourcing and Dating

A clipping which does not bear any indication of its source and date has no right to be in your files.

If you do not know the source of a clipping, how can you testify to its authenticity? If the clipping does not carry a date, how can you be sure that facts in it are current enough to still have validity?

When you record this important information on clippings, do not use a pencil. Record the information in ink.

For clipping your local newspaper, it's possible to have a rubber stamp made bearing the name of the paper. A revolving band dater might be used to mark the date.

If space for identification is limited on newspaper clippings, use abbreviations. Just be sure that they can be interpreted. KG 9-15-70 is an acceptable shorthand in our local history files for the **Kalamazoo Gazette**, Sept. 15, 1970.

When sourcing and dating magazine clippings, the information should be recorded on the first page of the article.

Preservation of Magazine Clippings

It is customary in certain libraries to cope with magazine clippings by fastening them into paper folders slightly larger than the clippings. The folders are often homemade from materials such as kraft paper although commercially prepared manila folders may be used. The magazine clippings are usually stapled in place although they may be secured by paper fasteners or even stitched on the sewing machine. The subject heading is indicated on the outside of the folder.

Such protective measures—or the alternate choice of mounting—may be justified if the magazine clippings are delicate, worn, or subject to very heavy usage. I have found, however, that when magazine clippings consist of entire pages, they stand up quite well without further treatment. Folding the pages in half will add to their bulk and reduce the possibility of tearing. The folding should be done so that the title of the article appears on the outside. Different procedures are essential, of course, if you clip just a small portion of a magazine page. Such small clippings are subject to damage unless they are mounted.

Preservation of Newspaper Clippings

It is possible for full-page newspaper articles to be housed in the vertical files without extra strengthening. The lengthy features that appear in the rotogravure sections are an example.

As far as smaller newspaper clippings are concerned, I have for years waged a one-woman crusade in favor of mounting all of them. Why? There are many reasons.

1. Small clippings are easily crushed under the weight of heavier objects.

2. Subject headings have to be squeezed into odd spaces or super-imposed on print. As a result, they are difficult to read.

3. Packs of loose clippings are difficult to leaf through when speed is important.

4. Unmounted clippings are easily lost because of their small size and unassuming appearance.

If a newspaper article is valuable enough to warrant marking, clipping, and sorting, it's worth the extra step of mounting.

Librarians have tried to substitute all sorts of procedures in place of mounting, but none of them are quite satisfactory.

Some libraries just insert the clippings, sorted by subject, into manila folders. Others put them into old mailing envelopes or commercially made clipping envelopes. One library handles its local history clippings by first putting them into small envelopes or small folders labeled with subtopics. They are then placed in a standard-sized manila folder headed with the main topic.

Folders and envelopes are perfectly satisfactory means of housing newspaper clippings TEMPORARILY. But they will not provide the protection which delicate clippings need to withstand handling by staff and patrons. Nor will they prevent the wear and tear which occurs when many clippings are housed together in packs in the vertical files.

In past decades a good many librarians relied on a device called the **U-File-M Binder Strip (178)**. It is still being manufactured. The **U-File-M** is a narrow piece of strong paper edged with small tabs. Both the binder strip and the tabs are adhesive backed. The binder strip may be cut to any desired length.

One method of using **U-File-M's** is to paste the binder strip along the left margin of a newspaper clipping. Subsequent clippings on the same subject can be added by moistening pairs of small tabs. In this way, sizable groups of clippings can be joined together. For extra strength the binder strip may be pasted on a piece of backing paper before the clippings are added. **U-File-M's** can also be mounted along the crease of manila folders. In fact, folders are available with premounted strips.

U-File-M's are successful in keeping related newspaper clippings together, but even with the use of manila folders, they cannot hope to match mounting in the protection offered to these fragile bits of paper.

Mounting newspaper clippings does cost money, but I feel that this investment is more than justified because it puts needed information into a format that will protect the material and make it easy to use.

Mounted material does consume more space than unmounted material. But what virtue is there in saving space if in doing so you are creating barriers in the way of your service to the public?

I am well aware of the financial facts of life in libraries. But there are ways of achieving mounting which will not break the budget.

Newspaper clippings selected for your general files can be mounted on a standard grade of typing bond. I have experimented with this technique for several years and find it workable. The light backing provided by this paper will support clippings over a period of years under normal wear. This should cover the typical life span of usefulness enjoyed by general newspaper clippings.

Some school libraries manage by mounting their clippings on kraft paper (ordinary wrapping paper).

If you cannot absorb the labor costs involved in mounting, enlist the efforts of volunteer groups. Girl Scouts, 4-H Clubs, women's groups, and school service organizations can be approached to take on this project.

Preservation of Local History Clippings

Local history clippings deserve particularly careful treatment because their value increases with time. The choice of proper mounts for these clippings is important because of this long-range usefulness.

The villain accused of much of the blame for paper deterioration is acidity. As well as being intrinsically weak, newsprint is high in acid-producing ingredients. Nothing available to the average library at this moment will remedy that situation. But libraries often aggravate the problem by mounting local history clippings on high-acid paper and placing them in folders with high-acid content.

For a long time it was believed that the rapid deterioration of modern papers was entirely due to the substitution of wood pulp for rag fibers. It was assumed that modern all-rag paper was as stable as its counterpart of centuries ago. But the W.J. Barrow Research Laboratory, working under the sponsorship of the Council on Library Resources, proved that the solution wasn't that simple. Their experiments seem to demonstrate that the alum-rosin sizing introduced in the 19th century is the major agent in boosting the acid content of modern paper. It appears to wreck its havoc on both rag and wood-pulp paper. This means that a quick switch to all-rag paper for mounts and folders will not automatically solve a library's preservation problems.

Fortunately, the research in paper longevity has resulted in the development of a "permanent/durable" paper which is said to have a life span of centuries because it is acid-free and is made of long fibers which give added strength to the paper.

One of the leaders in the development of long-lived paper is the Standard Paper Manufacturing Company (169). Its product is called **Permalife**. The Michigan State Library has just undertaken a project of mounting its important historical clippings on **Permalife** paper. Instead of trying to preserve the newspaper clippings themselves, the Archives at Western Michigan University are reproducing them on **Permalife** paper by means of the Xerox process.

Permalife stock is also converted into acid-free file folders and envelopes by the Hollinger Corporation (92). Many archivists use these Hollinger products to protect their rare holdings.

If you are making a real pledge to the future with your local history collection, investigate the advantages which permanent/durable paper would offer.

Whatever type of paper you finally choose for your local history clippings, insist on a good quality stock free of groundwood. Papers that contain groundwood are unstable. They quickly discolor and become brittle when exposed to light and air. Two additional characteristics which paper experts check are the paper's resistance to tearing and its endurance to folding. It would be profitable for you to check these points, too.

In choosing mounts, always keep in mind that thickness or weight are not the final determinants of a paper's longevity. Some libraries have had unfortunate experiences with mounting on construction paper which is bulky but short-lived. Weight and thickness are important, but the ingredients that have gone into making the paper are even more so.

At one time scrapbooks enjoyed great popularity among librarians as a means of preserving local history clippings. Scrapbooks are not unmixed blessings. In the first place, much of the paper used in making scrapbooks deteriorates rapidly. In the second place, it is usually necessary to provide a detailed index to a scrapbook in order to unlock the treasures it contains.

Trimming and Placement of Clippings

In preparing newspaper clippings for the mounting process, they should be trimmed closely.

Before it is cut away, the subject heading indicated on the clipping should be jotted on the back side of the mount. This will facilitate labeling later on.

If the date and source notes on the clipping are jeopardized by trimming, they should be transferred to the mount immediately.

Clippings must be fitted to the shape of the mounting paper. This often necessitates cutting columns into sections. A large group of clippings can be prepared ahead of time for pasting by cutting them to fit the mounting paper and then paper clipping them to the mounts. If an article is broken up into several sections, some libraries number the sections lightly before paper clipping them to the mount so that mix-ups in pasting can be avoided.

Precutting does save time since the paster can concentrate on pasting without having to pick up his scissors repeatedly.

In placing clippings on mounting paper, always be sure to leave room at the top of the page for the subject heading. Allow room also for the library's identification stamp.

Theoretically speaking, it is economical to mount more than one article on a sheet if they relate to the same subject. In actual practice, however, this isn't as easy as it sounds. In order to achieve this maximum use of each mount you will have to:

1. Be lucky enough to stumble on related articles as you clip.

2. Stockpile your clippings until you acquire articles which can be mounted together.

3. Check the files each time to see if there are any partially filled mounts.

As far as general clippings mounted on inexpensive paper are concerned, it is more wasteful to expend staff time hunting for unfilled mounts than to use a fresh piece of paper. If the mounted clippings circulate, the problem is magnified still more.

In a local history file where clippings are mounted on more costly paper and do not circulate, the practice of filling pages with multiple clippings becomes a more practical goal. Making full use of each mount will help to conserve storage space as well as paper. Hopefully, historical clippings will be mounted in chronological order on the pages so that they will present a sequential record of each subject. Pasting clippings haphazardly in empty spaces will give a very distorted view of the progression of events.

There is another way to economize on space and materials in preparing clippings for the general files. You can cut standard-sized mounts in half to accommodate small clippings. I like to use these smaller sheets with the longer sides placed vertically. In this way the mounts can stand tall in their folders and display their subject headings on a level with the full-sized mounts. They can also be placed two abreast in the folders, thus saving space.

Adhesives

When it comes to actually attaching clippings to their mounts, there are a variety of products which invite consideration.

Pastes and Glues

The best all-around adhesive that has come to my attention for mounting purposes is a "white glue" manufactured by Gane Brothers & Lane, Inc. **(78)**. It is called **"Yes."** Unfortunately, it is more expensive than ordinary library adhesives even though it can be diluted generously.

For other possibilities, consult the catalogs of the various library supply houses. They will list products which may be used for mounting.

The best way to find the most desirable paste or glue for your particular needs is to buy various brands in the smallest size offered. Actually working with these adhesives will enable you to test them for economy, lasting quality, ease of use, and physical effect on the materials to be mounted.

To do a satisfactory job of mounting clippings, paste and glue should be smooth and thin enough to flow easily over the paper. They must not, however, be so "watery" as to soak the clippings.

Most pastes and glues will need thinning to the proper consistency unless the distributor specifically indicates otherwise. There is no magic recipe for determining the proper amount of water to add. You will have to experiment until you achieve the proportions exactly right for your purposes.

Rubber Cement

Rubber cement is an appealing adhesive to many librarians because any excesses can be easily rubbed off a paper surface with fingers or an eraser. Furthermore, rubber cement does not wrinkle or curl even thin paper.

There are two methods of using rubber cement.

Applying cement only to the back of the material to be mounted creates a "temporary" bond. While the material will stick to the backing, it can usually be removed without damage at a later time. There are limits to this maneuverability as far as clippings are concerned. It is true that clippings of better quality paper can be easily peeled from their mounts. But once thin newspaper clippings have dried, they can be pulled only partially free before they tear.

Some librarians welcome the flexibility allowed by "temporary" mounting. They like being able to reposition items. They speak favorably of the possibility of reusing mounts once clippings or pictures have lost their currency.

Most libraries, however, are more interested in having a clipping stay put than they are in easy methods of removing it. For the rough and tumble life that most library resources lead, temporary mounting with cement is a risky business.

To obtain a "permanent" bond using rubber cement it is necessary to apply the cement both to the mount and the back of the item to be mounted. With this method you lose the option of moving a clipping or picture once the cement has set. While this two-coat application provides a firm seal for the present, a number of librarians have raised questions about the long-term permanence of rubber cement as a mounting agent. The judgment is that it will hold for some time but not indefinitely.

As a matter of fact, the label on one bottle which I have indicates that for "maximum permanence" it is necessary not only to apply coats to both surfaces, but also to add still another coat to one of the surfaces. This seems to indicate some doubt even in the mind of the manufacturer about the durability of rubber cement.

Rubber cement costs more by the gallon than most library pastes. It is used undiluted unless it thickens when exposed to the air. Then a special thinner must be bought. The need for multiple coats should also be counted in as a cost factor. When all these considerations are taken into account, rubber cement must be rated as a relatively expensive mounting agent.

Spray Adhesives

There are adhesive products on the market in aerosol cans which are sprayed on the backs of materials to be mounted. The manufacturers of some of these sprays claim that they can be used to provide permanent adhesion. The sprays I have tested do not live up to these claims. They are suitable for temporary mounting but they hold their bond only so long as they are not subjected to stress.

Pasting Techniques

When a liquid adhesive is to be applied to clippings, place them face down on a protective underlay. Sheets of old newspapers are good for this purpose. If the newspapers are slit open, soiled sheets can be easily thrown away—leaving fresh pages below.

A paste cloth can be used to smooth the clipping and make sure that the adhesion is complete. Soft paper towels make fine substitutes for paste cloths. As an added advantage, they do not have to be laundered as paste cloths do. They can just be thrown away.

Mounted clippings should be separated by sheets of wax paper until they are completely dry.

Clippings should be placed in a press or under weights while they are drying to prevent curling or wrinkling. This is not necessary if rubber cement is used.

All the outer edges of a clipping should be firmly fastened to the mount. Applying spots of adhesive only to the four corners leaves free edges that can easily catch on other materials and tear. Furthermore, a loosely mounted clipping will not draw as much supportive strength from the heavier backing paper. These warnings apply to other shortcuts such as stapling clippings to mounts or taping only the corners of clippings.

Adhesive Tapes

Cellophane tape becomes yellowed and brittle with age. In time it discolors the clippings and mounts on which it is used. Avoid this type of tape like the plague.

Some manufacturers claim to have solved these problems with a newer type of transparent tape that has an acetate base. The most widely distributed acetate tape is the 3M Company's **Scotch Brand Magic Transparent Tape.**

While acetate tape is slightly opaque, it does not interfere significantly with vision and it will allow photocopying.

Applying this tape to the outer edges of a clipping is a quick process, but the finished product looks a little untidy. This may not be a significant point where news articles are concerned, but it would be a factor to consider in mounting pictures.

The cost of non-yellowing transparent tape should be carefully weighed against other adhesives before employing it on a large scale as a mounting agent. Since it is essential to secure the entire outer edge of each clipping, a roll of tape disappears in a hurry.

Scotch Brand Magic Transparent Tape No. 810 is being used in an interesting experiment with important historical clippings at the Michigan

State Library. Because specialists maintain that the ingredients used in the manufacture of pastes and glues may contribute to the deterioration of clippings, the Michigan State Library is using strips of tape instead to fasten Michigan history clippings to their mounts. **Magic Transparent Tape** was chosen because it is reputedly acid-free and, as far as is known, will experience minimal deterioration and discoloration.

Mounting tapes are available which have adhesive on both sides. They produce neater results than ordinary tape because they remain hidden under the mounted material. However, my efforts to use double-faced tape have been frustrating. It takes considerable dexterity to apply the tape accurately to the edges of a clipping or picture. If you don't come close enough to the edge, a loose flap is left. If you overlap, the surplus must be trimmed away. To further complicate matters, materials secured with double-faced tape have a tendency to pull free from their mounts with hard usage. It should also be noted that double-coated tape is much more expensive than regular varieties.

Dry Mounting

If finances are available, the finest method of mounting is a technique called dry mounting. This process is achieved by means of a thin paper coated on both sides with a thermosetting adhesive. It looks something like wax paper. It is available in sheets or rolls.

The instructions call for first tacking a sheet of dry mounting tissue to the back of a clipping, picture, or map. The tacking is accomplished by means of a quick application of heat. Both pieces of paper are then trimmed together. In working with small newspaper clippings, you can often cut several units from a single sheet of tissue. Scraps can be pieced together to fit a clipping, but each separate section of tissue must be tacked in place.

The printed material and its underlay of tissue are next tacked to the mount. The "sandwich" thus created is sealed permanently through a combination of heat and pressure.

Tacking can be done by means of a special tacking iron or with an ordinary laundry iron. The final "baking" can also be done with a household iron. But if you are planning to do more than an occasional piece of dry mounting, you will want to consider investing in more efficient equipment.

It is possible to use a thermal copier for dry mounting, but keep certain reservations in mind. In the first place, the thermal copiers in common use are limited as to the size of materials they can accommodate. Stiff, heavy backings cannot be employed. Furthermore, many people in the field are convinced that a superior job of dry mounting can be achieved only by means of specially designed dry mounting presses.

These presses are available in several sizes. Dry mounting presses which are open on three sides will enable you to mount large items in sections.

For detailed information on mounting with a dry mounting press, write to Seal, Incorporated (162) for a free descriptive booklet. Seal will also furnish the names of companies supplying recommended mounting boards.

Dry mounting tissue is available from Seal, Incorporated and the Eastman Kodak Company. Seal, Incorporated produces several models of dry mounting presses.

Dry mounting can involve a significant investment of money in equipment and materials. It also can require a considerable investment of staff time in cutting tissue to proper size and "baking" the mounted items. But if properly done, the results are beautiful to behold—offering a smooth, neat, and lasting bond. Even if you can't afford this technique for all of your mounting requirements, give it thoughtful consideration for your local history collection where materials are processed for long-term preservation.

If you would like to experiment with laundry iron mounting, these are the steps to follow:

1. Set the iron at "silk" or "rayon."

2. Put clipping or picture face down on a surface protected against heat.

3. Place dry mounting tissue on back of item to be mounted.

4. Tack the tissue in place by applying the iron lightly to the center of the area to be used.

5. Trim tissue and attached paper to desired size.

6. Place the clipping or picture faceup on a sheet of mounting paper.

7. Tack two opposite corners to the mount. This can be done by carefully lifting a corner of the top layer and touching the iron to the tissue underneath.

8. Cover with a clean sheet of paper.

9. Iron with a slow, firm, circular movement over the entire area to be attached.

While experiments with electric irons may give you an introduction to dry mounting, remember that the results can't compare with those produced by a dry mounting press which provides even heat and steady pressure over the entire surface at once.

Lamination

In a world without budget burdens, the crowning treatment for clippings would be lamination. Unfortunately, wholesale lamination of clippings is beyond the means of the average library. If it is done at all, it should be reserved for the most precious of your holdings. This process is discussed in more detail in the chapter dealing with the preservation of maps.

Labeling

The final step in processing clippings is to record the subject heading and apply the identification stamp of the library. The subject heading should be placed at the top, left-hand side of the mount so that it can be read easily as the mount stands in its place in the file. Naturally, all subject headings should be printed in ink or typed on adhesive labels. Never use pencil!

If the source and date are difficult to decipher on the clipping itself, they should be repeated on the mount.

CHAPTER 6

VOCATIONAL MATERIAL

Interest in the ways of earning a living is a preoccupation that spans the generations. It ranges from the six-year-old who wants to be a fireman when he grows up to the 45-year-old who decides to change jobs in midstream. Added to this spontaneous interest is a demand created by career units in the school curriculum.

Any library—public or school—can make a big contribution to its users by maintaining up-to-date, well-organized files of career material.

GUIDES TO VOCATIONAL MATERIAL

The tools which are useful in selecting general vertical file materials can also be utilized to enrich vocational files. Sections on career aids are included in such lists as Ruth Aubrey's **Selected Free Materials for Classroom Teachers (14)** and **Free and Inexpensive Learning Materials (72)** from George Peabody College.

The **Vertical File Index (192)** will alert you to many important new publications. But a word of caution is in order. For some reason the **Vertical File Index** ignores new or revised titles in certain key vocational series.

In addition to these general guides, there are specialized listings which concentrate entirely on career and guidance materials.

Gertrude Forrester's massive bibliography, **Occupational Literature (70)**, has served as a launching pad for many career files. The volume has a twofold usefulness. It provides helpful annotations and ordering information to aid in the selection of career materials. In addition, the subject headings and cross references used to organize the bibliography can serve as leads to the librarian who is establishing a filing system for his own vocational collection.

While the 1964 edition of **Occupational Literature** is dated, the H.W. Wilson Company gives assurance that a new edition is scheduled for the fall of 1970 or early in 1971.

Another excellent list is published by the Department of Education of the State of Ohio. It is called **Sources of Occupational Information (139)**. A new edition was released in 1970. A copy of this compilation was furnished to our library free of charge.

For the initial plunge into a career collection, Irving Eisen and Leonard H. Goodman have selected **A "Starter" File of Free Occupational Literature (55)**. This guide lists 103 carefully screened pamphlets which give an initial introduction to approximately 500 careers. The emphasis is on non-rural middle-class career goals. The pamphlets are arranged by occupational fields and a detailed index by job titles is provided. While the list was designed for the counselor who wants to set· up a selective occupational library, it can be helpful to the librarian as well. It is available from the B'nai B'rith Vocational Service for $1.25.

Serial indexes or bibliographies of career and guidance materials are issued at regular intervals by several publishers. Four of the best-known services are singled out for consideration here.

Careers, Inc. publishes its **Career Guidance Index (33)** nine times each year for $6.00. It contains annotated references to free and inexpensive vocational materials.

Leads to free and inexpensive literature about occupations and counseling are also offered by the **Career Index (39)** which appears annually and is updated by four supplements each year. This index is sold by Chronicle Guidance Publications, Inc. for a net subscription fee of $11.00.

The B'nai B'rith Vocational Service compiles a quarterly bibliography called the **Counselor's Information Service (20)** which offers annotated listings of books and pamphlets relating to occupations and guidance. The annual subscription is $7.00.

Highly respected among guidance and personnel workers is "Current Occupational Literature," a survey which is found in every issue of **Vocational Guidance Quarterly (132)**. These lists prepared by the National Vocational Guidance Association include a wide variety of free and inexpensive publications on occupations. Career studies are rated according to NVGA standards. Vocabulary level is indicated. A yearly subscription to the periodical costs $5.00. The lists which appear in the **Vocational Guidance Quarterly** are compiled at three-year intervals to form the **NVGA Bibliography of Current Career Information (132)**. The 1969 edition of the **Bibliography** costs $2.00. Both the **Quarterly** and the **Bibliography** can be ordered from the American Personnel and Guidance Association.

Before investing in serial indexes or bibliographies, librarians will want to investigate them carefully. Publishers will sometimes furnish sample copies. Some services are overpriced for what they have to offer in the way of listings for general library use. If I were to make a choice among these serial bibliographies, my selection would be "Current Occupational Literature" in the **Vocational Guidance Quarterly**.

It is possible for a library to do an adequate job in the vocational field without subscribing to a specialized serial bibliography.

School librarians may find themselves in a favored position as far as these lists are concerned. Frequently, school counselors subscribe to such professional aids as the **Vocational Guidance Quarterly** or the **Counselor's Information Service**. Under such circumstances the school librarian can arrange to consult these guidance publications for ordering purposes.

The same fortuitous access may be possible with the **Educators Guide to Free Guidance Materials (54)**, published annually by Educators Progress Service. This listing of printed, filmed and taped resources has a section of career planning materials. At $7.50 it does not record enough occupational literature to justify purchase for that purpose alone. However, since many school systems buy the guide for use by teachers and counselors, it will be on hand for consultation by the school librarian, too.

Since it appears irregularly and is limited in coverage, the column, "Counseling Aids," in the **Occupational Outlook Quarterly (25)** does not qualify as a full-fledged serial bibliography. But it does furnish some leads to new career material. The **Quarterly** is issued by the Bureau of Labor Statistics of the U.S. Department of Labor. More will be said about it in the pages which follow.

SOURCES OF VOCATIONAL MATERIAL

United States Government

In their efforts to attract qualified employees, many federal units prepare pamphlets and leaflets about the career opportunities they offer.

The extent of this publishing program is demonstrated in the **Guide to Federal Career Literature (184)**, a 1969 directory of recruiting materials aimed at the college graduate. It records 246 publications from 46 different departments and agencies. The inclusions represent only the principal publications used in nationwide recruiting for college entry-level positions.

Some of the materials describing career possibilities in the federal service are for sale by the Superintendent of Documents. They are listed in **Price List 33A, Occupations, Professions, and Job Descriptions (150)**.

Large numbers of booklets are distributed free by the federal departments and agencies themselves. Here are a few of the governmental units which will provide free literature about job opportunities in their employ.

Maritime Administration
Veterans Administration
U.S. Department of Agriculture
U.S. Department of Commerce
U.S. Department of State

Of course, the most famous of all governmental recruiting materials is that issued by the armed forces of the United States. If there are recruiting offices in your community, a quick tour of them will stock your files generously. Otherwise, write directly to the headquarters of each service.

Since so many federal jobs fall under civil service supervision, it is important for public libraries and high school libraries to obtain the announcements of civil service examinations. These announcements are useful for alerting patrons to current openings. They have broader applications, also, since they give an overview of the nature of the work, the educational and personal qualifications required, and the salaries offered. This information is helpful to the library user who is trying to choose a future occupation.

In addition to announcements of individual examinations, the U.S. Civil Service Commission **(183)** publishes more extensive pamphlets about federal careers and entrance requirements. Some are general introductions to civil service. An example is the booklet, **Working for the U.S.A.** Others are geared to those who have special skills or training to offer. A recent leaflet described federal jobs for engineers, physical scientists, and mathematicians. Aids for helping candidates prepare for civil service examinations are also available.

Some of the booklets issued by the U.S. Civil Service Commission are distributed free and can be obtained directly from the Commission. Other Civil Service Commission pamphlets are sold by the Superintendent of Documents. They are listed in **Price List 33A (150)**.

Not all of the vocational material produced by federal agencies is concerned with employment opportunities in the United States government. Many excellent publications are offered which deal with a broader spectrum of occupational information.

A promising new series has just been started by the Manpower Administration of the U.S. Department of Labor. The series title is **Occupational Guides (110)**. The first two guides are devoted to optometry and oceanography. While the brochures contain loose supplementary inserts housed in a pocket, these extra parts can easily be stapled in place. Contact the Manpower Administration for free copies.

The Women's Bureau of the U.S. Department of Labor issues a series of occupational leaflets, **Careers for Women (198)**, which are especially designed for the needs of female workers. Although these leaflets are for sale by the Superintendent of Documents, single copies may be obtained without charge from the Women's Bureau.

The Small Business Administration **(165)** deserves a big thank-you for a unique series of booklets filled with practical advice for anyone hoping to establish a small business of his own. This group of vocational guides is called the **Starting and Managing Series**. Their prices range from 25 cents to 75 cents and they should be ordered from the Superintendent of Documents. Additional titles are added at irregular intervals. Watch for announcements in **Selected United States Government Publications (164)** or screen the publications lists which the SBA will send free to anyone who asks to be placed on their mailing roster.

The SBA also publishes a group of free guides called **Small Business Bibliographies** which cover such career activities as interior decorating and hobby shops. As well as offering leads to helpful literature, they are prefaced by a short but pithy survey of each business.

The Bureau of Labor Statistics is well-known to librarians for its invaluable publication, the **Occupational Outlook Handbook (25)**. This handbook which covers over 700 careers should be the cornerstone of vocational service in all libraries. It is comprehensive, reliable, and current since it is revised biennially. While multiple copies are feasible because of the handbook's relatively modest price, only one patron can make use of each copy at a time. Luckily, over 100 reprints **(25)** of articles from the 1970-71 handbook are available. Libraries with heavy career demands can obtain these reprints for their files and thus assure wide access to the information. Reprints are for sale by the Superintendent of Documents or any regional office of the Bureau of Labor Statistics.

To supplement and update the **Occupational Outlook Handbook** between editions, a companion periodical is issued. It is called the **Occupational Outlook Quarterly (25)**. Since the subscription price is only $1.50 a year, it is economically practical to obtain a second copy to clip for your vocational files. Reprints of some articles are available without charge from the Bureau of Labor Statistics **(25)**.

State Governmental Units

The importance of vocational materials which reflect conditions in a particular state cannot be overemphasized. In these days of super mobility, it might be argued that occupational literature keyed to the national picture is more significant than localized information. But conditions still vary sharply from one state to another and even from one locality to another. Statistics show that even in this move-happy civilization, many people spend their working lives in one state—yes, even in one community. Furthermore, regional differences become very important to the temporary resident while he is part of the local working force.

These facts make it urgent for the librarian to collect as much information as he can on the job picture in his state and his area.

The state employment service is a prime source to consult for such information. The coverage provided differs drastically from one state to the next. Some state employment agencies publish very general booklets on job opportunities in the state, particularly entry jobs for new young workers. Some compile detailed surveys of the employment outlook in various metropolitan areas, as well as the state as a whole. Training opportunities, wages paid, skills available, and unfilled jobs are all subjects of state publications.

A number of state employment services prepare series of career briefs reflecting regional factors. While some of these series are modest in size, certain states maintain very extensive sets. For example, the Department of Employment of the State of California publishes occupational guides for over 400 occupations.

Listed below are some of the states which produce career briefs.

Alabama	Mississippi
Arizona	New Jersey
California	Ohio
Colorado	Oregon
Idaho	Pennsylvania
Illinois	Utah
Indiana	Washington
Michigan	

As well as materials which reflect employment factors peculiar to the state, some state employment services publish vocational guidance information of a more general nature such as techniques of getting a job.

Contact the employment body in your state to discover what publications it can provide for your career files.

State merit agencies distribute information about career opportunities in the civil service systems which they administer. The title of the controlling body changes from state to state. It may be the state personnel board, a civil service commission, or a merit system council. Public libraries and high school libraries should arrange to receive announcements of examinations, as well as any other descriptive literature available about jobs in the state's civil service system.

Don't overlook the governmental bodies which license or certify members of such occupations as cosmetology, nursing, teaching, and mortuary science. Approach them for printed material on requirements for entering the profession or trade. Some regulating agencies even issue sample tests for applicants.

Local Governmental Units

Large cities sometimes release recruiting leaflets and examination announcements for governmental positions. If you live in a smaller community, it is more difficult to obtain printed material. Now and then you may find a windfall as we did when our police department distributed a detailed account of the work of a city policeman, as well as a description of the Police Cadet Program which the department operates. We also welcomed a booklet from the city personnel department which briefly outlined the different areas of employment within the City of Kalamazoo.

Be sure to watch the newspaper, too. Occasionally the ads which local governmental units insert are detailed enough to be worth clipping for your files.

In some localities bodies such as school systems, special study commissions, or community colleges will initiate studies of current and future manpower needs and availability. The printed results of such studies belong in your library.

Professional, Labor, Commercial, and Industrial Organizations

Many societies, institutes, and associations are eager to provide pamphlets and brochures describing career possibilities in their areas of activity. Some labor unions also distribute helpful material. Most of the publications are free.

A ready-made mailing list covering national associations, societies, and institutes can be found in the **Encyclopedia of Associations (57)** published by Gale Research Co.

Leads to organizations affiliated with various vocations can also be discovered in articles in the **Occupational Outlook Handbook (25)** and in the **Occupational Outlook Quarterly (25)**.

Libraries which own **The Encyclopedia of Careers and Vocational Guidance (58)** will find that at the end of the career studies in Volume II there are lists of agencies and organizations to write to for additional information.

The career briefs and monographs for sale by commercial publishers often contain clues to associations connected with a particular occupation.

Here are just a few of the organizations which will furnish descriptive literature for your files.

Air Line Pilots Association, International
American Advertising Federation
American Federation of Information Processing Societies
American Gas Association, Inc.
American Institute of Architects
American Society for Metals
American Textile Manufacturers Institute, Inc.
American Trucking Associations, Inc.
Association of American Geographers
Institute of Life Insurance
National Association of Food Chains
Water Pollution Control Federation

It is important to remember that national organizations are not the only groups active in distributing vocational literature. State associations may also be involved. To illustrate this point, the following groups in Michigan have made career material available.

Michigan Funeral Directors Association
Michigan League for Nursing
Michigan Society for Mental Health
Michigan State Medical Society
Michigan State Pharmaceutical Association

Even on the local level, associations may produce publications of value to your career files. Chambers of commerce often prepare lists of local industries, processors, and retail firms which are appropriate for career study as well as being a record of community activity.

Private Businesses and Industries

A number of large businesses and industries publish occupational brochures. They are usually devoted to recruiting for the companies themselves. Occasionally, they will present a detailed study of a career field or will survey occupational opportunities in the industry as a whole. Although they tend to be generalized and overly optimistic, these company publications can be useful, especially if they represent area firms.

Instead of concentrating on career opportunities in its own field, the New York Life Insurance Company has chosen as a public service to issue a series of free booklets on a broad variety of occupations. Each booklet is written by someone who has distinguished himself in a particular career. Write to the New York Life Insurance Company (135) for a full set.

The Bank of America National Trust & Savings Association issues a publication called the **Small Business Reporter (166)** which studies specific businesses as well as the techniques of business management.

The **Small Business Reporter** which comes out ten times a year costs $8.50 annually, but single copies of all reports are distributed free. Send for a list of available titles.

Educational Institutions

Colleges and universities sometimes publish brochures on the career areas in which they offer training. While the publications are usually concerned with the programs of instruction at the school, they often provide good general information about the vocation itself.

Until recently there were several well-known career series available from nationally recognized schools which were helpful additions to the career file. But these institutions have either abandoned their series entirely or stopped updating them.

Despite this mortality rate, don't give up on educational institutions as sources of career information. Pay particular attention to schools in your part of the country. Our files have been enriched by up-to-date vocational material from several Michigan colleges and universities.

Periodicals

Magazines are fodder for your vocational file since they often run feature articles on interesting careers. The information in such articles is likely to be very current. Magazines also tend to pick up off-beat occupations which are not normally included in more circumscribed sources.

Some magazine articles are useful not only for clipping, but also for the clues they offer to additional information. For example, when **Changing Times** prints articles on careers, they usually contain references to agencies or publications that can be of further help.

Reprints of vocational articles which have appeared in magazines are sometimes offered for sale. Send to **Changing Times** for a list of its current career reprints. For reprints from **Mademoiselle**, contact the Alumnae Advisory Center, Inc. (3). **Glamour** offers reprints of job features that have been published in the magazine, as well as special **Fact Sheets** on vocations. Unfortunately, the **Fact Sheets** I have seen are woefully outdated. The magazine reprints for sale by Chronicle Guidance Publications, Inc. will be discussed later in this chapter.

As has already been noted, free reprints are available for some articles in the **Occupational Outlook Quarterly**.

School librarians who want to add another dimension to their career files can ask students who have relatives in various occupations to bring in professional journals, trade papers, or union periodicals which these relatives receive. Such publications offer an insider's viewpoint not readily available elsewhere.

Commercial Publishers

The strong and continuing demand for career information has enticed many publishers into preparing series of vocational guides. Some are poorly done and infrequently revised. But a number of career series have established solid reputations over a period of years. Their names are library bywords almost on a par with Granger or Bartlett.

Some of the more widely recognized series will be mentioned here. Chronicle Guidance Publications, Inc. **(39)** is well-known in library and guidance circles for its **Chronicle Occupational Briefs**, a series of over 380 career titles. Except for a handful of longer presentations, the briefs run four pages in length. The publisher tries to release a minimum of 72 new or revised briefs per year. A special price is offered to those who buy a complete set of **Chronicle Occupational Briefs**, but it is also possible to buy the briefs singly. An annual subscription service is also available.

Another vocational series sponsored by Chronicle Guidance Publications consists of **Chronicle Occupational Reprints**. These are reproductions of career articles that have been published in trade magazines. A minimum of 20 are reprinted each year. They are available individually, by subscription, or as a complete set.

Careers, Inc. **(33)** features three interesting series. **Career Briefs** are eight-page introductions to an extensive range of vocations. **Career Summaries** are more compact sketches printed on both sides of card stock. To meet the needs of potential dropouts and slow achievers, Careers, Inc. has inaugurated a new series stressing semi-skilled occupations. Written in simple form and printed in larger type, this series is called **Job Guides**.

The publisher promises approximately 45 new or revised **Career Briefs** each year, as well as about 80 new or revised **Career Summaries**. Twenty-seven new **Job Guides** are anticipated each year. The publisher claims that all titles in these series are revised within four and one-half years.

Career Briefs, Career Summaries, and **Job Guides** may be ordered as complete sets, by annual subscription, or by individual titles. A comprehensive career kit and special subject kits are also offered.

Science Research Associates, Inc. **(160)** publishes briefs covering hundreds of occupational areas. Two major series are available. **SRA Occupational Briefs** are four-page surveys written for use by secondary school students and adults. **Junior Occupational Briefs**, written in a simpler narrative form, are designed for pupils in grades 6-9 but may also be used with the educationally handicapped. The briefs may be purchased in sets, but they are also available individually.

In addition, SRA publishes **Job Family Booklets** dealing with broad fields of work and **Guidance Series Booklets**, some of which cover the general vocational problems of young people.

A veteran name in career publishing is the Institute for Research **(95)** which has some 300 **Careers Research Monographs** for sale. These detailed studies give fuller coverage than the other career series already mentioned. The special attention paid to the historical background of occupations is one of the hallmarks of **Careers Research Monographs**. The

Monographs cost more than the briefs described earlier, but they offer a more comprehensive portrait of the career and a sturdier format.

The publisher provides a special discount if the complete series of **Monographs** is ordered. However, **Careers Research Monographs** may be purchased in smaller numbers.

While it is important for librarians to be acquainted with the giants in the vocational field, it's also important to be on the alert for literature from less widely known publishers. For example, Park Publishing House **(143)** issues a small but useful series of career studies. The eighteen titles which are available include such popular career areas as cosmetology, nursing, and dentistry.

While the B'nai B'rith Vocational Service **(20)** cannot be classed as a commercial publisher, this would be a good place to mention its career briefs since they often are grouped with the publications of the commercial firms. Although its list of titles is not large, the **Occupational Brief Series** of the B'nai B'rith Vocational Service has a special contribution to make. As well as covering the usual career facts, these briefs consider the opportunities available for minority groups and for women. Of interest primarily to Jewish youth are other B'nai B'rith pamphlets describing careers in Jewish communal service.

Special Purchase Plans

As has already been indicated, publishers of career briefs and monographs frequently offer discounts for large scale purchases. For example, Science Research Associates, Inc. which sells a single **SRA Occupational Brief** for 45 cents net will provide a full set of 400 for $83.50 net. The Institute for Research; Careers, Inc.; and Chronicle Guidance Publications advertise similar bargains. Reduced rates are also available from some publishers if you place a yearly subscription to their vocational publications. Careers, Inc. and Chronicle Guidance Publications operate under this provision.

These are tempting offers. They promise savings in money and in the time spent on ordering. However, these mass purchases may burden the library with a number of unwanted and unused items. How many calls do you anticipate in a given year for career literature on acrobats, gunsmiths, auctioneers, or art gallery operation? Yet these occupations are all included in well-known sets.

By ordering a publisher's complete output of briefs or monographs, you are inevitably going to acquire a substantial number of older titles which are in line for revision. This is another factor to weigh against the savings you are offered.

In addition to a simple discount for large orders or for yearly subscriptions, career publishers offer an assortment of unusual package plans. Depending on the publisher, these plans feature a mixture of the firm's briefs or monographs; career reprints; subscriptions to indexes of occupational and counseling literature; research reports; professional newsletters; posters; and even filing cases.

My reaction to package plans is that most of them are sculptured to the needs of counselors rather than librarians.

If you would like to know more about package plans, consult the catalogs of these publishers:

B'nai B'rith Vocational Service
Careers, Inc.
Chronicle Guidance Publications, Inc.
Science Research Associates, Inc.

EVALUATION OF VOCATIONAL MATERIAL

High on the list of requirements for good career material is currency. In this hyperkinetic world nothing is so stale as old vocational pamphlets. Salaries, educational requirements, job opportunities, and working conditions are constantly changing. New jobs are springing up which were unknown a few years ago. On the other hand, long-standing jobs have been virtually eliminated or drastically changed.

One of the sterling qualities of career pamphlets is that they are likely to be revised more frequently than books on occupations. It's a simple matter of economics. Pamphlets are cheaper and easier to revise. But don't take too much comfort in that fact. Librarians will still have to work zealously to keep their vocational files timely.

They must become very date-conscious. It is not enough to check the year of issuance of a career brochure. Old statistics can be concealed in a new publication. The significant factor is how recent the data within the pamphlet is. Beware of statistical statements or charts which carry no time identification. A comment that the average union minimum hourly wage for plumbers is $5.08 means little unless you know the year when this wage applied.

Receiving free material that is obsolete is merely annoying. The problem becomes really serious when expenditures of library funds are involved in the purchase of the career series issued by commercial publishers.

The publication dates of these briefs or monographs are easily determined when you are ordering them from a guide such as the **Vertical File Index**. Otherwise you will have to ask the publisher for a list of the titles in his series with the copyright dates indicated. In some cases you will have to be quite insistent. Even this will not protect you from the publisher who fakes a revision or who does a skimpy job of updating. These hard facts of life are good arguments for sampling a series before investing heavily in it.

As well as being watchful of new material, the librarian must constantly assess the occupational information already in the files. Career files should be weeded ruthlessly to eliminate outdated publications.

Occasionally there may be overriding reasons for keeping an older publication because of the specialized information it contains—usually a detailed history of the vocation. Under such circumstances the pamphlet should be clearly labeled with a warning such as this:

> NOTE: This pamphlet was· published in 1958. It is still useful for the history of the occupation.

Just as important as currency in a career pamphlet is a concrete and realistic approach. Vague generalities are of little aid to the patron who wants hard facts. Descriptions which gloss over disadvantages and exaggerate benefits are more harmful than helpful. These rosy surveys are likely to come from groups with a vested interest in promoting a particular career. Trade schools or business schools are often guilty of this promotional approach in the vocational material they distribute.

A topnotch pamphlet should be able to weather questions such as these:

1. Does it spell out the physical abilities and personality traits which are important to the job?

2. Is it explicit in presenting the kinds of demands the job makes on the individual?

3. Does it give a true picture of salary patterns, not just the higher ranges?

4. Does it depict what beginning jobs are like, rather than concentrating on the glamour positions at the top?

5. Does it pinpoint the real prospects for women and minority groups?

6. Does it retain an objective viewpoint, allowing the reader to make his own judgment about the job's desirability?

Style can play an important role in determining how extensively a vocational pamphlet will be used. The narrative approach may be appropriate for elementary school students or immature junior high schoolers, but it will only repel the older adolescent or adult who wants quick, precise facts. An informal style is acceptable but when it becomes too chatty or indirect, it is a handicap.

Libraries should stress materials that concentrate on a particular occupation rather than those which try to survey an entire industry. Broad studies of related occupations do have special pertinency in the lower grades. Fourth-graders may participate in a unit on aviation which considers all types of work involved in making and operating airplanes. This approach may also be assigned by a civics teacher at junior high school level when students are beginning their career studies. Occasionally a young man will be attracted by a spectacular industry like electronics or aerospace without having a precise job in mind. But aside from such scattered instances, the calls for career information that reach most libraries are for specific occupations. This means that a pamphlet on petroleum engineers is likely to be more popular than one covering all jobs in the petroleum industry.

As indicated earlier, it is essential to examine several selections from a career series before making a wholesale investment in it. It is also vital to calculate what proportion of your total vocational budget you want to commit to a single series. Restricting your vocational collection to one firm's publications is very much like buying the output of only one book publisher. Each series has its strengths and weaknesses. The types of careers covered can also vary from series to series.

If you are interested in more information about standards for occupational literature, you may want to obtain a copy of **Guidelines for Preparing and Evaluating Occupational Materials**, a product of the National Vocational Guidance Association. The **Guidelines** are included in the **NVGA Bibliography of Current Career Information**. They may be ordered separately (**132**).

PERIPHERAL INFORMATION

Don't be stereotyped in your thinking about supplementary resources which can be useful in career service.

College and trade school catalogs are a natural adjunct to vocational information.

The annual reports of corporations can furnish insights into company policies and potentials which are helpful to patrons considering jobs with those firms.

Materials on labor-related laws are pertinent. For example, pamphlets describing child labor laws, compulsory school attendance regulations, or provisions relating to the employment of veterans can be very useful.

Booklets on rehabilitation and employment of the handicapped have a contribution to make.

Reports of special training programs and job possibilities for minority groups will be of assistance.

Facts about scholarships, fellowships, student loans, and other methods of financing an education are important to career-minded library patrons.

Material on part-time or summer jobs also has a legitimate place in your files.

Information on service organizations such as VISTA, HOPE, the Peace Corps, and the Teachers Corps should be available since some of your patrons may decide to dedicate a part of their working lives to these programs.

While many of these supplementary resources will be physically separated from your vocational collection, they can still serve as an extension of it.

ORGANIZATION OF VOCATIONAL MATERIAL

A miniature career collection can be incorporated into the general vertical files by lumping the material under a subject heading such as "Vocations." As career resources swell, it is more practical to place them in a separate arrangement.

When an independent career file is established, some means must be found to make sure that folders and pamphlets will be returned to the proper cases.

A distinctive color may be used in lettering pamphlets, folders, and file drawers. Colored labels may also be applied to folders and drawer fronts. Some libraries employ colored stars or dots to distinguish vocational material, but this is a risky system. The stars or dots fall off easily. Furthermore, patrons are likely to pick at them absent-mindedly as they read.

Another way of isolating vocational material is to use a stamp with an identifying phrase such as "Career file." To make sure that it will be noticed, apply the stamp just preceding the subject heading on each pamphlet. The stamp should also be used on the folders in the career file.

If the index to the career file is typed on colored cards, it will not be necessary to use any preliminary words such as "Career file" or "Vocations" on the cards.

There are two basic types of filing arrangements for vocational materials. One is alphabetical, the other numerical.

Numerical plans are usually based on the classification system recorded in Volume II of the **Dictionary of Occupational Titles (188)**. The **Dictionary** is published by the United States Department of Labor.

This is a brief and edited sample of the classification code used in the **D.O.T.**

07	OCCUPATIONS IN MEDICINE AND HEALTH
070	Physicians and Surgeons
070.081	Pathologist
070.101	Surgeon
070.108	Anesthesiologist
	Cardiologist
071	Osteopaths
071.108	Osteopathic Physician
072	Dentists
072.101	Oral Surgeon
073	Veterinarians
073.181	Veterinary Livestock-Inspector
074	Pharmacists
075	Registered Nurses
075.378	Nurse Anesthesist
077	Dietitians
077.081	Research Nutritionist
078	Occupations in Medical and Dental Technology

Numerical codes such as this are based on an elaborate classification of job families. Their prime purpose is to keep related occupations in close physical proximity. In fact, the principal argument for using a numerical approach in library files is that it offers a quick overview of jobs that share certain common elements. The excerpt from the **Dictionary of Occupational Titles** shows that anyone who is inspired by the thought of healing people or animals can find a variety of potentially appealing jobs under the broad category of "medicine and health." This correlation of jobs is particularly attractive to vocational guidance counselors.

Numerical arrangements require the use of an alphabetical index to locate specific jobs. If you faithfully follow the system in the **Dictionary of Occupational Titles**, you can use Volume I of the **Dictionary** as a ready-made index since it includes an alphabetical list of job titles with a notation of the corresponding classification number.

Another type of numerical arrangement has been attempted by school libraries which have assigned Dewey Decimal Classification numbers to career pamphlets. Usually pamphlets treated in this manner are housed in pamphlet boxes on the open shelves.

After working with both numerical and alphabetical files, I am wholeheartedly in favor of the alphabetical system. The numerical classification used in the **Dictionary of Occupational Titles** offers a tidy way of presenting job relationships, but it does not reflect the manner in which requests for occupational information reach the library. Most patrons want information on a precise job. They are not concerned with the nice interplay between occupations. There are books and pamphlets which are deliberately designed to give broad surveys of major job families. The entire occupational file doesn't need to be organized to offer still another overview.

A strong argument against a numerically arranged file is that it can't be approached directly. In order to trace a particular job, the librarian or patron must first turn to an alphabetical index to discover the proper code designation. Then the code designation must be traced in the files. This procedure is especially troublesome in libraries where patrons serve themselves.

For libraries which rely on the numerical system in the **Dictionary of Occupational Titles**, there is also the problem of dealing with brand-new occupations since the **Dictionary** is revised only at intervals of several years.

For most libraries the alphabetical arrangement of career material is the simplest and most productive plan. There are two methods of developing an alphabetical arrangement.

1. The terms used can describe the trade or profession. Examples are "Optometry," "Truck driving," and "Surgery."

2. The terms used can describe the worker. Examples are "Optometrist," "Truck driver," and "Surgeon."

I recommend using the name of the worker as the subject heading in your files. There are many worker titles which will not gracefully convert into fields of work. It's easy to change the term "Actor" into "Acting" and "Banker" into "Banking," but what would you do with the following titles?

      Airline stewardess
      Waitress
      Curator
      Actuary
      Ticket agent
      Credit manager

The usual treatment would be to bury the material under general subject headings such as "Air transportation" or "Restaurant work." The direct, immediate access offered by worker titles would be lost.

Broad industry surveys pose no problem in files where worker titles are employed. A monograph on career opportunities in the chemical industry as a whole can be headed "Chemical workers."

In setting up an alphabetical filing system, librarians can turn to Volume I of the **Dictionary of Occupational Titles** for possible headings. As well as standardizing job titles, the **D.O.T.** includes succinct descriptions of the occupations which are helpful in assigning subject headings. This reference tool is particularly useful in dealing with occupations for which there are many names. In the alphabetical arrangement in Volume I the **D.O.T.** uses the most common title as its main entry. Alternate names are listed under this entry. There are cross references from the variant titles.

An abridged and somewhat modified version of the **D.O.T.** list can be found in Gertrude Forrester's bibliography (**70**).

The **Occupational Outlook Handbook (25)** is another handy guide to subject headings.

For the small collection, limited lists such as those in Forrester or the **Occupational Outlook Handbook** may be simpler and quicker to use.

Some school counselors argue for vocational files that are oriented to the courses taught in the institution. They feel that this helps the student evaluate the career fields open to him as the result of following various courses of study.

If the school librarian thinks that such an approach would be helpful in his library, it should be carried out by means of a supplementary index showing the relationship. It would be unwise to arrange the career pamphlets themselves under school subjects.

Help in determining curriculum-career relationships may be obtained from the **Missouri Filing Plan for Unbound Materials on Occupations (85)**. This plan was designed for the actual placement of career material under school subject areas. But it can easily be converted into an index correlating occupations with curricular fields.

For the librarian who is desperately short of time or who panics at the thought of organizing a career file, there are commercially prepared shortcuts.

Wilma Bennett has developed an **Occupations Filing Plan (18)** which is sold by Interstate Printers & Publishers, Inc. It features an alphabetical arrangement by fields of work. The headings are adapted from the **Dictionary of Occupational Titles** but they have been broadened in an attempt to keep related jobs together. The **D.O.T.** code numbers are not used.

Subject headings and cross references are listed in a book from which you can select appropriate terms for your files. However, if you want to expedite the process, you can order a set of 1,148 prepared labels which are all ready to paste on your file folders and cross reference guides.

The book alone sells for $3.95. The book plus a set of printed labels is $14.95. You may order these materials on approval.

As well as filing aids, the book also contains a short discussion of occupational information.

Keep two facts in mind when considering the Wilma Bennett plan.

1. The subject headings are given in terms of the trade or profession rather than the worker.

2. The plan attempts to keep related jobs together under broad headings rather than isolating each job as a separate unit.

Chronicle Guidance Publications, Inc. also offers a ready-to-use filing system for career material (39). It consists of 300 manila folders which are arranged by a numerical classification based on Volume II of the **Dictionary of Occupational Titles**. Direction cards are available which provide an alphabetical approach to the code numbers used in arranging the folders. A complete set of the labeled folders costs $35.00.

Science Research Associates, Inc. (160) has created a filing system of its own which is centered around six major occupational fields. While it is keyed to job family relationships, it is not based on the **Dictionary of Occupational Titles**. The SRA publicity calls this system an alphabetical filing plan, but it departs drastically from the straight alphabetical arrangement which librarians know. The six major fields which form the framework of the plan are not alphabetized. They are assigned code numbers and are arranged by that number. Under these major headings fall the job families which, in turn, incorporate individual job titles. It is true that these subdivisions are arranged alphabetically, but only within each area of relationship. The subdivisions are numbered according to this internal alphabetizing.

Printed file folders utilizing the SRA system are for sale. The net price for a complete set of 212 folders is $17.50. An alphabetical index to the filing plan must be purchased separately.

Before investing in a commercially prepared filing plan, try to communicate with librarians or counselors who have had experience with the system. If you have trouble in establishing a contact, write to the publisher for the names of libraries or schools using the plan.

CHAPTER 7

LOCAL HISTORY: WHY, WHAT, AND HOW

Smaller libraries rarely aspire to specialized subject collections. Their staff members are happy to achieve good general coverage. But there is one area in which any public library—no matter how small—has a responsibility to provide a specialized collection. That area is local history.

Even school libraries are not exempt from this obligation. If instruction is offered in local history or civic affairs, the library automatically acquires a need to gather material that pictures the community.

It's true that there are other agencies on both local and state level which are concerned with regional historical material. Genealogical societies, historical societies, universities, archival centers, and state historical commissions are among the bodies with a vested interest.

But the existence of these groups does not minimize the obligation of the local library to assure the preservation of community history.

Agencies and organizations at the state level are not always willing to expend time and space on the localized minutiae that are so important to depicting a given locality. They must, of necessity, take a broader approach. While they would snap up the diary of an early pioneer in your area, they are not likely to want to bother with the programs issued by the amateur theatrical group in your community. Yet 25 years from now when that theatrical group celebrates its silver anniversary, those programs will be an important aid in planning the festivities.

Even the existence of a historical or genealogical society on the local level does not always guarantee the adequate preservation of community materials. The group may restrict itself to narrow fields of interest. It may not want to be concerned with more current items. Rapid turnover in officers and in membership may cause efforts at collecting information to be sporadic and diffuse. Furthermore, the results are not always accessible to the general public.

The public library finds itself nominated by logic and default to play a major role in the field of local history.

It is qualified for this participation because it can:

1. Offer continuity to the collection of historical material.

2. Unify diverse efforts to preserve local history items.

3. Represent the entire range of local interests and needs.

4. Furnish personnel trained and experienced in organizing and using information.

5. Provide a central depository open to all citizens.

Don't ride off to do battle alone on the basis of this list of qualifications. Before initiating a local history collection, your first move should be to contact interested groups and individuals in the community to see what is already being done.

Cooperation rather than competition should be the key word. If the high school library has done a superlative job of collecting material about the origin, staff, students, academic programs, and extracurricular activities of the institution, there is no reason for the public library to duplicate all of these materials so long as they are available to the general public. However, a librarian should never hesitate to duplicate any type of material for which there is a steady demand or which he needs to execute good reference service.

If you represent a small library, the second step to take in preparing yourself for historical specialization is to stop feeling apologetic about what small libraries can contribute. This is one area in which smaller libraries have several advantages over their larger counterparts.

In the first place, residents in small towns think of the librarian as a neighbor. They will often turn over to him business or family items which they would hesitate to give the librarian in a big impersonal institution. In the second place, the librarian in a smaller community can keep alert to everything going on in the area. He's aware of governmental, organizational, and private developments which would slip by unnoticed in a larger city. Therefore, he can always be on the spot to acquire materials which will give a comprehensive picture of his community's past and present. In like fashion, local agencies and groups find it easy to remember the library when they have pertinent material to dispense. This happy situation does not prevail in larger cities where the library may be overlooked in the complexities of urban life.

There is an urgency in collecting historical materials today which is more intense than ever before. When families lived in 12-room houses and stayed in the same location for generations, the materials that feed historical collections accumulated undisturbed in attics or barns. With the advent of small homes, apartment-dwelling, and frequent moves, these accumulations of old materials are being consumed in bonfires or being sold to the junkman. With small home-owned businesses giving way to chains and conglomerates, the records of local firms are also disappearing.

Every library has a duty to help in preserving vital local information before it vanishes forever. Even if the library does not have ideal equipment or specialized personnel to handle these resources, it does offer a better fate than destruction in a bonfire or deterioration in a damp cellar.

Is a local history collection worth the effort? Ask the people who turn to a typical collection. There is the businessman who is trying to find early pictures of his factory to use in advertisements. There is a doctor reconstructing the controversy which raged around a progressive health officer in the younger days of the city. There are citizens studying issues

116

and candidates in an effort to acquire ammunition for campaign use. There is the genealogist hot on the trail of an early ancestor. There are the visitors hoping to discover the story of the house on the hill that looks just like a castle. There is the newspaper reporter preparing a special feature on Lincoln's visit to the city. There is the graduate student writing a paper about the effect of the Civil War on the local economy. There is the newcomer to the community studying growth patterns and land-use projections in an effort to determine the best place to buy a home. There is the history buff trying to find out how "Whiskey Alley" got its name.

All of the people who figured in these true examples would testify to the importance of a local history collection.

THE INGREDIENTS OF A LOCAL HISTORY COLLECTION

Any good historical collection should have a sound nucleus of books. If a history has been written of your county or of your city, obtain copies. Histories of your state which pay explicit attention to your community should be represented. City directories are obligatory inclusions. So are collections of phone books for your area. Yearbooks of local high schools and colleges are important. A strong argument can be made for including the books written by local authors even if they don't deal with the community.

Yes, books are essential. But don't sit back smugly once you've arranged for their acquisition. You've only scratched the surface. Most ingredients of local history do not come neatly packaged in tidy volumes. The raw materials of local history must be assembled from a bewildering assortment of items that can range from the yellowed handbill for a local fair to the financial statement of a local bank. These odds and ends are like pieces of a jigsaw puzzle which fit together to present a revealing picture of the community. No book can hope to incorporate the intricate and continually evolving record captured in these miscellaneous materials.

In collecting the miscellany that forms the blood, muscle, and bone of a local history collection, there is one golden rule to follow: Treasure the past but don't forget the present. Tomorrow's history is being made today. The bits and pieces you collect about current activities in your community will be choice historical items 50 years from now. If you doubt this, remember that many things which cause historians to exalt were considered trivia at the time of their origin—playbills, political posters, postcards, etc.

This means that even the library in a newly established community can't close its eyes to its historical obligations. There may be no past to preserve except for general area history, but there is a present which will become history in the future.

To illustrate the variety of materials which are qualified for collection as historical records, here is a selective checklist. It is far from comprehensive, but it is indicative.

County, city, village, or township governments

Charters
Ordinances
Directories of officials
Annual reports
Special surveys or studies of housing, recreation, etc.
Zoning and planning reports
Agendas or minutes of meetings
Sample ballots
Organizational charts and booklets describing the functions of local government

School systems

Annual reports
Minutes of boards of education
Directories of teachers
Superintendents' bulletins
Curriculum guides and studies
Studies of future needs for buildings and capital improvements
Brochures issued when new buildings are opened
School census reports
Student publications
Publicity and programs for student activities such as plays and concerts
Commencement programs
Evening school announcements
Sample report cards

Businesses and industries

Company histories
Charters
Annual reports
Financial statements
Account books
House organs
Sales catalogs
Advertisements
Speeches describing business activities
Copies of key patents in the firm's development

Political parties, candidates, and interested citizens' groups

Posters depicting candidates
Publicity leaflets
Studies of candidates or campaign issues
Crucial speeches
Records of county meetings of political parties
Ads and program notes for rallies and picnics

Service, social, and hobby groups

Compiled histories of the club or organization
Newsletters
Rosters of members and officers
Constitutions and bylaws
Minutes of meetings
Program notes of theatrical or musical groups. Exhibition catalogs
of art or photography groups
Literature for fund-raising campaigns

Religious institutions

Anniversary publications
Newsletters
Lists of members
Birth, baptismal, marriage, death and burial records
Minutes of meetings of church officials
Records of clergymen who served the institution
Groundbreaking or dedication brochures
Sermons centered around local events or people
Funeral orations for prominent citizens

Personal papers and memorabilia

(These must either represent prominent citizens or be old enough
to justify inclusion because they give the flavor of an era long past.)

Diaries
Correspondence
Account books
Scrapbooks
Photographs
Marriage, birth, or death records
Wills
Land grants, deeds, bills of sale
Diplomas

A few sources of historical material deserve a special word of
explanation or endorsement.

Older citizens in your community possess memories of times past
which will die with them unless you record these recollections. Probably
the simplest means of capturing their comments is with a tape recorder.
The tapes themselves should be preserved, but the recollections can also
be transcribed for inclusion in your vertical files. Historical interviewing
is a delicate process requiring tact, perseverance, and a good knowledge
of local history.

Graduate students working on research projects involving local history
can be approached for a duplicate of their completed work. They usually
are flattered to receive the request.

Museums, historical associations, or genealogical societies in your area may publish pamphlets or newsletters devoted to subjects of local interest. If significant papers are read at meetings sponsored by these bodies, ask for copies of the presentations.

The area newspaper is one of the kingpins in your collection. It is a treasure house of local news which will mellow into basic history. The use of hometown newspapers will be discussed in greater detail in a later section. In addition to the local newspaper itself, watch for the market surveys which are published by many newspapers to attract advertisers. These brochures usually feature charts, statistics, and photographs of the region served by the paper.

Pictorial materials have a role to play in the enrichment of your local history files. Photographs and postcards add another dimension to your resources since they capture images in a concrete, detailed fashion that cannot be duplicated in words. A postcard showing the corner of Main Street and First Avenue in 1905 is a historic find which will increase in value with each passing year. More will be said about pictorial materials later in this chapter.

Local maps also are important in the historical collection. Seek them out and preserve them, whatever the subject matter. Surveyors' maps, maps showing school boundaries, maps of real estate developments, soil surveys, geological maps, street maps, zoning maps, lake surveys, maps of local college campuses, maps showing locations of landmarks—all of these are grist for your mill. The physical treatment and organization of maps is considered in another chapter.

As you develop your resources, you will inevitably discover that items of great significance to the historical panorama of your community are in the firm possession of other institutions or individuals. Since you can't own the originals, the alternative is to obtain reproductions. These can be made by a commercial photographer, a camera fan on your staff, or by means of a duplicating machine. If you employ these machines, be sure that the duplication process is one which will stand the stresses of time. There is still uneasiness about the life span of copies made on many of these machines.

EVALUATING MATERIALS FOR INCLUSION

Don't be too restrictive in your interpretation of what constitutes local history. You cannot arbitrarily stop at the city incorporation lines. The first settler in the area may have taken up residence at the other side of the county. Can you ignore him? The resort that flourished at a nearby lake years ago may have been the focal point of summer social life for the town's residents. Will you dismiss it because it was outside your boundaries?

Major emphasis should center on your own snug little community, but its story can't be told without referring to its periphery.

Similarly, it's wrong to be too parochial in your judgment of the type of material which reflects local history. Some historians suggest that the songs, games, and dances prevalent in the early days of a settlement are as historically significant as the establishment of the first blacksmith's shop.

Seemingly frivolous materials can earn a place in your collection by satisfying the curiosity of succeeding generations. For example, in our library we carefully preserve a copy of the popular song, "I've Got a Gal in Kalamazoo," because our city is featured in the lyrics.

The firm standards applied to most library acquisitions in relation to style of writing and quality of printing may have to be waived when it comes to local history materials. Here content takes precedence over form. A pamphlet that covers an obscure episode in the region's past should be coveted despite awkward grammar and poor paper.

Historical gifts may necessitate decisions on the part of the librarian which would tax a Solomon. Some of the material presented by local residents will be useless junk. The librarian must exercise great tact in handling such offers. The right to dispose of inappropriate or unneeded items is one that he must preserve zealously.

If you are a novice at historical collecting, enlist the help of an expert in evaluating questionable items. You can always discard surplus material at a future date, but you can't replace a treasure once it has been tossed out. One of the specialists in our state says that his motto is: "In case of doubt, don't throw it away."

Sometimes groups of historical records will be offered to the library on an indefinite loan basis with the stipulation that they may be reclaimed at any time by the club or institution. This is a risky arrangement. It makes the library answerable for theft or mutilation, but does not give it complete control over the materials. Furthermore, members of the contributing body seem to have no qualms about carrying off sections of the records for study or revision. Many times this is done without notifying the librarian. Sometimes the borrowed items are not returned.

This type of temporary deposit is to be discouraged. However, if the records are an important part of community history and the alternatives are destruction or complete inaccessibility, a library may be forced to compromise its stand.

Libraries may find themselves having to cope with gifts of historical materials which are very massive, very specialized, or very valuable. Should they be kept or not? To deal with this problem you must first establish guidelines for your collection. How far do you want to go in preserving the correspondence of distinguished residents? Do you have the space and staff to handle the business papers of local firms? Do you feel qualified to accept responsibility for a diary which is truly a collector's item?

Once you've established your guidelines, you can turn to other institutions to absorb materials which are beyond your scope. Items which you find burdensome will often be welcomed with open arms by state historical societies, state archivists, historical museums, or university libraries.

TECHNIQUES FOR BUILDING THE COLLECTION

A local history collection is like a magnet. Once established, it attracts contributions to itself.

Publicity helps to speed the process. Make speeches at every opportunity about your collection and its goals. Arrange for newspaper, radio, and TV coverage of interesting new acquisitions to the collection. Such exposure inspires further gifts. Send letters to local clubs, businesses, institutions, and government agencies asking to be placed on the mailing list for their publications. Since so much important material originates with governmental bodies, cultivate contacts in key offices who will alert you when new information becomes available. Encourage staff members to participate in societies which have an interest in the history of your community.

Each contact with a patron using the history collection is really an ad for additional materials. The businessman who uses your files to compile a history of his company for an anniversary celebration will be glad to see that you get a copy of the finished brochure. The amateur historian who is tracing the history of plank roads in the area may bring you photocopies of additional information unearthed in another library.

In your search for materials, don't overlook the importance of incidental clues. For example, newspaper articles about local interests are often based on information which can be obtained in its original form. If a feature article about the need for new parks mentions a study of recreational facilities made by the local Rotary Club, follow up this lead by requesting a copy of the study.

At the same time, don't forget the necessity for an orderly pattern of routine acquisition. Maintain a checklist of periodically released items so that you don't miss materials which will be impossible to obtain later on. You can review this checklist at set intervals to discover gaps in your receipts. While such checklists are usually organized on the basis of the issuing body or the title of the publication, it is possible to set up a chronological file to jog the librarian's memory. A "tickler" file arranged by the months of the year will remind the staff that February is the time to watch for the annual public report prepared by the school board.

The burden of keeping up with publications about the area rests very heavily on the shoulders of the librarian. Most of these materials are produced locally for local consumption. They will not turn up in the standard indexes or lists of publications. Most of them are designed for short-term use and the supply is quickly exhausted. You must be constantly on the alert for them and act promptly to obtain them.

Carefully worded questionnaires are useful devices for soliciting information for the library's local history files. One popular project is to ask prominent citizens to fill out a form devoted to biographical data. A photograph can be requested at the same time. Most people feel complimented to be chosen for this attention. Forms may also be used to solicit the histories of business establishments and clubs.

While techniques of acquisition are important, probably the most significant step in building a history collection is to assign the project to a staff member who is enthusiastic about the undertaking and who is knowledgeable about local history or willing to become so.

ORGANIZATION

An alphabetical subject approach is the best means of organizing local history files. Dewey Decimal Classification is completely inappropriate because of the intricate content of the resources involved.

Since the emphasis in these files is on details and specifics, the subjects chosen must be precise and finely honed. If your municipality has adopted a sister city in another part of the world, this concept must be immediately conveyed by the subject heading you select. If your city conducts a "Pioneer Days" celebration each year, there should be a subject heading which mirrors this fact. The more exact your subject headings, the fewer cross references you will need and the less guesswork you will have to do in serving your patrons. Fine subject designations also cut down on unnecessary handling of precious historical resources.

Major divisions should be provided in your files for local, county, and state information. (The approach to state materials will be covered more fully later in this chapter.) These resources should be filed first by location and then by subject.

When quantities of newspaper clippings are involved, there are additional decisions to make. Should the clippings under a topic be kept in simple chronological order or should they be broken up into sub-topics? Are clippings on community parks more useful in straight order by date or subdivided under the names of individual parks? The first approach gives a progressive picture of the development of parks in your area. The second arrangement enables you to quickly locate material on each park. Your choice should be based on the nature of the requests which you receive for information.

While it is out of print and there are no plans for its revision, libraries which have access to Miriam Ball's **Subject Headings for the Information File (17)** will find its delineation of state, county, and city headings useful. It served as a guide for our local history collection in its earlier days but as our holdings increased, we outgrew this list. We now create our own headings which are infinitely more varied and minute than the Ball listings.

An index to the subject headings used in your local history files is essential. The complexity of these headings makes a written record indispensable. Generous cross references will help to unravel the complicated pattern.

Your vertical files may be a way station for some material. For example, the minutes of the city council may be housed there until a year has elapsed. The accumulated minutes can then be bound, cataloged, and placed on the open shelves. Rather than attempting to give prime file or shelf space to a long run of annual reports from the parks department, you might keep only the current edition in your vertical file. Previous reports can be shifted to a separate storage room from which they can be retrieved when needed. Having the latest edition in the vertical files will alert you and your users to the existence and nature of the publication without usurping undue space in your service area.

Special gift collections pose peculiar problems of organization. If your library is housing the papers of a family, company, organization, or institution, you will have to make allowances for the unique character of these holdings. Archivists and historians warn that these collections should be kept intact. A record should be made of the collection and its contents but let good sense be your guide. If the papers are those of the town's most famous resident, there may be good reason for providing an itemized approach. But shortcuts are possible with papers of lesser importance. The records of the Ladies' Literary Society might be noted in the catalog by a single card indicating the name of the group, the character of the holdings, and the period of time covered. For reasons of inventory control, the number of items in the collection should be indicated.

Rather than attempting to assign an artificially concocted Dewey number to these special collections, a simple location note or symbol should be added to the catalog card. One suggestion is that a Cutter number might be used, based on the person or organization in original possession of the papers.

Since it is important to preserve the unity of these special collections, access to individual items of interest will have to be provided by adding subject cards to the catalog; inserting notes at appropriate places in the vertical files; or photoduplicating the pertinent portions. The records of the local Men's Club, for example, may detail the campaign which its members conducted for a municipal swimming pool. While this material is important as part of the history of the Men's Club, it is also important as part of the story behind the construction of the swimming pool. Access from both angles should be provided.

The complexity of local history materials points up the need for organizing holdings thoroughly and carefully. Too many libraries have relied on the memory of a single staff member as a key to these resources. Librarians do move away or retire or die. For the sake of continuity, your local history collection must be able to stand on its own two feet despite changes in staff.

HOUSING AND PRESERVATION

In a public library the local history collection should be housed in a separate room or concentrated in a clearly defined area of the general room. This will serve to dramatize the collection and point up its special nature.

If your building can boast of air conditioning and well-filtered air, the historical materials you own will be assured of a better chance at longevity. Shielding them from sunlight and adapting fluorescent lights to eliminate ultraviolet emanations will also help to retard physical deterioration.

Steel files and acid-free storage boxes may be used to protect historical materials from dust, light, and physical manhandling. Files equipped with locking mechanisms provide extra security.

Archivists prefer storing important papers flat rather than standing them in vertical files. But even the most enthusiastic archivist admits that boxes stacked flat in piles are difficult to consult. Why not compromise? You can cling to the convenience and accessibility of upright storage for all materials except the few delicate or precious pieces that justify flat containers.

Be generous in your use of folders in the vertical files. Do not overload them. Attempting to economize will invite damage to the contents.

To provide additional protection for valuable or awkward items, envelopes of cellulose acetate can be used. Paper envelopes fastened inside file folders are also good storage devices for unusual items. Be sure that the paper envelopes and folders are made of acid-free stock if you are concerned about long-term preservation.

Marks of ownership and location should be applied with great discretion and care to avoid defacing important historical resources. Some historians even urge that marking of valuable material be restricted to the envelope or folder housing the item. Certainly every effort should be made to avoid marring the face of pictorial material which might be needed for duplication in books, magazines, or newspapers.

If paper clips are going to remain on material for long periods of time, substitute plastic clips for metal ones to avoid discoloration.

To protect very fragile items from wear, it may be desirable to make photoreproductions of the material which can be used for ordinary consultation.

More information on the physical management of historical maps, pictorial materials, and clippings can be found in the special chapters on these subjects.

Because your local history collection is a promise to the future as well as a tool for the present, mass circulation cannot be justified in public libraries.

If you cannot resist the pressures for circulation, try to accumulate duplicates of frequently requested materials. Photocopies of popular items can also be made for circulation. Providing a duplicating machine for public use will help to compensate for circulation restrictions.

School libraries may be more liberal in their circulation policies since their local history materials do not represent a commitment to the community as a whole. In addition, the school librarian can assume that the public library will act as a backup to his collection. If, however, the school library is the major depository for information on the history of the school, careful consideration should be given to protecting this collection from the hazards of random circulation.

SPECIAL RESOURCES

Newspapers

The history of your community cannot be adequately told without the help of the local newspaper. It is like a group diary, recording events and thought in your area.

One method of presenting the contents of your local paper is to clip significant articles and file them by subject in the local history files. This system provides quick, easy access for the user but it has certain disadvantages.

1. Clippings take up a great deal of room.

2. Clippings are vulnerable to damage, theft, and deterioration.

3. The physical process of clipping is time-consuming. If clippings are mounted, even more time is consumed.

4. The sheer bulk of articles makes it almost impossible to clip all stories of possible interest.

The cost of this operation can be lowered by utilizing volunteers such as retired people to do the mechanical processing of clippings. Mounting expenses may be curtailed by letting clippings age a while before pasting them. Many times summary articles will appear which will permit the discarding of preliminary clippings.

A clipping program is most easily managed in smaller communities where local news is fairly limited. In larger cities articles of local interest are so numerous that the cutting and mounting of clippings becomes an operation of massive proportions.

The processing of clippings is discussed in detail in Chapter 5.

To avoid the problems associated with clippings, some public libraries have resorted to indexing the local newspaper instead. Since newsprint deteriorates so rapidly, these libraries usually microfilm their newspaper holdings for use with the index.

The index consists of cards topped with subject headings. The date and page of each article on the subject is entered below the heading. There are two techniques for adding entries to the index. One method calls for pulling subject cards one by one as the indexer proceeds from article to article. Under the second system, the indexer first types all the new entries on a sheet of paper before turning to the index file. If there is sufficient staff time to support this nicety, it helps to record a few key words from the headline to give a clue to the contents of each article. Noting the exact column in which an article appears is a refinement which also will depend upon the time available.

Clerical help can be employed in some phases of the indexing operation. For example, the librarian can mark subject headings on the articles in the newspaper which are to be covered. The typing of entries on the index cards themselves can then be turned over to a clerk or student assistant.

The indexing method, if combined with microfilming of the newspaper, is a great space saver, but this approach has its drawbacks, too.

1. Many people dislike using microfilm. They find it difficult to read.

2. Indexing reveals only the general content of articles. To trace a particular fact, it is often necessary to put reel after reel of microfilm on the reader.

Despite these disadvantages, indexing may be the only choice possible as the municipality and the local newspaper grow larger and larger.

It's a common predicament for libraries to find themselves with newspaper runs covering many decades when absolutely no clipping or indexing was attempted. Most libraries have all they can do to cope with the current year's paper without tackling this backlog. And yet those early newspapers are studded with vital information about the region.

To tap this resource, try to enlist the efforts of interested citizens in your community. History buffs or retirees with academic backgrounds may be delighted to tackle these intriguing old papers under the supervision of the library staff. The indexing they do may not be perfect, but it will be infinitely better than having no subject approach to these papers at all.

To quiet any skepticism, let me point out that our museum which is a part of the local library system is currently sponsoring a project to index the early years of the **Kalamazoo Gazette**. The indexing is being done by inmates at one of our state prisons.

If you are not ready to tackle a major indexing of back issues of your local paper, you can build up a partial index by asking patrons and staff members to jot down the location of any helpful newspaper articles which they are lucky enough to stumble upon.

Pictorial Materials

To preserve a visual image of his community, the librarian must make a conscious effort to build up the pictorial portion of his local history collection. He cannot rely on gifts alone, as important as they may be.

He must make the rounds of dime stores, drug stores, and newsstands to locate picture postcards depicting the community. He should also canvass local restaurants, hotels, and motels since they often furnish postcards to customers which feature pictures of their establishments.

He should make arrangements with the editor to obtain copies of historically significant photographs which have appeared in the local newspaper.

Any major events taking place in the community should alert the librarian to picture leads. When a local industry has an anniversary celebration or the Chamber of Commerce organizes a street fair, the library can contact the sponsor for copies of photographs taken in connection with these activities.

Because this is an age of constant and devastating change, every library should initiate an organized campaign to preserve the present-day community on film. The demolition of an ancient structure, the leveling of an impressive hillside, the relocation of a monument, or the remodeling of a government building should send the librarian or his agent scurrying to photograph the edifice or terrain before the face of the city is changed forever.

In fact, one of the finest projects the library can organize is a systematic photographic inventory of the city. A local camera club or a budding young amateur photographer can be enlisted to carry on this undertaking. Public buildings, parks, monuments, historic houses, factories, stores, and schools are among the landmarks which should be included in this photographic survey.

One word of caution! Photographs taken for library use must be fully identified and carefully dated.

Photographs which reach the library as unsolicited gifts can be mixed blessings. Among them may be treasures that will add luster to the collection. But the album that features pictures of the family pets and Uncle Willy from Toledo will have to be evaluated very critically. Are the local landmarks and residents depicted really significant enough to justify inclusion in the library's files?

Oftentimes the big stumbling block in making full use of gift photographs is that the scenes and people shown are not identified. Older residents of the community can be of inestimable help in solving these mysteries.

In order to squeeze the greatest benefit from your collection of photographs and postcards, make sure that they are indexed thoroughly. You may be keeping pictures of dwellings either for their historic importance or their indication of architectural trends. The indexing might be expanded to include references to these pictures from the name of the original owner, the style of architecture, or the location.

Special Indexes and Directories

Special card files or indexes can add greatly to the scope of your local coverage.

Some libraries maintain obituary indexes to death notices which have appeared in the newspaper.

An index to street name origins is extremely useful.

A card file recording early cemetary inscriptions is an intriguing possibility. The location of each gravestone should be indicated on the cards. This is a project which might be carried out by the local historical society or even by an American history class in the community high school.

An index to early county records of marriages, births, and deaths would be a boon to researchers.

A card directory of local clubs and organizations serves a double purpose. It can be helpful in furnishing current information about officers and meetings. Superseded cards can be preserved to form a historical record of these groups.

In an effort to provide a centralized approach to all of their holdings in the area of local history, some libraries have developed a single index for pamphlets, photographs, maps, periodical articles, clippings, and parts of books. The various types of reference aids may be distinguished by file cards of different colors. If a library chooses, instead, to list everything about a given subject on a single card, symbols must be added to the entries to identify the nature of each resource.

Resource indexes do not need to be limited to the holdings of your own institution. A record of community information available through other agencies and individuals is an excellent backup tool. Where are the birth records housed? What early church documents are kept at the First Presbyterian church? Which resident is an expert on the history of railroads in the area? What materials with local implications are in the state library collection? These are all bits of knowledge which may prove invaluable.

State History

The emphasis which you place on local affairs should be supplemented by special attention to materials about your state. There are good reasons for this focus.

Being a part of a local community obligates a library to record that community's present and its past. Similarly, being situated in a particular state obligates a library to interpret that state to local residents.

Furthermore, the events which have shaped your state have also molded your city. The history of the one is the history of the other.

In acquiring material about your state, concentrate on what is currently being published. Leave the pursuit of rare old items to the historical library.

While discussions of the state's past are obviously a part of "state history," don't ignore the publications which consider present-day economy, culture, government, population, etc. These accounts are initially helpful in answering reference questions about current developments. They are also the history of tomorrow.

Because of the mass of material available, the average library will have to be selective in its choice of publications about the state. It should concentrate on the more basic items. Since major libraries in the state will be collecting and preserving state information, there is no compulsion for the local library to acquire anything that does not fall into its normal pattern of reference service. Interlibrary loans and photocopying arrangements will satisfy the occasional requests that involve highly specialized materials.

Official state publications are basic ingredients for your files. The **Monthly Checklist of State Publications (120)** is one way to keep abreast of current state releases although it is not all-inclusive. Our Michigan State Library issues a periodic list of state documents which it has received. It also serves as a clearinghouse for supplying documents to local libraries. You will want to check with your state library to see if it provides similar services.

129

Judging from our experience, it is possible to be placed on the mailing lists of many state agencies although some are haphazard about fulfilling their obligations.

Clues to new state publications can be obtained from newspapers since they often report the printing of documents that are of interest to the general public.

A good method of surveying the agencies which might have publications of interest to your patrons is to obtain an organizational chart of the state government. The secretary of state may be able to provide such a chart. The official handbook or manual of your state will also give an overview of agencies and their responsibilities. These manuals are referred to in a variety of ways. Some are familiarly known as "the red book" or "the blue book." **State Administrative Officials Classified by Functions (170),** which is **Supplement II** to **The Book of the States,** will also introduce you to key governmental bodies in your state.

State historical commissions and state historical societies are particularly good prospects for bolstering your files since they usually have extensive lists of publications relating to state history. Many are inexpensive but authoritative booklets which will be first-rate additions to your collection. Museums and universities are also likely to sponsor historical publications.

A helpful guide to historical organizations can be found in the **Directory of Historical Societies and Agencies in the United States and Canada (4),** a biennial publication of the American Association for State and Local History.

Valuable materials about the state may be the natural by-product of activities carried on by private agencies or business firms. Our experiences in Michigan are typical. Our library profits from the studies of the state's economy issued by a Michigan foundation, the W.E. Upjohn Institute for Employment Research. We are also pleased to have in our collection a survey of Michigan cities made by the Consumers Power Company to attract new industry to the state.

Don't forget the federal government in your search for state information. Typical of its contributions is an excellent series of pamphlets on the natural resources of each state which is the work of the U.S. Department of the Interior. Another important series concentrates on the climate of the states. It is issued by the Environmental Science Services Administration of the U.S. Department of Commerce. These studies are for sale by the Superintendent of Documents.

For further leads to federal publications about the states consult **Price List 87, States and Territories of the United States and Their Resources (150)** and **Price List 70, Census Publications (150).**

You will also want to investigate the commerical publishers who specialize in state history. In our state, Hillsdale Educational Publishers, Inc. **(91)** concentrates on Michigan interests. Franklin Publishers, Inc. **(71)**—headquartered in Milwaukee, Wisconsin—publishes historical booklets covering several midwestern states, plus New York. Comparable firms exist in other parts of the nation. They often exhibit their wares at educational meetings or state library conventions.

On the national level, Teachers College Press launched a **Localized History Series (107)** which originally was expected to cover all 50 states. There is some doubt at this time as to whether the series will continue to that goal. At present 28 states are represented. While conceived as manuals to help students study their own communities, each booklet devotes considerable attention to the history of the state.

As well as states, the series also features booklets on some large cities, watersheds, and ethnic groups.

The price for each booklet is $1.50.

Newspapers represent an important source of state information. Subscribing to a newspaper from the state capitol or the largest city in the state will enable you to supplement the state clippings from your local paper.

If you're lucky, you may find that some group or agency within your state has published a bibliography which includes free and inexpensive materials about your state. In Michigan we are very fortunate. Our state library publishes a quarterly called **Michigan in Books** which, despite its title, also offers good coverage of new pamphlets about Michigan. Our state library has also produced comprehensive bibliographies about Michigan from time to time. Your state library may provide similar lists.

The Library Extension Service at the University of Michigan also issues a source list of free and inexpensive materials about our state which is revised periodically. Educational institutions in your state may duplicate this service.

CHAPTER 8

MAPS

Among the resources of any self-respecting library should be a representation of maps. Too often we tend to think of maps in terms of travelers only. Maps are also valuable to businessmen, government officials, historians, speakers, students, and people with friends or loved ones in other lands. Yes, they're even of interest to treasure hunters.

Here are some examples of map use taken from actual library experience which illustrate the variety of services these resources can provide.

1. To pinpoint the location of communities for businessmen who are trying to arrange for shipments to distant points.

2. To verify street names for the local post office in its attempt to forward poorly addressed mail.

3. To help the convention-goer who wants to find a hotel within walking distance of the auditorium.

4. To assist the timid driver in finding the easiest way to get to Greenfield Village or the Chicago Art Institute.

5. To locate places of current interest. "Just where did that earthquake strike that I heard about on the 12 o'clock news?"

6. To give aid and comfort to people with ties abroad. "Where is this military base my son mentioned in his letter from Vietnam?" "Can you locate this settlement in Africa where my daughter will be stationed with the Peace Corps?" "Where is the town in which my pen pal lives?"

7. To help the historian who wants to determine the precise spot where the first city hall stood or to trace the bed of an early railroad that once served the city.

8. To reinforce the hobby interests of patrons such as the rock collector who studies geological maps or the sailor who looks for nautical charts or the scuba diver who uses the shipwreck maps of the Great Lakes or the hiker who searches for new trails to conquer.

9. To help government officials plan the future of the area. Old maps showing the composition of buildings razed many years ago helped our city officials determine what kind of support they would need for a projected parking ramp.

10. To add interest to the speech of a clubwoman who wants a large map of Brazil for her talk before the Ladies' Study Circle.

11. To provide a decorative background for the businessman who wants to build a window display around imported gift items.

12. To serve as a model for the climatic map of Africa which Johnny needs for his notebook in order to get an "A" in social studies.

13. To dramatize the printed word for the reader who has just finished a book about General Custer and wants to know exactly where the famous last stand took place.

14. To assist the English teacher who wants to spice up her bulletin board with pictorial maps showing the location of literary landmarks.

Do you really need individual maps if you have some good atlases in your library? The answer is a resounding yes! Single maps are like zoom lens cameras which zero in on details and small areas that the generalized maps in atlases overlook. They can concentrate on special subjects such as housing characteristics which are not covered in the broad overview taken by most atlases. Furthermore, single maps can be readily circulated and displayed.

MAP SELECTION

Selecting maps need not be a harrowing project. Don't worry too much about the fine distinctions between types of maps such as physical, political, economic, pictorial, historical, social, statistical, etc. Just concentrate on acquiring the maps for which you have a demonstrated or projected need. Don't become frantic about the complex technicalities of different map projections. Just turn to reputable sources.

Map scholar, Lloyd A. Brown, has a word of comfort for the novice. He says, "A map is supposed to convey a picture. If it does this clearly, without confusing the reader, the chances are it is a good map. And if a map is drawn to scale, with clean lines carefully laid down, with parallels of latitude and meridians of longitude indicated, the chances are it will be a fairly accurate map, though not necessarily so. Whether we realize it or not, all of us are capable of editing a map or chart which is badly done. Good maps are almost never badly printed!" (23)

There are some easy guidelines which even the beginner can follow in selecting maps. Be alert to these key characteristics in the maps you consider adding to your collection.

1. *The reputation of the publisher.*

2. *The date of the map.* In these days of rapid change, the more recent the map, the better. Of course, currency loses its importance in the case of reproductions of early maps. Your patrons, for example, might be interested in the concepts of the world shown in reproduced maps of the 16th century. And as far as maps of your own community are concerned, older maps are precious acquisitions.

3. *The geographic area covered.* Does the map properly emphasize the area in which you are interested?

4. *Detail included on the map.* Does it show railroads? Does it include counties? Does it indicate park and forest areas? The details to be checked will depend upon your purpose in acquiring the map.

5. *Size of map and scale of miles.* How large is the map? How many miles are represented per inch on the map? The fewer miles covered per map-inch, the more intimate the coverage.

6. *Use of color.* Are the variations distinctive enough to isolate physical features and political units? Are some shadings so dark that they make it difficult to read place names?

7. *Text designations.* Are identifying names clearly printed? Are they sparse or are they generously supplied? Are adequate explanations and instructions provided? Are text portions of the map in English or in a foreign tongue?

8. *Indexing.* Does the map carry its own place name index? If not, is there a separate index available? The importance of having a good index can't be overemphasized. Not only does a detailed index help you locate points on the map, but it also serves as a midget gazetteer when you're trying to track down an elusive town that evades identification.

9. *Special features.* Some maps carry extra bonuses such as mileage charts or enlarged inserts of important areas.

10. *Physical preparation.* Is the map flat or folded? Or is it in rolled form? Is it cloth-backed? Does it have a protective plastic coating?

11. *Price.*

MAP SOURCES

How do you go about building up your map collection? Even the newly minted librarian knows that a subscription to that old stalwart, the **National Geographic Magazine**, will bring maps neatly tucked in the pages of the periodical. Four map supplements are usually included each year.

The removable maps are carefully compiled and are valuable additions to your collection. Happily, all **National Geographic** maps are clearly dated. Unhappily, a name index is rarely provided on the maps themselves.

It should be easy to fill in gaps or duplicate popular items. Many people in any given community subscribe to the **National Geographic Magazine.** Since this is not a periodical which people dispose of lightly, there should be basements or attics loaded with back issues and their accompanying maps. Patrons are often glad to share this bounty with the library.

The National Geographic Society publishes a list of all the maps which it has for sale currently. With rare exceptions, these maps are duplicates or modifications of the maps sent to subscribers to the magazine. Some of the maps distributed with the magazine can be purchased in enlarged form. Many **National Geographic** maps can be ordered in a protective plastic format.

Separate indexes have been prepared for certain maps. They are available for an extra fee.

Commercial Publishers

Where do you turn once you've decided to venture beyond the security of **National Geographic** maps? There are many commercial map publishers eager to sell their wares and some of these wares cost a pretty penny. This is particularly true of the wall maps designed for classroom use. Many are handmounted on muslin or linen. They frequently are attached to wooden rods or spring rollers. They may even be mounted on stiff backings such as masonite. The publishers offer plastic coatings or overlays which are markable and washable. Some maps boast of special features such as raised relief for feeling as well as seeing. It's quite common for maps designed for school use to fall in the $20 to $50 price range.

What is your position in relation to these maps? If you are employed in the media center or instructional materials center of a school, there are good arguments for purchasing as many of these maps as the budget will allow. However, you may want to weigh the merits of map transparencies as against those of wall maps.

Map selection in a school should, of course, be geared to curricular needs. Since so many of the wall-type maps being produced today are aimed at school use, it will be an easy matter to find maps which fit neatly into the teaching patterns in your school. Their sturdy format will absorb the buffeting of being shifted from classroom to classroom. Protective coverings will enable instructors to write or mark on the maps for more creative teaching.

If your school library budget cannot bear the heavy weight of such an investment, there often are special funds in administrative or departmental accounts to take over the burden.

If you are interested in maps for classroom use, write for catalogs to such firms as:

American Map Co., Inc. **(7)**
George F. Cram Co., Inc. **(42)**
Denoyer-Geppert **(47)**
Hearne Brothers **(90)**
Nystrom **(137)**
Weber Costello **(195)**

On the other hand, public libraries should be extremely cautious about investing in expensive, school-oriented maps. The demands a public library faces are much broader than those of a school library which can restrict its map buying to curricular requirements. Can you really justify spending your map budget on a few high-priced maps rather than on a variety of maps to meet a variety of needs?

Investing in expensive maps places a heavy responsibility on the librarian who is working with a modest public library budget. To warrant the initial outlay, he must make sure that his selections will keep their informational value over a period of years. This automatically curtails the choices he can make. A costly political map depicting a part of the world where boundaries are unstable is a poor investment. Maps which feature changing factors such as airline routes or rail networks are not worth heavy raids on the library budget.

Maps in which a library has sunk sizable sums can turn into white elephants. Librarians often hesitate to discard them even when they become dated. It seems wasteful to throw away anything that expensive. Unfortunately, the same exaggerated prices which impede weeding also prevent frequent replacement with new editions.

Added to these problems is the fact that some maps designed for school use may be troublesome to public libraries because of their format. Roller maps, for example, are difficult to store and circulate.

Luckily, there are some useful series available from commercial publishers at modest prices. Relatively inexpensive maps depicting the world, regions of the world, and selected countries can be obtained from:

American Map Co., Inc. **(7)**
Geographia Map Co., Inc. **(80)**
Hammond, Inc. **(87)**
Rand McNally & Co. **(155)**

Some commercial publishers specialize in city maps and street guides that sell for moderate amounts. Among these are:

Dolph Map Co., Inc. **(51)**
Geographia Map Co., Inc. **(80)**
Hagstrom Co., Inc. **(86)**
H.A. Manning Co. **(109)**
R.L. Polk & Co. **(148)**

Public libraries have a special obligation, of course, to collect city maps and street guides for the area in which they are located. These resources have a twofold contribution to make. They can be useful now to direct people where they want to go. They will be equally useful in the future as historical records of the community.

Find out what firm specializes in publishing maps for your area. It may be a small local business. Or it may be a company with statewide or regional emphasis. Check the yellow pages in phone books for listings. See what maps are for sale at local newsstands or bookstores. Contact the public utility firms to see what maps they find useful.

Typical of such specialized publishers is the Fred F. Johnson Company **(99)** which concentrates on metropolitan area maps and street guides for the Midwest. These maps are available in the form of inexpensive folding maps or as wall maps on heavy paper with hanging rods. The wall maps range from $17 to $20.

Here my reluctance about costly maps for public libraries vanishes abruptly. Good wall maps of your local community are an excellent investment. And price be hanged! In fact, you would even be justified in investigating the city-county maps published by Hearne Brothers (90) for each state except Alaska. These 4' x 5½' cloth maps with a cellulose acetate finish are mounted on spring rollers and sell currently for an impressive $152.50.

Foreign publishers deserve the attention of any library building up a map collection. Expert cartography and low production costs combine to make some of their maps real finds. Many of these maps offer minute coverage of areas which are unavailable elsewhere.

My one real argument with certain foreign publishers also applies to many map sources in the United States—namely, a reluctance to date maps. In ordering maps from some countries there is also the possibility of encountering place names which have not been Anglicized—as, for example, "Wien" for "Vienna."

Don't shy away from maps produced in other countries. Some reputable foreign publishers with outlets in the United States are:

John Bartholomew & Son Ltd.
Maps distributed by American Map Co., Inc. (7) and
Frederick Warne and Co. Ltd. (194)
Foldex Ltd.
Maps distributed by American Map Co., Inc. (7) and
Gallup Map & Stationery Co. (77)
Hallwag
Maps distributed by Crown Publishers, Inc. (43)
Kummerly & Frey
Maps distributed by Rand McNally Map Store (155)
Michelin
Maps distributed by Michelin Tire Corporation (116)

Foreign publishers even have special resources to offer the school librarian. Excellent wall maps appropriate for classroom use are available through agents in our country such as Nystrom (137) and Denoyer-Geppert (47).

In dealing with commercial map publishers, whether in our country or abroad, the initial procedure is to write for lists or catalogs of their publications which you can study. Be sure to include an explicit request that publication dates be indicated for the maps. Perhaps all you will get is a general statement about the firm's policy of revision, but that will at least give you a guideline for judging currency.

Sample a publisher before investing heavily in his maps. Order one map. Examine it for content and for quality of printing. Make sure that it lives up to the claims made in the publisher's catalog or advertisement. If the map is not dated, conduct spot checks to see if recent changes or developments have been incorporated. These tests are essential before you make a wholesale investment in a map series.

United States Government

Our federal government is a major producer of maps. These maps are authoritative, well-printed, and cheap. What map-hungry librarian could ask for more?

To harvest this bountiful crop of United States government maps, your first move should be to obtain a copy of **Price List 53, Maps, Engineering, Surveying (150)**.

It is important to understand the purpose and limitations of this price list. It concentrates on maps which are for sale by the U.S. Government Printing Office. The entries include such practical items as climatic maps of the United States and such exotic listings as reproductions of original Civil War maps.

But beware! This price list records just a portion of the output of federal maps. Map experts estimate that more than half of the United States government maps are *not* available through the Government Printing Office.

Some are sold only through the individual mapping agencies themselves or through their authorized agents. This is true of the following important map producing units:

Geological Survey **(81)**

Coast and Geodetic Survey **(40)**

U.S. Naval Oceanographic Office **(187)**

U.S. Army Topographic Command **(182)**

Lake Survey District, Corps of Engineers **(103)**

To learn more about the publications of these agencies, contact them directly for catalogs and lists of their maps and charts.

Still other maps are distributed free of charge by the governmental agencies which compile them. This is true of the maps issued by the Bureau of Reclamation **(27)** to show the status of reclamation projects and federal dams.

It is also true of the extensive series of national forest maps sponsored by the Forest Service of the U.S. Department of Agriculture. These maps can be obtained from Forest Service Regional Offices. A list of the Regional Offices is available from Forest Service headquarters in Washington, D.C. **(69)**.

As you must suspect by now, there is no quick and easy way to keep abreast of United States government maps.

The **Monthly Catalog of United States Government Publications (119)** is disappointing as a source for locating maps for the average library. There is a separate heading, "Maps and charts," in the indexes but the listings are few and often are devoted to highly technical and specialized items. The final blow is the catchall referral which often appears at the end of the index entries, instructing the reader to *"see also* names of localities— *also* subjects." These vague directions are of little help to the novice map-hunter.

One compensating feature of the **Monthly Catalog** is that it lists some of the map catalogs issued by the various governmental agencies.

Your best strategy would be to familiarize yourself with the federal map series which are most closely allied to normal library needs. To keep up with the agencies that issue only an occasional map, you will need to have your antenna tuned to leads offered by government lists, professional publications, and other librarians.

The most famous of United States government maps form the **National Topographic Map Series,** available from the U.S. Geological Survey **(81).** These magnificent maps are sometimes called the "mother maps" or "master maps" of the country. The detail shown is awesome. Not only do they indicate the shape and elevation of the land surface, but the large-scale maps pinpoint such specific features as gravel pits, oil fields, cemetaries, and schools. The ultimate aim of the Geological Survey is to cover the United States, Puerto Rico, Guam, American Samoa, and the Virgin Islands with these maps.

There are free index maps which designate the quadrangles in each state which have been mapped. Don't stop with the index map for your own state. Ask for a complete set.

You certainly will want to order the quadrangle map for your area. The price for the standard quadrangle map is a startlingly low 50 cents. Consider expanding your coverage to the neighboring quadrangles. In this mobile civilization our local patrons are often concerned with the possibility of vacation homes, business investments, or camping trips in outlying regions.

You will also want to investigate the special maps, some of them wall-size, which are available for certain major cities and for national parks and monuments.

Complete information for obtaining topographic maps is included on each index map.

The Geological Survey also offers for sale selected individual maps from the **National Atlas of the United States** which is scheduled to be published in 1970. These separate sheets cover such topics as natural vegetation, sunshine, water resources, population, and territorial growth.

The Coast and Geodetic Survey **(40)** is another federal agency which has an active publishing program. One of its specialties is nautical charts. Many boatmen claim that United States government charts are the finest in the world. If your library is located in a coastal region, you will want to consider buying the charts for your area.

Of special interest is the new series recently initiated by the Coast and Geodetic Survey for recreational boaters. These guides are called **Small-Craft Charts.**

Even if you do not choose to invest in these nautical charts, your library should have descriptive material on hand for boaters who want to purchase their own. Ordering details for the navigational guides of the Coast and Geodetic Survey are given in the **Nautical Chart Catalogs** which you can obtain free of charge.

The Coast and Geodetic Survey also has for sale an extensive collection of aeronautical charts covering the world. They are designed for flyers but are popular with non-pilots as well. Of greatest interest are the sectional and local charts which cover the various parts of the United States. They cost 40 to 55 cents. Once again, your library should be able to supply ordering data even if you decide not to buy the charts themselves.

Libraries in the vicinity will want to be aware of the charts of the Great Lakes and certain related water areas which are published and sold by the Lake Survey District **(103)** of the U.S. Army Corps of Engineers. A free catalog is available which tells where and how to buy these publications. Other districts of the Corps of Engineers have developed maps of large rivers or other waterways under their jurisdiction. Contact the Corps of Engineers in your district for a listing of charts and maps pertinent to your section of the country.

Well worth your attention are those maps in the **U.S. Army Topographic Command Map Series (182)** which have been approved for public sale. They range from a huge railroad map of the United States in four sections to a 26" x 49" map of Burma. They are inexpensive and well-done.

A comprehensive list of all the other federal offices which are involved in some form of map making would be overwhelming. It's best that we stop with just a few more examples which indicate how naturally the activities of a federal agency can culminate in the production of maps.

For example, the Bureau of the Census produces maps based on the special types of information it collects. Typical of its output are a map showing Japanese and Chinese in the United States and another depicting mineral industries in the United States by counties These maps can be bought from the Government Printing Office.

The Federal Power Commission publishes maps showing principal electric power facilities and natural gas pipelines in the United States.

The National Park Service has developed a set of eight color maps designed for park visitors. The packet, entitled **National Parks of the United States**, can be purchased from the Superintendent of Documents.

Through the years a long series of county soil maps have been developed for inclusion in the soil survey reports issued by the Soil Conservation Service of the Department of Agriculture. However, these maps are bound right into the reports and are not available separately. Furthermore, many of the older soil survey reports are out of print. If you are lucky enough to obtain a soil survey report for your area, treasure it. The text and the map will be important additions to your local coverage. **Price List 46, Soils and Fertilizers (150)** contains a list of the surveys which are currently in print.

The lesson demonstrated by this detailing of maps is simple: If you don't find any clues to the map you want, write to the federal office most intimately involved with the subject. Chances are good that the agency has compiled some sort of map or chart related to your needs.

State Governments

Governmental map publishing isn't limited to the federal level. State agencies also are aggressively involved in map making.

The best-known example of this is the official highway map issued by the various states. These maps are important because of their detailed, authoritative coverage of roads and communities within the state. The place name indexes are useful in locating very small communities. Many maps offer additional features such as:

Mileage charts

Hunting and fishing information

Insert maps of cities

Summaries of traffic regulations

Points of interest for travelers

Lists of campgrounds and parks

State symbols such as the official bird, tree, flower, seal, and flag.

The title of the issuing agency varies from state to state. It might be the state highway department, the department of transportation, the department of public works, or the department of commerce.

Most states update their maps frequently and are very gracious about distributing them. As new editions of these maps are released, many of them are recorded in the **Monthly Checklist of State Publications (120)**. However, there is often a time lag. Furthermore, inclusion in the **Checklist** is not automatic. It is wise to inventory your state road maps at least once a year to determine how up-to-date your holdings are. Even asking to be placed on permanent mailing lists is not a perfect solution since some states do not maintain such lists.

Some librarians are convinced that they receive a faster response to their requests for state highway maps if they write to the agency responsible for tourist promotion or economic development rather than to the governmental body in charge of highways.

Closely related to the state highway maps are the turnpike or toll road maps published by many states. In some instances they may be issued by the state agency in charge of all highways. More often they are put out by the turnpike commission or authority itself. You can turn to the **Monthly Checklist of State Publications** for listings of turnpike maps. You can also appeal to the tourist office in any state. Turnpike, toll road, or thruway maps can earn a place in a public library collection by helping the traveler who wants to make careful plans ahead.

Many state highway agencies will provide—either free or for a fee—maps of counties and cities within the state. For example, the Michigan Department of Highways furnished our library with maps of street systems for communities in the state. These are prints of their own working maps. They do not have name indexes, but for very small localities these maps are the only resource we can find.

Wyoming offers another example of the extensive mapping program carried on by state highway bodies. The Wyoming Highway Department has a printed list of county and city maps which it offers for sale.

The **Monthly Checklist of State Publications** will furnish leads to some of these maps which cover regions within a state. However, since your major interest in these maps will center around your own state, the best procedure is to write to your state highway authority to ask what maps of cities and counties are available for distribution.

Roads are far from being the only focal point of mapping activities on the state level. The possibilities are endless. You will want to study the various departments and commissions within your state to see which jurisdictions have a natural affinity for map making.

Terminology varies from state to state, but certain key words should alert you to possible leads. Agencies charged with responsibility for the following areas are prime prospects for your map gathering.

Mining and mineral industries
Geology
Agriculture and soil study
Natural resources or conservation
Water resources
Lakes and streams
Waterways
Forestry
Lands
Parks
Wildlife
Fisheries
Tourism
Commerce or economic development
Planning
Railroads
Public utilities
Education
Taxation
State history
Aeronautics

Here is an illustration of the riches that can be yours if you take the time to investigate state-sponsored maps. The Department of Natural Resources in my State of Michigan has mapped about 2,500 lakes within the state. The 18" by 24" maps are for sale to the public at only 50 cents each. Free county indexes are available, listing the lakes for which maps have been printed. What a bounty of information this offers to libraries within the state!

Fortunately, there are tools to aid you in tracing state bodies which are potential map sources. If you should want to collect maps from states other than your own, a good beginning list of contacts is available in the booklet, **Sources of State Information and State Industrial Directories (35)**, prepared by the Chamber of Commerce of the United States. For a comprehensive survey of the units of government responsible for specific activities in each of the 50 states, turn to **State Administrative Officials Classified by Functions (170)** which is a supplement to **The Book of the States.** To get a concentrated look at agencies in your own state, use the official handbook for your state.

Local Governmental Units

Local governmental units—county, city, township, village, school— are also involved in map making. Road commissions, planning bodies, engineering departments, park boards, county surveyors and assessors are all good prospects for map hunting. School districts often issue maps depicting boundaries and buildings. In large cities transit authorities may distribute detailed maps showing bus and subway routes.

Transit system route maps are valuable to visitors and, therefore, concern any library which has patrons traveling to the cities covered. Aside from such uses, the maps issued by local governmental units rarely are of interest to any libraries except those in the immediate vicinity. But to these area libraries they are of utmost importance both for current reference value and future historical use. Establish firm liaison with the various governmental agencies in your bailiwick. Often the maps they publish are not widely publicized, particularly if they were designed primarily for internal use. It may take some ingenuity and persistence to obtain such maps, but the rewards are worth the effort. Under certain circumstances you may even be justified in paying for photographic copies of maps for which no duplicates exist.

Foreign Governments

In their efforts to promote good will and help prospective tourists, many foreign governments gladly provide free maps of their countries. This is a boon to libraries as well as travelers.

Maps may be obtained from such sources as the embassies, consulates, information services, and travel bureaus of these nations.

Lists of agencies representing foreign countries are found in:

1. **The Congressional Directory (41).**

2. **Information Services and Embassies in the United States of Members of the United Nations (181)** issued by the Office of Public Information of the United Nations.

3. **Guide to Foreign Information Sources (35)** published by the Chamber of Commerce of the United States.

Remember that foreign governments are interested in much more than tourist maps. Canada, for instance, issues a list of maps available from government sources which reveals that Canadian authorities are engaged in printing much the same broad range of maps as our officials. You may not want to acquire specialized foreign maps for your library, but you will want to be able to guide businessmen, investors, students, and prospective emigrants in their efforts to acquire them.

Businesses and Associations

Businesses and associations offer rich possibilities for acquiring maps. For a broad collection of city maps, write to the chambers of commerce in the metropolitan areas you want represented. Occasionally, you'll receive a reply indicating that maps are for sale only. But by and large, these organizations will happily furnish you with free maps. As added lagniappe they'll probably toss in lots of descriptive brochures, too. A public library will want to approach the chambers of commerce in all cities within its own state. Beyond that point it should contact chambers of commerce in cities across the nation which its patrons are likely to visit or where they are likely to have business dealings.

The major petroleum and refining companies publish frequently revised maps which are useful additions to your map holdings. Go on a treasure hunt to your local gas stations or write the national headquarters. Don't forget that oil companies with outlets in other countries may even have foreign maps available. For example, the Humble Oil & Refining Company **(59)** which distributes Esso gas has a series of 14 maps of European countries for sale for 25 cents each. Kenya Shell Limited **(102)** offers maps of Africa.

Because boating is big business today, some oil companies also publish charts or maps of interest to leisure-time sailors. For example, Texaco, Inc. **(174)** distributes without charge a collection of 10 cruising charts which cover coastal and inland waters of our country. Phillips Petroleum Company **(147)** offers a similar series of seven cruise guides depicting popular boating waters in different parts of the United States. Mobil Oil Corporation **(118)** not only issues four free **Mobil Cruising Guides** but also publishes an accompanying handbook called **America's Waterways** which contains many excellent leads to charts and maps from other sources.

Reflecting their professional interest and know-how, the American Association of Petroleum Geologists **(5)** has just launched a new series of geological highway maps. The intent is to present the general geology of various sections of the country in an interesting and colorful manner, simple enough to be understood by the general public but detailed enough to be useful to science students and geologists. In all, eleven regional maps are projected, covering all the states except Alaska and Hawaii. Three have already been published. The price of each map is $1.50.

The state and city affiliates of the American Automobile Association have a wide range of maps for free distribution to their members. They would be useful additions to a library's map collection. There are maps which cover cities and counties in the United States. There are also maps of foreign areas available through the AAA World-Wide Travel Service. If you can find staff members, trustees, or cooperative patrons with memberships in the AAA, persuade them to share these maps with your library.

As well as profiting from such extensive map publishing programs, the librarian should be alert to the occasional map distributed by a business or association as a natural outgrowth of its activities. One example is the **Map of Malaysia** offered by the Natural Rubber Bureau. If these maps are issued by nationally known organizations or firms, leads may be discovered in periodicals or in bibliographies of supplementary sources.

When it comes to local businesses and associations, you will have to rely on a mixture of luck, grapevine information, and constant inquiry. It's helpful to know that city maps are frequently distributed as publicity items by banks, savings and loan associations, and realty companies.

Pictorial Maps

A special word of consideration must be given to pictorial maps since they are a unique hybrid—half picture, half map.

The interest in these maps stems largely from teachers and students with an occasional request from a local business or club planning a display or program.

School libraries should consider building a respectable collection of such maps, directly keyed to the school curriculum. Public libraries will have to gauge their involvement in terms of demand.

Here are some sources which have pictorial maps for sale:

American Map Co., Inc. **(7)**

Denoyer-Geppert **(47)**

Friendship Press **(75)** Beware! Some pictorial maps from Friendship Press are designed for children to color and decorate with accompanying pictures.

Hagstrom Co., Inc. **(86)**

Hammond, Inc. **(87)**

National Council of Teachers of English **(126)**

Perfection Form Co. **(145)**

Occasionally, it is possible to stumble upon a pictorial map which is yours for the asking without any investment of money. Libraries in Michigan experienced such a stroke of luck when the National Bank of Detroit published a colorful pictorial map, **Historical Tour of Greater Detroit**.

LISTS AND CATALOGS

There is no good clearinghouse of information about all kinds of maps. The lack of such a central source makes it all the more urgent for you to collect as many catalogs and lists as you can. It has already been pointed out that such guides are helpful not only for library purchasing, but also for the patron who wants to obtain personal copies of maps.

Special Libraries for February, 1970, included an article titled "Published Sources of Information about Maps and Atlases" **(173)**. While it is scholarly in tone, it does contain an extensive list of map publishers and sellers in our country and elsewhere who produce a current catalog or list of publications.

The Library of Congress has compiled five intriguing lists which should be a delight to both the map-lover and the historian. All are for sale by the Superintendent of Documents except for the third which is available free from the Library of Congress.

1. **A Descriptive List of Treasure Maps and Charts in the Library of Congress.** 1964. 30 cents

2. **Civil War Maps: An Annotated List of Maps and Atlases in Map Collections of Library of Congress.** 1961. $1.00

3. **Facsimiles of Rare Historical Maps: A List of Reproductions for Sale by Various Publishers and Distributors.** 1968.

4. **Land Ownership Maps: A Checklist of 19th Century U.S. County Maps in the Library of Congress.** 1967. 70 cents

5. **Maps Showing Explorers' Routes, Trails and Early Roads in the United States: An Annotated List.** 1962. $1.25.

The National Archives and Records Service describes some of its unique holdings in a list called **Civil War Maps in the National Archives.** The list which was published in 1964 can be purchased for 75 cents from the Superintendent of Documents.

What makes these inventories especially important is that most of the rare maps which are listed as being in the Library of Congress and the National Archives can be photoduplicated. This means that if you find entries for exciting maps covering your area, you can obtain photographic copies.

HOUSING OF MAPS

Obtaining maps can be a problem. Coping with them in the library poses still other problems. Because of their specialized nature, their diversity of size and physical make-up, and their lack of hard protective covers such as books have, the treatment of maps calls for some deep thought on the part of the librarian.

The first decision you will have to make is how to house your maps. Housing can be as simple or elaborate as your needs and budget indicate. Factors which will influence your choice include:

1. The format of maps in your collection.

2. The size of the collection.

3. The purpose and use of the collection.

4. The nature of your library quarters.

Most map authorities agree that the best housing for maps consists of storing them flat. Folded maps may eventually weaken and tear along the creases. Rolled maps are likely to deteriorate if left rolled for long periods of time.

The equipment most commonly suggested for map storage is a horizontal metal filing case with large shallow drawers. There is still considerable disagreement among map librarians and equipment manufacturers

146

on the most desirable size. The happy medium seems to be a drawer that is not so large as to be unwieldy and wasteful of space, but one that is not so small that it necessitates excessive folding of maps.

Walter W. Ristow (156) of the Geography and Map Division of the Library of Congress feels that the trend is toward drawers two inches deep, with inside dimensions approximating 43 by 32 inches. This size can accommodate maps up to 40 x 30 inches in size.

The cases usually come in units of five drawers each. They can be stacked. A two-unit combination will provide a convenient counter-height surface upon which to examine maps.

Horizontal cases are available from firms which supply libraries, offices, architects, and engineers. They may be labeled as map cases, blue-print cabinets, or flat files. Although fiberboard cases are available, those constructed of metal are by far the best choice if you can afford them.

In selecting a map case, be sure that the drawers are carefully aligned and that they operate in a smooth and easy fashion.

Some map cases offer extra features such as:

Drawer stops to prevent accidental spillage.

"Lock-out" devices to hold drawers in open position while the contents are being examined.

Hinged metal weights at the front to hold maps in place.

Fabric covers for dust protection and for securing maps more firmly.

Metal hoods at the backs of drawers to keep maps from curling up.

Drawer dividers to aid in housing small maps.

While map cases are the most desirable form of horizontal storage, other equipment can be used, especially when funds are limited. Some institutions have employed map-sized boxes of heavy cardboard or plywood which have hinged fronts for easy access. These boxes have been made to order. You may be able to discover packing boxes which can be converted to similar use.

Single-drawer flat files constructed of fiberboard are obtainable from such suppliers as Fidelity Products Co. (62).

Folders made of sturdy materials such as heavy red rope paper may be used to store maps when filing cases are unavailable. If the folders are constructed with overlapping flaps or in envelope form, they will offer added protection from dust and damage.

It is quite possible that flat storage of maps, no matter how highly acclaimed, may not answer all or any of your needs.

Suppose that you have maps on sticks or spring rollers which can't be stored flat? The large map firms and many school supply houses sell special cases or racks for spring roller maps. Suppliers serving architects and engineers offer roll files which are large enough to hold maps. But librarians have often skirted these commercial offerings to come up with solutions of their own to this dilemma.

Some are quite conventional such as storing rolled maps on open shelves; in long shallow drawers; on top of cases; in roomy cupboards;

or laid on pairs of wooden pegs. On the other hand, some methods display a great deal of ingenuity.

Libraries have experimented with placing rolled maps in vertical containers much like giant umbrella stands. There have been attempts to adapt the traditional newspaper rack for storage of rolled maps. Other solutions have been to build diagonal shelves in a cabinet or employ a sloping rack spaced with dowels to support the maps.

A popular technique for storing rolled maps is to fasten a screw eye to the end of the inner map stick and suspend the map from a hook attached to a low ceiling, to the underside of a high shelf, or to a specially constructed crossbar. Some libraries attach a screw hook to the end of the map stick and hang the maps from a rod or heavy wire. This method is less desirable since an exposed hook on a portable map can be a hazard.

If you're tempted to try some of these ideas, please keep certain admonitions in mind. Standing a map on end may eventually result in warping the map stick. Storing roller maps horizontally on pegs or by any other method which exerts pressure on the map itself may cause wrinkles where the support depresses the map. Hanging a map by a single screw eye tends to cause the map to droop spirally unless it is tightly bound. Maps stored this way should be tied at both ends. Another solution is to insert screw eyes in both ends of the map stick and suspend the map from both screw eyes.

Unfortunately, there is no one simple answer to all the problems of storing rolled maps.

As we have just seen, horizontal map cases do not meet all of the needs of the library which prefers to keep some of its maps on sticks or spring rollers. Even for the housing of sheet maps, you may decide that horizontal filing is not the answer for your library, despite the recommendations of the map experts.

Some libraries cut maps into sections, mount them on a flexible backing, and insert the folded maps in protective covers so that they can stand on the open shelves with corresponding books. Others have turned to cases with narrow vertical compartments in which they file maps mounted on heavy cardstock. Some libraries use pamphlet boxes for special sets of maps. This is true of our reference department where we have a duplicate collection of official state road maps which we keep near our service desk for quick consultation.

I even know of a school librarian who punched holes in the reinforced edges of his sheet maps and hung them by shower hooks from clothes hangers. The oversized hangers which cleaners use for draperies are preferable for this sort of use. Spring clothes pins offer another means of attaching the maps to the hangers.

The vertical file provides still another alternative to horizontal map storage. It's true that unless oversize files are used many maps will need to be folded several times. This raises the possibility of hastened deterioration. But there are mitigating factors which may make the use of letter or legal size vertical files very attractive.

1. Most of the maps which the typical library possesses are not rare or precious maps. They are free or relatively inexpensive maps which can be replaced easily. In fact, they should be replaced frequently to keep up with changes in this frantic world.

2. If maps are circulated, they usually must be folded anyway so that the patron can carry them.

3. When maps stand folded and upright in a vertical file drawer, the cover or title section of the map offers a quick preview of the nature and contents of the map.

4. Smaller maps are less likely to be overlooked among their big brothers if they are housed in ordinary vertical files.

5. It is easier to remove and refile maps when they are stored in vertical files rather than in horizontal arrangements.

6. Standard vertical files are cheaper than good map cases.

There are some highly specialized types of equipment on the market which can be used to provide vertical storage for maps. The best-known is the plan file which has long been in use by architects, engineers, and surveyors. It is a large, steel container filled with sturdy pockets which, in turn, would hold folders full of maps. Other types of vertical containers suspend maps by holding devices which attach to the maps themselves. These unique pieces of equipment are of interest to the map scholar but of more dubious value to the average librarian.

ARRANGEMENT AND CATALOGING

Your map collection will earn its keep only if you can find the map you want when you want it.

The arrangement you choose for your maps is an important factor in determining how close you will come to achieving this goal.

Libraries with very small map collections sometimes add their maps to the vertical file folders used for pamphlets on the same subject. In other words, pamphlets, clippings, and maps on Bermuda would be in one folder. The only exceptions made are for maps which are physically unmanageable for such inclusion. This merger of materials is particularly appealing to school librarians who are anxious to bring all their resources on a given topic together for quick consultation by teachers and students.

Public libraries with modest collections often file their maps under the "M's" in the alphabetical sequence in their vertical files. With this approach all maps stand together under the heading, "Maps," and are then subdivided.

As map resources grow, it becomes more practical to isolate them. Trying to cope with large numbers of maps in the general pamphlet files can be awkward and frustrating.

Even separate map files do not solve all of the many problems facing map librarians. They've been arguing furiously for years over the best method of organizing maps. University libraries and public or special libraries with strong collections often classify their maps. Most of them feel that Dewey is inadequate for this purpose. As a result, many classification schemes have been presented modifying Dewey or starting from scratch. Some of these classification schemes are quite elaborate and far beyond the needs of the smaller general library.

Elementary and secondary school librarians have also dabbled with the classification of maps. Some of them attempt to use Dewey call numbers which will correlate with the book collection. Others have assigned arbitrary number symbols of their own to the various continents and countries.

A common element in all of these classification schemes, whether unassuming or complex, is the feeling that maps should be arranged regionally. This means that they should be organized first by continent, then by country, and finally by units within the country. One of the arguments advanced for this concept is that it brings together as closely as possible those maps which people use most frequently in relation to one another.

It is true that teaching units are often organized by major geographical areas. It is also true that a traveler planning a lengthy trip may occasionally want to survey broad geographical reaches. But years of experience in both school and public libraries have left me convinced that the bulk of requests involving maps center on a single country, or city, or river rather than on a series of interrelated geographical regions. I would like to argue for a simple alphabetical arrangement of maps, using the names commonly associated with the various geographic entities.

A straight alphabetical arrangement offers a direct and immediate approach. It eliminates the need for mechanical symbols to designate class divisions. These artificial symbols only interpose an extra barrier which needs to be interpreted before finding what you want. Furthermore, mechanical schemes are subject to breakdowns when changes such as the creation of new countries occur. Nor will they always expand comfortably with your collection.

For most libraries an alphabetical arrangement is the most practical means of handling maps.

A few libraries have in essence said, "A plague o' both your houses." They have not attempted to arrange maps either alphabetically or by a classified approach. Instead they have assigned sequential numbers to the maps much like the accession numbers used with books. The maps are arranged by these numbers. Such libraries rely entirely upon catalog entries to relay the contents of their collection. While there are merits to this plan, it does have drawbacks for the busy school or public librarian who must produce maps for immediate use while a crowd of customers clamor for attention at his elbow. The system does serve to emphasize the importance which cataloging can assume in manipulating maps.

A map catalog can function not only as a finding device, but as an inventory record and ordering tool as well.

Should you try to establish a catalog for your maps? The decision depends on the size and nature of your collection and the time you have available. If your map holdings are very small, there is little need for a catalog. As collections become larger and more complex and more valuable, a catalog can be an important aid in controlling them. Sometimes a happy compromise can be reached, limiting cataloging to the map resources which can justify this treatment and can benefit from it. In our reference department we have a map catalog. However, we do not catalog the set of official state road maps which we keep for quick reference use because the coverage and origin of these maps is so obvious. Nor do we catalog the gas station maps or official highway maps which we tuck in our boxes of travel brochures.

All libraries, large or small, should attempt to keep some record of the maps which are a permanent part of their local history collections.

Map cataloging differs sharply from book cataloging in certain respects. In book cataloging the author is the key bit of information. In map cataloging the cartographer or engraver is often unknown. Titles are also of less importance since they usually are little more than a statement of the geographical area covered by the map.

The basic cataloging information about a map is the area covered. It takes precedence even over the kind of information depicted on the map. In other words, a map about railroads in Scotland is significant, first of all, because it is about Scotland and only secondarily because it is about railroads. If you are attempting to set up a very simple sort of catalog for your maps, you may settle for a single subject card bearing the heading, "Scotland—Railroads." If your catalog is more ambitious, you may make a second card referring from railroads to Scotland.

For the average library there is no need to go beyond the making of subject cards for maps. Leave the more complex cataloging to large, specialized libraries. For your purposes the geographical area is the main entry. In fact, it should be the only entry except for occasional cross references. The only deviation might be a series entry for important sets of maps.

A prime bit of map knowledge which must appear on catalog cards is the date. This is of great significance in determining pertinency of information recorded on the map. A street map dated 1920 obviously will be of no value in directing a patron to a new subdivision, but it might be of great assistance to the historian trying to chart city growth. Unfortunately, dates are frequently omitted from maps. In such instances, you will have to guess at the date of issuance from clues such as population figures on the map. Your catalog cards should use brackets and question marks to indicate conjectural dates. If no hints at all are discernable from the map, you should at least record the date of receipt. The urgency of establishing a time relationship for maps is an added reason for stamping each map with the date of receipt as soon as it arrives.

Your catalog cards should indicate the source of each map. In some cases the distributor is as important as the publisher, or even more so. This is true of the free street maps distributed by local businesses.

The price or free status of maps is also useful information, especially if the cards are consulted before replacements or new editions are ordered.

Map size is an added item of interest which often appears on catalog cards. Many libraries also record the scale of the map. Scholarly libraries even note the type of projection, although this technical information is of little significance to smaller libraries. If a map is published in sections, you will want to record the number of sheets.

If you have maps in several locations, it will be necessary to mark your catalog cards with place symbols. There is no set formula for these symbols. You can make up your own. "PB" might stand for maps in pamphlet boxes and "H" for maps suspended from hooks.

Maps which come in large sets—such as the U.S. Geological Survey maps—pose a special cataloging problem. A cataloging shortcut is available for many of these extensive sets. Frequently there are index maps or diagrams published for the maps in the sets. In such instances you can type a single catalog card for the set as a whole and mark the index map to show your particular holdings. If a library owns just a handful of the maps in a given set, it would, of course, be better to catalog them individually.

Some libraries, particularly school libraries, incorporate their map cards directly into the main card catalog. In this sort of amalgamation, it is necessary to mark each card with a word or symbol showing that it refers to map holdings. The clue might consist of an abbreviation, "M" or "Ma," or the word, "Map," typed or stamped on the upper left-hand corner of the card.

It would be presumptuous of me to try to establish a master map card for you. The choice of inclusions is a highly individual matter based on circumstances peculiar to your own library. All I can do is to show you what a catalog card *might* look like. You may want to delete items of no significance to your library. You may want to add other descriptive information of value in your own unique situation.

Location | Heading
symbol
if needed | Title. Publisher or source. Edition and date. Price (if desired)
Scale. Size. Number of sheets.
Descriptive notes.

152

Suitable housing, a sensible pattern of arrangement, and a good map catalog aren't enough to assure that maps will be easy to find. The maps themselves must be carefully and clearly marked. In addition to the subject heading, the notation should include any necessary location symbol. The date of issuance should be a prominent part of the label.

The type of housing you use will determine the location of the heading. For example, maps in horizontal cases are usually marked on the reverse side of the map at the edge nearest the front of the drawer. The letters should face the front so that they can be read easily. They should start at the left-hand corner. Maps housed in vertical files should be labeled in the upper left-hand corner in the same manner that pamphlet material is marked.

PRESERVATION OF MAPS

Maps, being the fragile creatures they are, have called forth a great body of literature on their care and preservation.

Except for select items in a local history collection, the average library is concerned with the ordinary, utilitarian type of map. This means that we can ignore the real intricacies of map preservation and concentrate on a few basic principles and techniques.

What about the folding of maps? In his book, **Conservation of Library Materials,** George Cunha expresses this opinion: "A single fold does little harm to a map. Double or triple folds are particularly damaging where the creased edges meet and should be avoided." **(44)**

Clara Egli LeGear, one of the great names in map circles, had this comment to make: "Unmounted maps which are too large for the files may be folded, preferably with the grain of the paper. They should be folded a minimum number of times to fit the files. A fold made with the grain of the paper is sharper and smoother than one made against it, and is less likely to break. The grain is comparable to the warp in woven fabrics and runs in the direction of lesser resistance to folding. To accommodate extra large maps, right-angle or cross-folding may be necessary, but some libraries prefer to dissect such maps. A little trim from wide margins may obviate folding map sheets which are only slightly larger than file drawers. Trimming should, however, be done with discretion. Maps to be mounted on cloth should be sectioned and hinged if folding is required. Cross-folded paper maps break eventually at the weakened points, and unsectioned mounted maps crack in the folds." **(106)**

The sectioning and hinging which Clara LeGear mentions is a technique which calls for mounting a map in pieces with about a ¼-inch space between the sections to allow for folding.

Even when storage cases are used which minimize the need for folding, some libraries go one step further in attempting to protect their maps. They enclose them in heavy paper folders within the map drawers. These folders prevent any damage to the maps that might be caused by sliding them in and out of the drawers. They also help to keep the maps from slipping around within the drawers. Since the contents are indicated on the outside of each folder, map librarians claim that this facilitates the finding of maps and cuts down on unnecessary handling of these resources.

It is recommended that the folders for horizontal files should be at least two inches shorter and narrower than the inside drawer dimensions of the cases to allow for maneuvering.

For the preservation of important items such as rare maps of your locality, acid-free folders should be considered. The Hollinger Corporation (92) produces such folders.

Is storing maps in rolled form really bad for them? Some map experts think it is very bad. In fact, they suggest removing the maps from their rollers and cutting them so that they will fit in storage drawers. However, one authority argues against this treatment because cutting up maps may impair their legibility and reduce the chances of using them for accurate measurements of distance.

Most public and school libraries will continue to use rolled maps if they find this format convenient. It is only when a map of permanent significance is involved that the damage caused by rolling will become of prime importance to them. Usually, this concerns a historical map of the community.

For maps that are deteriorating or subject to heavy use, some type of reinforcement is indicated. This often takes the form of strengthening the edges, folds, and areas of strain with adhesive cloth tape. A more permanent solution lies in mounting the maps. Since this process involves a considerable investment in materials and time, it would be foolish to consider mounting maps which can be easily replaced or which have only passing value.

The time-honored method of backing maps has been to hand mount them on muslin or linen. This method of mounting maps is a time-consuming and messy process. It requires great skill and a large working area. If you are curious about the process, there is a detailed description in Clara LeGear's **Maps: Their Care, Repair, and Preservation in Libraries (106)**.

Luckily, there is an alternative to this laborious method of wet mounting. Seal, Incorporated manufactures a dry backing cloth called **Chartex** which serves as a very satisfactory reinforcement for maps. It makes a sturdy but pliable mount which does not dry out or become brittle with age. Since **Chartex** is applied dry to a dry map, there is no expansion or shrinkage to cause curling or buckling. Best of all, it is such an easy process. An ordinary electric hand iron may be used to apply **Chartex**. However, a dry mounting press is preferable if you have access to one. **Chartex** is available from firms which handle photographic, school, and library supplies. Write to Seal, Incorporated (162) for a descriptive handbook and a free sample.

Many other materials have been tried through the years for backing maps. Cardboard is one. However, map experts point out that there are perils in using cardboard. In time, poor cardboard becomes brittle and cracks with handling, breaking whatever is mounted upon it. If you do decide to use a stiff paper backing to mount your maps, be sure to choose stock of good quality.

Libraries wanting stiff mountings for their maps have also experimented with plywood and wallboard. These materials offer sturdy support, but they may create storage problems.

Even window shades have served as a base for maps. Can you think of a cheaper way to get a roll-up map? Brackets to hold window-shade maps can be mounted on a small piece of wood. With hanging devices such as hooks or screw eyes inserted in the top of the board, the entire display unit is ready to travel wherever it is needed. It has been suggested that two rubber suction cups might be substituted for the hooks, but my experiences with rubber suction cups have not been happy ones. Window-shade maps are particularly suited to school library use.

Mounting may help to solve the problem of the small map. Not only are small maps likely to be completely lost among the larger sheets in a map drawer, but they are also vulnerable to crumbling and creasing. Filing them separately by size only creates another place to look. By mounting these small maps on large backings, they will be able to hold their own among the big maps. It may be a temptation to just dispose of small maps as nuisances, but sometimes these diminuative publications are the only resources available for offbeat places or specialized information.

Frequently, there is a need to protect the surface of a map. Varnish and shellac have been discredited except for maps which are expendable, because with time they turn brown and brittle.

Clear acrylic sprays are available which offer a degree of protection from dirt and moisture. There are certain precautions to take in using such aerosol devices. Experiment with the best distance from which to spray in order to prevent too much penetration. Don't try to put on too thick a coat in one application. Two or three thin coats are better than one thick one. Before spraying an important map, make a test run to determine the compatibility of the spray with the paper and ink.

Plastic film which has been coated with a pressure sensitive adhesive can also be used to make a protective covering for maps. A protective backing sheet conceals the adhesive until the film is ready to apply. A bond is established by rubbing the film briskly against the map. The application of pressure sensitive plastic film to large surfaces can be quite tricky, really calling for the cooperative efforts of two people.

The solution may lie in a new product called **Book-Lon** which is a self-adhesive plastic film with an added talent. It features a "delayed action" adhesive. After application the film may be adjusted until the user is satisfied. The film sets itself permanently after 6 to 24 hours. It can be ordered from library or school supply houses.

Pressure sensitive plastic film is often called "cold laminate." It should not be confused with true lamination which offers the ultimate method of protecting map surfaces.

The process of lamination utilizes heat and pressure to bond the map to a protective plastic film. Laminate may be applied to one side only, but better protection is offered by sandwiching the map between two layers of film. A cloth reinforcement may also be added.

Since a laminated map is protected from air, moisture, and dirt as well as being strengthened against tears, its life expectancy soars.

Map curators still worry about the acid which is left in the paper even after lamination. They claim that this acid will continue to cause deterioration over a long period of time. But except for precious local history maps, this long-term fear need not concern the average librarian.

Happily, lamination offers a perfect solution for the map which can't be mounted because of important material printed on the back. Laminated maps also boast of surfaces which can be marked and later wiped clean. This is important in teaching.

Lamination can be done on a laminating or dry mounting press. Smaller items of a flexible nature can be laminated on thermal copy machines.

While results are less professional, lamination can even be applied with an ordinary laundry iron. For a detailed description of laundry iron lamination suitable with any flat illustrative material including maps, consult Dr. Herbert E. Scuorzo's article, "Plastic Picture Protection," in the **Grade Teacher** for September, 1963.

If you are interested in lamination, contact photographic, school, or library supply houses for equipment and materials. In ordering laminating film remember that if you're willing to pay a premium price, it now comes in matte finish as well as the regular glossy finish.

Lamination is not an inexpensive undertaking, but it is a boon to libraries which can afford it.

CHAPTER 9

PICTORIAL MATERIAL

Many librarians who enthusiastically cultivate other supplementary sources carefully avoid any commitment to pictures. They are frightened by the physical and organizational requirements of such collections.

What a treasure they're missing! Pictures have a definite contribution to make to the informational services of a library.

Don't be browbeaten by accounts of the complex methods and equipment employed by very large libraries. No matter how Spartan your treatment of pictorial materials has to be, they can still add a new richness to your resources. In the beginning stages, they can even be housed with pamphlets on the same subject if no better arrangement is possible.

If you are dubious about the contribution which pictures can make to the reference function, look at these examples of picture use in a public library.

Period costumes for a local theatre group staging *Oklahoma*.

The exact colors in the traditional depiction of Uncle Sam for a commercial artist planning a full-color advertisement.

A fireplace for a new recreation room which would look "colonial" but not old-fashioned.

Danish Christmas decorations for a December club meeting featuring the community ambassador to Denmark.

Not only do pictorial resources earn their keep by helping to answer reference questions, but they also serve as valuable raw materials for building effective exhibits and displays. In addition, they can be used to dramatize speeches and oral reports.

PICTURE SELECTION

The first step on the road to a good picture collection is to gather materials energetically but with discretion. Pictorial resources need to be subjected to some of the same critical evaluation that is applied to books. Not all colorful magazine illustrations are suitable for inclusion in your files. Nor does every attractive bit of publicity that comes through the mail deserve a permanent place in the picture collection. Processing, housing, and maintenance involve the expenditure of time, money, and space. The touchstone of judgment should be the extent to which a particular picture will meet the needs of your community.

The decision becomes particularly crucial when mounting is involved. Some librarians sharpen their powers of selectivity by letting clipped pictures "ripen" a while before they make a final evaluation about their suitability for mounting.

The larger your collection becomes, the more discriminating you will have to be. Almost any picture of a reindeer is precious when you've been struggling along with none. But when you have acquired ten or fifteen, you'll want to concentrate on keeping only the best.

Aesthetic considerations really take a back seat in the selection of materials for most subject areas in the picture collection. The clarity of the image, the authenticity of the portrayal, and the demands of your public have priority.

Artistic standards do come to the fore when choosing reproductions of paintings and other art objects. Here the artistic quality of each reproduction becomes important.

Color enhances most pictures and usually increases their value to the user. For your collection, choose color representations if you can find them.

PICTURE SOURCES

The process of acquiring pictures is one that will vary with the librarian's ingenuity and his budget.

With a Pair of Scissors in Hand

You can cut your way to an effective picture collection!

Magazines offer the most obvious way of expanding picture files. There are many published today which feature illustrations potentially useful to a picture collection. You can think of a dozen without stretching a brain cell. Among the most evident are:

American Home	Life
Arizona Highways	Look
Audubon	National Geographic
Better Homes and Gardens	National Wildlife
Family Circle	Natural History
Holiday	Travel
House Beautiful	Travel & Camera
House & Garden	Woman's Day

Some affluent libraries actually maintain extra subscriptions to magazines such as **National Geographic** for picture clipping purposes. But you can do very nicely without such expenditures. First of all, establish a pattern of screening any magazines your library is discarding to salvage any usable illustrations. Secondly, start a campaign among your patrons to contribute back issues of magazines to the library. Don't be scornful of duplicates. It is good insurance to keep two copies of heavily pictorial magazines since you will often find desirable pictures on both sides of a page.

In schools where paper drives are common, school librarians can arrange to have promising runs of magazines set aside temporily until they can be assessed by the library staff.

While you are gleaning pictures from periodicals, don't overlook the house magazines which many companies publish. **Aramco World Magazine (11)** which is distributed bimonthly by the Arabian American Oil Company features excellent photographs of the Middle East. **The Grace Log (84)**, produced by W.R. Grace & Company, also is noteworthy for its striking photographs. **The Lamp (104)**, a quarterly published by the Standard Oil Company (New Jersey), contains many colorful illustrations. Most spectacular of all is the **Sabena Revue (157)** which is issued twice a year. It is studded with photographs of different parts of the world that are truly works of art. The first three publications, like most house magazines, offer free distribution. Even though the **Sabena Revue** carries a price tag of $1.50 per copy, it has been sent to our library without charge.

Also worth clipping are the pictorial magazines distributed by foreign governments or organizations to publicize a country's attractions or explain its way of life. An excellent example is **In Britain (93)**, a free monthly publication issued by the British Travel Association. It features superb photographs, both in color and in black and white. Prints of photographs for which the Association holds copyrights may be purchased from its Photographs Library. Another example of these foreign periodicals is **Deutschland Revue (49)** which is published quarterly by the German National Tourist Association. The photographs it contains are good possibilities for the picture file. While a subscription charge is indicated in the masthead, we have always been able to obtain free copies.

Newspapers offer some potential for clipping, especially when it comes to the colored illustrations in the Sunday supplements. Sometimes these supplements will furnish full-color pictures of people in the news which would be impossible to find elsewhere. Newspaper illustrations of local personalities, landmarks, and events are of special importance, too. The big drawback to newspaper pictures is the poor quality of the paper.

To increase the odds for locating choice newspaper and magazine illustrations, alert your staff to hard-to-find subjects so that they can be watchful during their leisure-time reading.

Librarians traditionally raise their hands in horror at the thought of anyone cutting up books. But this heretical behavior opens another avenue for acquiring pictures for your files. When books containing good illustrations become candidates for discarding, they should be screened for clipping. It's only fair to point out that a book scheduled for discarding may be in such bad condition that the pictures will be worthless.

Some large libraries with ample budgets buy copies of pictorially noteworthy books solely for clipping. This is beyond the realm of possibility in most libraries, except for inexpensive paperback volumes.

Pamphlets are prospects for picture cutting. Many of them incorporate excellent illustrative material. As a sample, I can point to the magnificent photographs reproduced in **Edible Wild Mushrooms (Extension Bulletin 357)** from the Agricultural Extension Service of the University of Minnesota. It's a good move to get duplicate copies of pamphlets you want to clip so that one copy can be retained intact for its textual value.

The richly illustrated travel booklets from chambers of commerce or state offices are worth screening for pictures. So are the brochures issued by the national tourist agencies of various foreign countries.

Even seed and nursery catalogs might contribute to your files.

Your scissors can also come in handy for salvaging the pictures of authors which appear on book jackets. While duplicate jackets are no longer freely distributed by publishers, plastic-covered jackets usually survive circulation well enough to justify clipping when the books are discarded.

The prospects for creating a picture collection by clipping are broad and exciting if you don't allow yourself to become stereotyped in your thinking. Almost any illustrated or decorated piece of paper is a possibility. For example, calendars often carry distinguished illustrations. Christmas cards can be clipped for art reproductions or symbolic representations. Greeting cards for other occasions deserve your attention, too. Even well-designed wrapping paper is worth saving for interpretations of holiday trademarks. You'll understand what a blessing these simple items can be if you've ever had to produce several versions of a Thanksgiving cornucopia for a harried artist.

Despite its importance, clipping is not the only method of building a picture collection. There are many sources which offer "ready-made" pictorial material.

The Business World

To expand the horizons of your picture collection you will want to investigate the resources offered by businesses and industries in an effort to sell their products and build good will. What makes these materials particularly appealing is that most of them are free.

Typical of such productions is the set of historic plane pictures offered without charge by United Air Lines (179). Also in the world of aviation, Cessna Aircraft Co. (34) distributes a free set of nine colored prints of the planes they manufacture, plus a diagram of the main parts of an airplane. The Ford Motor Company (68) furnishes free charts depicting the making of automobiles, as well as a pictorial history of measurement. Field Enterprises Educational Corporation (63) sells wall posters enlarged from **World Book**, **Childcraft**, and the **World Book Atlas**.

The trade associations representing various business and industrial interests are also active in distributing pictures and charts. Among the groups that have material available are the National Dairy Council, the American Petroleum Institute, the National Cotton Council of America, and the American Gas Association, Inc.

Special Interest Groups

Organizations active in special fields such as health, recreation, conservation, and history are potential sources for pictorial material.

Representative of their output are the beautiful horse painting and the chart of horse anatomy offered free by the American Quarter Horse Association (9).

The National Safety Council (131) has a tremendous collection of safety posters which are available for a small charge. The National Wildlife Federation (133) sells a set of wall charts on the flora and fauna of North America. The American Medical Association (8) has health posters for sale. The AMA also sponsors watercolor prints of various parts of our country which are very inexpensive. The American Classical League (6) sells posters in color which emphasize the Greek and Latin languages. The Bicycle Institute of America (19) distributes free copies of small posters on safe bicycling. The National Audubon Society (124) will furnish a catalog listing the charts and other pictorial aids it has for sale in the area of nature study.

Posters can also be obtained from your local chapter of the American National Red Cross and the American Cancer Society.

For pictorial material about your own state, be sure to check with the state historical society to see what it has available. As an example, the Minnesota Historical Society offers for sale a packet of 17 pictures on the military posts of pioneer Minnesota.

Museums and Galleries

Since art is a visual experience, it is only natural that pictorial reproductions of artistic works should be a major emphasis in most picture collections.

Some of the most distinguished museums and galleries in the United States offer excellent pictorial copies of major works of art. It's true that some of the large-scale reproductions meant for framing are relatively costly. But these institutions also publish small color prints and postcards which are well within the means of any library.

Among the museums and galleries which have extensive lists of reproductions for sale are:

Art Institute of Chicago (12)
Detroit Institute of Arts (48)
Freer Gallery of Art (74)
Metropolitan Museum of Art (115)
National Gallery of Art (127)

Libraries should acquire the catalogs of reproductions which are issued by these museums and galleries. Not only are they useful as ordering tools, but they also serve as authoritative guides to important artists and works of art for the librarian building a new picture collection.

It should be noted that art museums are not alone in their distribution of pictorial material. Museums of other types have developed picture collections correlated to their specialties. Typical of these institutions is the Field Museum of Natural History (64) which has picture sets for sale covering various aspects of nature and Indian life.

United States Government

To anyone who thinks of the federal government as a statistic-oriented establishment, it may come as a surprise to learn how deeply it is involved in the production of pictures, posters, and pictorial charts. In fact, it is one of the best sources you can tap because the pictorial material is well-planned, well-printed, and cheap. We've already touched on the offerings of the National Gallery of Art and the Freer Gallery of Art, but that's only a beginning.

To take advantage of this bonanza the first move is to obtain a free copy of **Price List 81, Posters and Charts (150)**. Don't rely exclusively on this publication since there is always a time gap between editions. Furthermore, it does not list all items produced by governmental agencies. Watch **Selected United States Government Publications (164)** for new listings. Write for descriptive literature when you have reason to believe that a federal agency is actively engaged in picture production.

So broad is the participation of federal agencies in picture publishing that it is difficult to single out any one office as being the most outstanding. Here is a random sampling.

The Bureau of Sport Fisheries and Wildlife, Department of the Interior, has just initiated a new series of wildlife pictures in beautiful natural color. The first set is entitled **Wildlife Portrait Series No. 1** and may be ordered from the Superintendent of Documents for $2.00.

Man's space efforts are recorded in pictures originating with the National Aeronautics and Space Administration. Sets of pictures and posters are for sale by the Superintendent of Documents. Other pictures worthy of saving are incorporated in the free material which NASA distributes to schools and libraries.

Trees, forests, and fire prevention are the subjects of a group of charts and posters developed by the Forest Service of the Department of Agriculture **(69)**. Single copies are available free.

Our armed forces are also active in producing pictures and posters. The U.S. Marine Corps and the U.S. Navy both have released prints of paintings in their military art collections. The U.S. Air Force has developed four sets of full-color lithographs depicting its activities through photographs and paintings. The Department of Defense also has made available for public sale posters on armed forces insignia and armed forces decorations and awards. It even offers a poster on the dangers of drug addiction. All these materials are for sale by the Superintendent of Documents except for the Navy series which is sold directly by that branch of the service **(185)**.

The National Archives and Records Service **(122)** is a good place to turn for historic materials. For example, it offers faithful facsimiles of such celebrated documents as the *Emancipation Proclamation*. It can even furnish photographs of Abraham Lincoln and Robert E. Lee taken by the renowned Mathew Brady. As guides to its specialized holdings, the NARS is developing a series of select lists. Two have already been published and are available free of charge. **Select Picture List Number One:**

The **Civil War** covers photographs related to that conflict which are for sale by the National Archives and Records Service. **Select Picture List: The Revolutionary War** is devoted to black and white photographic copies of works of art related to the American Revolution. These copies may be purchased from the NARS.

This sprinkling of federal publications only hints at the wealth of pictorial resources available from the United States government.

Commercial Publishers and Distributors

Any library seeking to broaden its picture resources should become acquainted with the wide range of materials for sale by commercial sources. Approach them with a judicious mixture of enthusiasm and caution. Some offerings are modest in price, but others are very expensive. Some can be put to a wide variety of uses while others are designed entirely for classroom instruction.

Certain publishers specialize in the fine arts. For over 50 years a firm called The University Prints (190) has been providing art reproductions at low cost. It offers over 6,600 small prints for only a few cents apiece, most in black and white but some in color. They cover architecture, painting, and sculpture as well as minor arts such as costume.

Artext Prints, Inc. (13) also operates in the area of the fine arts, featuring color prints of various sizes including color miniatures which average 3 x 4 inches. Imported color postcards are offered, too.

The New York Graphic Society Ltd. produces small color prints which the publisher suggests should be ordered through your local art store.

Art posters and travel posters are available from some commercial suppliers.

Because pictures of famous personalities are a particularly troublesome area, the Gale Research Company (76) inaugurated the **International Portrait Gallery**, a collection of 750 portraits of the world's influential people. The pictures are black and white. At this moment the series is selling for $125.00. A supplemental collection of 750 additional portraits is to be released in 1970. A **Black Portrait Gallery** featuring 750 important black personages is also scheduled for 1970 publication.

Of particular interest to school libraries are the innumerable sets of study prints developed to fit instructional needs. Some of these prints may be candidates for purchase by public libraries, but they should be carefully screened to determine what contribution they can make to a general purpose library. Prudence is doubly important because most sets are far from being cheap.

Among the publishers who are active in this arena are:

Audio-Visual Enterprises (15)
Encyclopedia Britannica Educational Corporation (56)
Fideler Visual Teaching (61)

Instructional Aids, Inc. **(97)**

Society for Visual Education, Inc. **(167)**

Regional interests deserve emphasis in any library. If you're lucky, you may find one or more commercial publishers in your state who specialize in historical or contemporary pictures of your part of the nation. For example, in Michigan we have a firm called Hillsdale Educational Publishers, Inc. **(91)** which sells prints and postcards with a Michigan flavor.

Picture Postcards

Librarians can profit by repeating that old bromide, "Drop me a postcard," to all of their vacationing friends. For travel postcards can become a valuable adjunct to the library picture collection. They record natural wonders, historic landmarks, and city scenes that are often impossible to find pictured anywhere else. Many times such postcards are for sale only at the site. That is why it is so important to cultivate the assistance of staff, friends, and library users in feeding the postcard collection.

Postcards which depict the local community are worth their weight in gold.

Postcard reproductions of works of art have already been mentioned in this chapter. They can be used to reinforce weak spots in your collection of larger reproductions.

Lists

Clues to pictorial resources will be found scattered through the supplementary source guides mentioned in Chapter 1.

Sometimes leads occur in unexpected places. For example, the **NVGA Bibliography of Current Career Information (132)** contains a listing of posters, charts, and pictures relating to vocations, education, and personal development.

Three little booklets which concentrate on picture sources are sold for 60 cents each by Bruce Miller Publications **(117)**. While these booklets may be of some help to the beginning picture collector, I cannot recommend them without reservation. The booklets are:

1. **Sources of Free and Inexpensive Pictures for the Classroom**. 1968.

Many entries are to illustrated booklets rather than to separate pictures and posters.

2. **Sources of Free Travel Posters and Geographic Aids**. 1965.

Entries for descriptive literature far outweigh those for pictorial material. Many references are to the travel bureaus, information services, and diplomatic agencies of foreign governments. Librarians usually have access to these addresses in other sources. Note the date of publication!

3. **Sources of Free Pictures**. 1967.

Many entries in this list are to illustrations in periodicals.

HOUSING

Cardboard containers, wooden crates, pamphlet boxes and other oddities have been commandeered to house pictorial materials. It's better to have a picture collection stored in a stray carton than to have no picture collection at all.

Libraries which have a choice usually turn to steel filing cases. Some attempt to make do with letter size files although larger drawers are overwhelmingly preferred. While legal size files offer a greater horizontal capacity, they are still limited as to "head room." Much more flexibility is provided by an oversize file which can accommodate considerably larger mounts.

For example, Steelcase, Incorporated (172) manufactures a three-drawer cabinet with inside filing capacity 18¼ inches wide and 15¼ inches high. These inside dimensions provide three more inches of width than legal files, six more than letter files, and four and ¾ more inches of height than either.

Naturally, such extra-large cases are going to be more costly than more commonplace equipment. However, they promise efficient, easily accessible storage for larger pictures which might otherwise have to be stacked on shelves.

Because of the weight which a drawer full of mounted pictures represents, it is wise to inquire about optional vertical file equipment such as sway blocks or dividers which help to support heavy or bulky materials. A clever and inexpensive trick to help in preventing sliding and buckling in picture files is to place strips cut from rubber matting on the bottom of the drawers.

While many libraries attempt to house postcards in their regular files, others turn to special card files which are designed for the Lilliputian dimensions of the postcard. These files are small enough to store on top of other cases or on tables.

Giant-sized resources such as posters and large charts call for special handling. They can be folded and inserted in regular files but folding creates unsightly creases that diminish their display value. Folded paper is also subject to more rapid deterioration. These awkward objects may be rolled, but in that state they are hard to store and difficult to flatten for exhibition. A better solution is to store them without folding in horizontal facilities such as map cases, portfolios, or long shallow boxes.

Librarians with a flair for woodworking have designed swing-out units which house large items vertically. These structures usually involve a door which pulls forward. It is fastened securely to the base of the case but is free at the top except for a chain. Sturdy leaves or dividers may be provided inside the case to support and separate the contents.

There are libraries which use a wide variety of storage equipment to house their pictures. These are usually extensive collections of many years standing. Letter size files, legal size files, oversize files, card files, and horizontal units are all represented. Resources are assigned to the file which best suits their physical makeup.

On the other hand, vertical files of a single uniform size are used for the bulk of pictorial holdings in many libraries. Unmounted pictures, small mounted pictures, and larger mounted pictures stand together in the drawers. Only jumbo visuals such as posters are isolated for special storage, with some libraries also providing separate housing for postcards. The arrangement of materials under a given subject often follows this sequence:

1. Small mounted pictures

2. Larger mounted pictures

3. An envelope or other device containing unmounted pictures

This system is employed not only in smaller libraries but also in some major collections. It works best, of course, with larger file drawers.

For the average library, this combined housing of pictures provides the most practical type of storage. If the librarian is skeptical about interfiling mounted and unmounted pictures, they can, of course, be arranged in two separate alphabets.

Some school libraries carry this trend toward the merger of resources to its ultimate point. As far as is physically possible, all materials—whether they are pictures, pamphlets, clippings, maps, transparencies, or flannel board sets—are gathered together in vertical files by subject. The theory is that a teacher or student hunting for resources will need to turn to only one spot to find this hoard of study aids.

More by necessity than choice, small public libraries may also house pamphlets, clippings, and pictures side by side in the same file drawers. This can create problems because of the diverse physical nature and organizational requirements of these items. Separate folders for pictures and pamphlets may help the physical situation. But joint housing makes it impossible to allow for desirable variations in subject headings between picture resources and pamphlet resources.

While filing cases are important to the organization and protection of the picture collection, there are also internal devices which help to facilitate the accomplishment of these goals.

Unmounted pictures are customarily housed in envelopes, pockets, or folders.

Folders open at the top and on both sides are awkward to use because the irregularly shaped pictures are likely to spill out at both ends, giving a ragged appearance to the files and exposing the clippings to damage.

A popular substitute is a homemade container open at only the top and the right-hand side. These storage units can be made from kraft paper folded in half lengthwise and taped shut at the left side.

Commercial sources will supply vertical file pockets which are closed on both sides. For subjects on which there are a great many unmounted pictures, file pockets of the expanding variety are most suitable.

Containers resembling large correspondence envelopes are also sold by the library and office supply houses for use with unmounted pictures.

In making your choice among these possibilities, remember that containers open at the top can be time-savers because they permit easy refiling of materials.

Libraries which house all of their pictures in common files often place the envelope or pocket containing unmounted pictures behind the larger-sized mounts on the subject. In such a progression, there is good reason to match the size of the container to the large mounts which it follows. This coordination will aid visibility and add to a sense of order in the files.

Plastic containers are still another device used in the storage of pictures. Some of the commercially published study prints used by school libraries come already equipped with plastic envelopes or pockets. School librarians themselves have constructed containers of cellulose acetate or other plastics to protect pictures and keep small groups of related visuals together. The edges are sealed with **Mystik** cloth tape or with plastic electrician's tape. These pockets and envelopes have been found useful for storing pictures in vertical files or on open shelves. They can be used to circulate the pictures, thus continuing their protection.

File guides in the picture files serve as handy road signs. Use them generously. Guides of heavier materials such as pressboard not only aid in locating pictures and separating categories, but they also offer physical support to the pictures.

As well as using file guides in their picture files to designate subject headings or letters of the alphabet, some libraries record cross references on them in addition.

PHYSICAL PREPARATION

If variety is the spice of life, librarians have certainly added considerable flavor with their physical manipulation of picture collections. I am not disturbed by this wide diversity. The test of any approach is not whether it conforms to what other libraries are doing, but whether it works well for *your* library. My goal will be to introduce you to various possibilities and let you choose the methods which hold the most promise for your circumstances.

To Mount or Not to Mount

Librarians run the gamut from those who proclaim that any picture worth saving is worth mounting to those who have collections composed almost entirely of unmounted pictures.

The arguments for mounting are these:

1. Mounting protects the picture.

2. It adds to the attractiveness and effectiveness of the picture.

3. It makes the picture easier to use.

The opponents of wholesale mounting make these points:

1. Mounting is expensive and time-consuming.
2. Mounted pictures take up more space.
3. Users prefer to choose their own backing colors for bulletin board displays.

Most libraries compromise, incorporating both mounted and unmounted pictures in their files. The ratio depends upon two factors: the budget and the librarian's interpretation of what is of permanent value.

Some librarians use their unmounted collections as a proving ground from which pictures graduate to the mounted state. If certain pictures circulate well or if they fill gaps that have developed in the mounted collection, these illustrations are then singled out for backing.

My personal reactions to the mounting controversy are mixed. While I campaign for the mounting of all newspaper clippings, I realize that there are moderating factors at work in the handling of pictures. The items which libraries choose for their picture collections are usually printed on better paper than news clippings. In most libraries unmounted pictures are not mixed with heavy, odd-sized pamphlets as newspaper articles are. Picture mounts are likely to be heavier than news mounts and therefore more of a storage problem. In short, the mounting of pictures is desirable but not mandatory. Let the popularity and uniqueness of the picture be your guide.

Choosing Mounts

Type of Mount

The high-water mark of individuality among librarians is demonstrated in their selection of mounts for pictorial resources. Just note this list of materials which practicing librarians have recommended for mounting various types of pictorial holdings!

Cover paper	Poster board
Bristol board	Kraft paper
Chipboard	Illustration board
Mat board	Show-card board
Tag board or manila tag	Railroad board
Construction paper	Lined pulpboard
Poster paper	Binders board

Even with this splintering of opinion, there are still a few basic guidelines which can be followed. First of all, select mounts that will be substantial enough to protect the pictures but not so bulky as to clog valuable storage space.

In the second place, it is wise to standardize your selection. If you operate an elementary school library which has only a small picture collection, you may be able to experiment with all sorts of novel materials in reinforcing the pictorial holdings. But in a public library or a school district resource center with a picture collection numbering into the hundreds, there is a real need for a uniform type of mounting which will permit mass processing.

Choosing the perfect mounting paper is a complex chore. Your first task will be to decide upon the variety of paper you want. Then you will have to determine the ideal weight or thickness for your purposes. Here you can become bogged down in a maze of paper trade terms such as points, ply, basis weights, and weights per M.

If there is a paper processor or wholesale paper merchant in your town or in a nearby city, the best procedure is to seek his advice. Explain your needs. Ask what he recommends to meet them. You may find that you can make better arrangements with a local firm than with national suppliers.

My own preference for mounting standard-sized pictures is a good grade of cover paper.

Large items such as posters and charts pose a special problem. If they justify the cost, oversized materials can be mounted on a sturdy backing such as manila tag. If you decide to use makeshift mounts such as stray pieces of cardboard, remember that you can expect no guarantees of longevity. Poor grades of cardboard, despite their thickness and seeming show of strength, soon break and crumble.

For important posters or charts, linen or muslin backings may be applied if you have the skill, time, and space to engage in this complicated process. **Chartex** would be a much easier mount to employ for these extra-large items. The use of these special backings is discussed more fully in the chapter on maps.

Mount Size

When it comes to mount size, librarians once again go riding madly off in all directions like Stephen Leacock's famous character. There is no consensus as to the ideal size or sizes to use in mounting pictures.

Librarians seem to be guided in their choice of backing dimensions by such diverse factors as these:

1. The physical measurements of storage facilities which are available.

2. The size categories into which most of their mountable pictures fall.

3. The aesthetics of various mount sizes and shapes.

4. The need for economical division of mounting paper purchased in large uncut sheets.

Some libraries use a single mount size for all pictures except posters and charts. Others employ a variety of different backing sizes.

The advantages of using a single mount size are that it eliminates the need for individual decisions and also simplifies filing. On the other hand, the one-mount method is criticized as being wasteful of backing paper and blind to aesthetic principles.

Since there is no agreement among librarians about mount sizes, what is the best policy to follow?

Utilize the space your storage facilities offer to the fullest extent. Get out your ruler and determine what is the largest mount your files will accept. Don't take anything for granted. I've discovered, for example, that there is a variation in the inside drawer dimensions of even such standardized items as letter and legal size metal files. This deviation is evident among different makes and sometimes even among different models from the same manufacturer. The variation is slight but it is significant enough so that a mount which will slip into one file will not fit into the next one.

Make sample mounts in the largest size your files will house and experiment in using them with expendable pictures. If this maximum-sized mount is not pleasing to your artistic eye, trim it to more attractive dimensions. Don't forget that a mount should look good with both vertically and horizontally placed pictures.

If your basic mount is sizable, you may find that it does not flatter small pictures. In this case, it is desirable to provide an alternate mount of smaller dimensions. In trying to find the easiest method of accomplishing this, many libraries just cut their larger mounts in half. Others provide an in-between size which they feel is more attractive and more practical.

Over a span of decades our library has been faithful to two mounts: 10 inches by 11½ inches and 11 inches by 14 inches. But this formula is not necessarily the answer to your needs. Your physical facilities and your artistic judgment should dictate your choice of mount size.

As has been indicated, some libraries order mounting paper in large uncut sheets for reasons of economy or because it allows them flexibility in mount sizes. If you have quantities of uncut sheets, try to obtain access to a power paper cutter. It will do a faster and much more professional job. These paper cutters are found in many printing establishments.

Mount Color

In mounting a picture, you are in essence creating a "frame" for it. From the artistic viewpoint, the color of this "frame" should be individually selected to best complement the picture. Unfortunately, the strictures of time and money do not always permit this coordination.

Even if you are forced to standardize your choice of mount color, it is still possible to present your pictures in an attractive manner.

Remember that the backing color you choose should emphasize the picture rather than dominating it. Your purpose is to "sell" the picture, not the mount. Mounts in the neutral tones will provide this subtle background and at the same time blend nicely with a wide range of illustrative material. Tan, gray, brown, buff, and cream are frequent library choices. Black and white are also popular.

In making color selections librarians should keep in mind that very light mounts will soil more rapidly than darker ones.

Most public libraries hold to a single color for all their mounting. This makes for a simpler and quicker operation.

Some school libraries have been more adventurous, using a variety of colors in their mounts. Their selection is usually directed toward finding a backing that will harmonize with tones in the picture. However, with holiday subjects they are likely to give precedence to the spirit of the occasion. As a result, Christmas pictures are often pasted on red or green mounts while orange figures prominently as a backing for Halloween illustrations.

No outsider can determine which color or colors will be most suitable for your collection. Once the practical considerations have been met, this becomes entirely a matter of taste.

Trimming

No matter how steady your hand is, a pair of shears is not the ideal tool for trimming pictures in preparation for mounting. A manual paper cutter will do a much neater and faster job. Be sure that the model you choose is big enough to handle large pictures efficiently.

If a paper cutter is unavailable, a razor blade in a special holder or a sharp cutting knife such as the **X-acto Knife** or the **Lewis Safety Knife** may be substituted. A steel-edged ruler, a steel straightedge, a T-square, or a steel carpenter's square can be used to guide the blade.

As you trim, don't neglect to salvage any text which serves to identify or explain the picture. In the case of a magazine picture, this includes the name and date of the periodical.

It has been suggested that leaving a narrow white margin around pictures makes them stand out more clearly from their mounts. Another recommendation has been to leave a substantial margin on heavily used pictures to facilitate their removal when mounts need replacement. But these procedures are not the usual rule. Most libraries trim pictures closely before mounting.

Pictures which are destined to remain unmounted will, of course, profit considerably from a wide margin since this surplus will serve to protect the picture itself from wear and tear.

School libraries which mount pictures for use in opaque projectors face special trimming requirements. The usual aperture on such projectors is 10 by 10 inches. This means that the picture must be trimmed to fit these limits if it is to be seen in a single exposure.

Picture Placement

It's usually best to place only one picture on a mount. Occasionally, two or three small pictures on the same subject may be grouped. This has added justification when all the pictures are from the same source.

The key rule for placement is that the bottom margin must be slightly wider than the upper to give a proper sense of balance. As far as side margins are concerned, libraries usually try to center the picture between them rather than attempting to create an off-center effect.

Holding to horizontal mounting so far as is possible will make it a bit easier to leaf through pictures in the files or in a pack on a table. But this temporary convenience is not important enough to justify placing a picture in an awkward, unattractive position on a mount. If a picture looks better in a vertical arrangement, it should be pasted with the long side of the mount turned vertically. Of course, there are pictures which *must* be pasted vertically because of their height.

You can rely on your innate sense of proportion or a trusty ruler when you determine the precise location of a picture on its mount. But some librarians have developed ingenious devices to expedite this process. One of the most intriguing is a homemade scale suggested by Carl J. Giganti **(82)**. He states that this instrument can be made by "taking a white card the same size as the card being used and marking it off, along the four edges very accurately, with the zero in the middle. With this device, one can use it either vertically or horizontally and note at a glance whether the picture is properly centered." A version of this homemade scale is shown below.

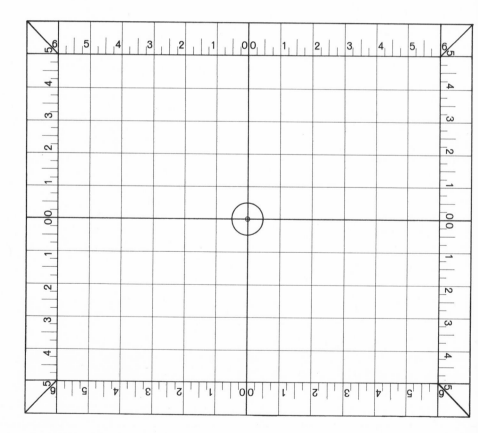

After finding the desired spot for your picture on the mount, make light tick marks or corner lines on the backing paper to guide you once you've applied adhesive to the picture.

In attempting to deal with as many pictures as possible within the confines of the regular files, libraries often turn to an accordian type of mounting for large pictures or panels. The illustrative material is pasted in sections on two or more mounts. The mounts are joined together by hinges of adhesive cloth tape or pressure sensitive book tape. The tape should be applied when the mounts are closed so that there will be adequate leeway in the hinge to allow flexing.

Attaching Pictures to Mounts

To a large extent, the discussion of techniques for mounting clippings in Chapter 5 is pertinent for pictures as well.

The same problems persist in the use of rubber cement, tape, and spray adhesives. Similarly, the liquid adhesive I have found most satisfactory for mounting newspaper articles is also my favorite for pasting pictures. It is a "white glue" called **"Yes"** which is manufactured by Gane Brothers & Lane, Inc. (78). As was indicated in the chapter on clippings, **"Yes"** is more expensive than many library glues and pastes but it does a commendable job.

If you can afford the necessary equipment and materials, dry mounting is the ideal method of attaching pictures. Properly done, it creates a perfect bond which is neat, smooth, and secure. This process is described in more detail in Chapter 5.

In attempting to find a bargain treatment for pictures, libraries have been known to resort to stapling their pictures to mounts. This method should be avoided no matter how tight the budget. As well as being unattractive, it is hazardous. Staples frequently tear loose, mutilating the picture in the process.

Tipping pictures with paste or glue at the four corners is another economy move which is unacceptable. This attachment is not strong enough to absorb the wear which most library pictures receive. Like stapling, it leaves the edges of the picture loose so that they are vulnerable to snagging. One argument advanced for tacking is that the picture will be easy to remove when the mount is worn. My feeling is that pictures fastened in this manner are likely to succumb faster than the mounts.

The only proper way to mount a picture is to see that it is attached firmly and fully on all four sides.

The strongest seal is one in which the adhesive is applied to the entire back of the picture. But this practice is far from being universal among libraries. While they make sure that the picture edges are secured, many libraries elect not to coat the whole picture with paste or glue. Instead, the adhesive is applied only to a strip along each edge. A token dab may be given to the center. Usually this procedure is adopted to save on adhesives or staff time, but the decision may stem from a fear of wrinkling or curling.

Oversized materials or those with extra thickness present a special problem. They are likely to demand overall pasting to compensate for their spread or weight.

Pictures prepared for showing in an opaque projector need individual consideration. The intense heat generated by this machine will loosen many adhesives. If you are furnishing mounted pictures for prolonged exposure in an opaque projector, it would be wise to test your adhesive for resistance to heat. Otherwise, you will have to resign yourself to cheerfully repasting the pictures each time they come loose.

Pictures printed on thin, absorbent paper sometimes present a problem because they may begin to curl even while a liquid adhesive is being applied. One solution is to cover the back of the picture with a clear plastic spray before attempting to use paste or glue. The spray will slow the absorption of the adhesive, giving you time to position the picture.

To insure a tight, even attachment, a paste cloth or paper towel may be used to smooth the picture after it is placed on the mount. Some librarians prefer, instead, to apply pressure with a brayer. The most knowledgeable technician I know recommends a tongue depressor or a bone folder. She claims that it's easier to control the amount and direction of pressure with these instruments than with a brayer. Tongue depressors should be sanded before use if they exhibit rough spots.

Pictures should be placed under weights until they are thoroughly dry. If they are stacked, wax paper should be used to separate the sheets.

Edging

Because of the expense and effort involved in mounting large posters and charts, many libraries resort to partial reinforcement by placing cloth tape or some other variety of tape along the edges on the reverse side.

Protection of Picture Surfaces

The best form of picture protection is "hot" lamination. This is an expensive process although its fans argue that the extended life span of pictorial materials helps to amortize the original investment.

School libraries with access to laminating equipment usually reserve this treatment for their most precious or popular pictures. Some of the commercial study prints used in school libraries come with laminated surfaces.

As of this moment, "hot" lamination does not play a significant role in public library picture collections.

"Cold" lamination involving the use of plastic film coated with a pressure sensitive adhesive is another method which school libraries use to protect pictorial resources. Public libraries occasionally use "cold" lamination but on a very selective basis. For more information on lamination, see Chapter 8.

A more modest type of protection from moisture and dirt is achieved by coating picture surfaces with clear acrylic spray.

School libraries sometimes make use of transparent covers into which they slip pictures before they're taken to the classroom. Vinyl picture covers such as those sold by Demco **(46)** permit pictures to be passed from hand to hand with no fear of damage.

Identification and Labeling

Any textual information that will help to clarify the significance of a picture should be placed on the mount along with the picture itself. Without this descriptive material, a picture loses much of its value. You may have a perfectly spectacular picture of Indians in full tribal dress, but unless the picture is accompanied by a caption identifying the tribe and the occasion, your picture is little more than a pretty decoration.

While most libraries are content to rely on the information which is printed with the picture, some do added research on their own. In mounting reproductions of paintings, for example, such libraries will search out the life dates of the artist and the school of art to which he belongs.

Usually the printed explanation accompanying a picture can be transferred directly to the mount. On occasion you may find it necessary to retype the information if the format of the original is poor or if you want to edit the comment.

Sometimes libraries prefer to place longer descriptions on the back of the mount. However, titles or brief captions should always be pasted on the front.

Source and date of publication are vital facts which should be recorded somewhere on the mount, perhaps on the picture caption or even on the subject label. Do you question the need for this citation? Knowing the source can be essential to an author who wants permission to reproduce a particular picture in his book. The date is equally important to the set designer trying to find typical room interiors of the 1940's.

When it comes to the location of subject headings on picture mounts, librarians line up like two opposing football teams. One side insists that subject labels should be placed on the *front* of the mount. This will permit mounts to be filed so that the pictures face the user. As a result, it is easier to consult the pictures while they are still in the drawers.

Other librarians are convinced that subject headings should always be recorded on the *back* of the mount. They argue that subject headings deface the front of the mount.

I'm inclined to agree with the supporters of back labeling. The subject heading is not an integral part of the illustration or the explanatory text that accompanies it. It is merely a device to help locate the picture. Placing a subject label on the front of the mount does detract from the attractiveness of the finished product without adding anything to the message conveyed by the picture.

There is no escaping the fact that back labeling requires mounts to be filed with the pictures facing the rear of the drawer. This causes a measure of inconvenience because pictures must be removed from the files to be studied. However, this removal also has its advantages. The drawers are quickly freed for others to consult. Packs of pictures run less chance of being bent and torn when they are examined away from crowded drawers.

Subject headings should be applied to the upper left-hand corner of the mount *as it will stand in the drawer.* The use of the left corner is appropriate because we are conditioned to turning our eyes to the left for books and catalog cards.

Usually all full-sized mounts are placed horizontally in storage files. This means that vertically pasted pictures will be turned sideways. To prevent further dislocation, be sure that all vertically mounted pictures face in the same direction before applying subject headings, Otherwise patrons will have to do a good deal of head bobbing as they examine a group of pictures.

The subject heading may be written directly on the mount in ink or it may be typed on gummed or pressure sensitive labels.

Many libraries prefer to print or type subject headings for mounted pictures entirely in capital letters. Their hypothesis is that taller letters are easier to see. To further augment the legibility of their labels, some libraries use large-print typewriters.

When gummed labels or pressure sensitive labels are used, it is wise to leave a small margin between the label and the edge of the mount. Labels placed at the very edge are likely to separate from the backing. Libraries which record subject headings on the front of mounts may avoid this peeling by using labels which fold in the center to fit over the top of the mount.

All pictorial material should be stamped on the back with the ownership symbol of the library.

Unmounted pictures pose peculiar labeling problems because of their physical characteristics. Their labeling is a haphazard affair in most libraries. The usual procedure is to record pertinent information either in margin areas on the front of the pictures or in free spaces on the back. A mixture of these locations can really slow up the filing process. One major library applied gummed labels to all of its unmounted picture clippings in an effort to provide a uniform location for subject headings. Most libraries, however, would hesitate to make this investment in a resource which they obviously think of as temporary and expendable.

The labeling of unmounted pictures is customarily done with pencil. When headings are faint or blurred, the handling of these awkward materials is made even more difficult.

Because of their format, postcards are immune to any controversy over front or back labeling. They must always be sourced, dated, and headed on the back of the card.

ORGANIZATION

Division of pictures by broad subject categories is a common practice. This is ironic because there is nothing so specific as a single picture capturing a single idea or moment in time.

What could be more definite than an illustration of a motorcycle? Yet many libraries will hide it under a broad class heading such as "Transportation" or "Motor vehicles."

There are serious drawbacks to this generalized approach to the picture collection. It presents no problem when a student rushes in to say, "My teacher told me to get 25 pictures on architecture." But when specific items are needed, this type of organization puts obstacles in the way of finding them. If intricate subdivisions are not provided, it means leafing through stacks of pictures to find the desired illustration. If detailed subdivisions are employed, they are often so involved and awkward that they become stumbling blocks themselves.

Why should it be necessary to look under "Physiology" for a picture of an ear or under "Games and amusements" for illustrations of the Olympic Games? Is it really sensible to put fireplaces under "Architectural detail—Fireplace?" Is the best place for pictures of military tanks really under "Armament?" These subject assignments are all recommended in a standard list of subject headings for picture collections.

It is generally acknowledged that when out-of-school adults consult pictorial materials, they are usually looking for very specific topics. With changes in teaching patterns, this has become increasingly true of school-affiliated patrons, too. In libraries which encourage the public to serve itself, there is even more incentive for establishing a direct approach to the subject content of pictures.

I must hurry to point out that there are areas in a picture collection which almost demand broad class groupings. Paintings offer one example. Sculpture is another. Depictions of famous and infamous people also fall into this pattern. The inclusions in these areas are so complex and varied that they would be difficult to handle separately. In effect, they are almost distinct collections within a collection. I know of one large library which even provides separate housing for its picture holdings on paintings and people.

The happiest solution to the problem of subject assignment for the picture collection lies in compromise. Stick to direct, specific subject headings whenever possible. Group pictures under broad generic headings when it is illogical to disperse them.

School libraries may decide that arrangement by curricular units is more appropriate for their needs, but even the strongest advocate will run into trouble with this plan. Many pictures are pertinent to two or more units. Should the cotton gin go under "Inventions" or "Textiles?" Should a picture of a pony express rider be placed under "Frontier and pioneer life," "Postal service," "Transportation," or "Communication?" What sounds gloriously simple in theory becomes complicated in practice. The saddest feature of this plan is that pictures which could add sparkle to a certain unit may be entirely overlooked because they're buried in the resources for another unit.

A published list of subject headings employed in the highly respected picture collection at the Newark Public Library has appeared in many revisions through the years. A sixth edition is now available, edited by William J. Dane. **The Picture Collection: Subject Headings (45)** is a helpful guide in establishing subject heading terminology and in discovering useful cross references. But it is based on a "scheme whereby small and fragmented topics are grouped under major headings." Be prepared to edit this list to fit your own philosophy and your own needs.

Clues to subject headings may also be gleaned from the **Readers' Guide** and from other more specialized indexes such as the **Art Index.** **Sears List of Subject Headings (163)** is useful in determining related topics.

Standard reference books may be of assistance in verifying correct entries for such items as artists' names, mythological citations, and botanical terminology.

There should be a separate card index to the subject headings employed in the picture collection. When all picture holdings are not filed in one consecutive series of drawers, the index cards should reflect this fact. The location of various picture resources on a given subject should be indicated. This might be done by a number code, assigning a separate numerical designation to each special storage unit. Or it might be done by a simple cross reference: Castles SEE ALSO Postcard collection.

Referral cards may be inserted in the card catalog, directing the patron to the pictorial resources available on a certain subject. A typical card might read like this:

Trees

Consult the picture files for illustrated material.

Such referral cards are useful in school libraries where there is need to identify all library holdings on a particular unit.

For the public library this approach to pictorial resources is not a fruitful one. A picture collection in a public library is a highly specialized service. When a patron comes to the library looking for picture material, he is intent on finding just that. His inclination is to head for the picture files, not for the card catalog.

School libraries employ more elaborate means to promote use of their picture holdings. They often classify and catalog pictorial resources as though they were books. This is most likely to occur with sets of study prints and with substantial items such as posters and large wall charts. The entries in the catalog may be distinguished by the use of colored cards or by color-banded cards. Usually a symbol such as "P" or "Pi" precedes the classification number.

CIRCULATION

Most libraries concern themselves with the total number of pictures borrowed on any one subject rather than with each individual item. For circulation purposes pictures are treated as sets rather than isolated entities. Thus a group of three pictures on skiing might be recorded only as "3—Skiing."

While this does not provide indisputable identification of the pictures which are in circulation, it may be the only practical procedure to follow. Because pictures are often borrowed in large packs, an attempt to tally each item separately would be a staggering task. So librarians make a simple notation and say a little prayer. Remember that the finer your subject divisions are, the closer you can come to pinpointing the exact nature of items in circulation.

Smaller libraries are likely to use the same type of circulation slip or card for all of their supplementary sources. These devices are discussed in Chapter 2.

Some libraries have turned to a fixed card system in the circulation of pictures. Each envelope reserved for picture circulation is assigned its own number. The number is repeated on a charging card which is kept with the envelope until it goes into circulation with a group of pictures. At the time of circulation the librarian records on the card the number of pictures taken, the subject of the pictures, the date due, and the patron's identification. Cards may be housed with general circulation records under the date the material is due or they may be placed in a separate tray until the envelopes are returned. The card pictured on page 180 is typical of those used with this system.

PICTURES		#3
9-15-70	John Smith	6
	103 Main St.	Birds

When school libraries assign Dewey decimal numbers to sets of study prints or to large posters and charts, they usually equip these resources with cards and pockets so that they can be circulated like books.

Various types of carrying devices have been used in the circulation of pictures. Old mailing tubes may be saved for transporting charts and posters. Paper envelopes are appropriate for circulating mounted or unmounted pictures. These can be used mailing envelopes or specially purchased envelopes. One library wraps mounted pictures in heavy paper for circulation. School libraries sometimes resort to plastic pockets or holders.

Some libraries even make picture envelopes of cloth. Our library uses denim carriers which were sewn in the workshop of a state mental hospital. They have an overflap which fastens securely with twill ties. The inside is reinforced with a rectangle of corrugated cardboard which fits loosely against the back of the envelope. A date due slip is pasted to the cardboard.

In making or buying envelopes, remember that they should be one or two inches longer and wider than the pictures they will contain.

Be sure that the identification mark of the library appears on all carrying devices.

Because of the misuse to which pictures are subjected when they are exhibited, some libraries attach a list of suggestions for safe display techniques to the carriers in which the pictures circulate.

When pictures are charged out, the date they are due should be indicated on the carrying device. The number of pictures taken should be recorded there also.

PHOTOGRAPHS

Photographs about the local community form a very special kind of picture collection. Extra care is necessary to insure the survival of historically important photographs since they are vulnerable to light, harmful chemicals, excessive heat and humidity, careless handling, and dirt or dust.

Envelopes will help to protect them. Under optimum conditions each important photograph should be placed in a separate container. In choosing paper envelopes, avoid high-acid paper and center seams. Be sure that any adhesive used in making the envelopes will not adversely affect the photographs. Experts also recommend seamless envelopes of cellulose acetate. To make the files more orderly and easier to use, it's best to hold to a single envelope size except for extra-large pictures.

While it is essential to know the exact content and history of each photograph, it is risky to attempt writing all of this information directly on the back of the picture. Writing may raise ridges on the face of a print. Authorities recommend that any necessary penciling be restricted to the outer edge of the reverse side.

Some libraries type the descriptive material on a separate strip of paper which is then applied to the back of the print. The adhesive used with this method should be free of harmful chemicals.

Another solution is to file the photographs numerically. Under this arrangement only a number needs to be penciled on the back margin and repeated on the envelope if one is used. Complete information about the photographs can be recorded on numbered cards. A subject index will provide access to the pictures.

Historically significant photographs are usually preserved unmounted in their original state. If you find it necessary or desirable to provide backing for such prints, exercise great caution in selecting the mounts and the method of adhesion. Experts frown on rubber cement and water-base adhesives because of their potentially harmful effects. Dry mounting tissue is the most highly recommended mounting agent. A good description of the dry mounting of photographs appears in a booklet, **The Fourth Here's How**, which is sold by the Eastman Kodak Company for 95 cents. Detailed information about the dry mounting of photographs is also contained in **Better Mounting**, a free pamphlet available from Seal, Inc. **(162).**

While photographs are usually mounted on card stock, **Chartex** dry backing cloth can be safely used to provide flexible reinforcement for prints.

Because of their extreme sensitivity, negatives pose even more of a problem for libraries than prints do. They should always be stored in jackets. Filing them by a numerical code will eliminate any unnecessary writing on the delicate film.

FOR FURTHER READING

Library picture collections are discussed in **How to Organize and Maintain the Library Picture/Pamphlet File (83)** by Geraldine N. Gould and Ithmer C. Wolfe. The emphasis is on school libraries.

While it is very brief and directed to the needs of teachers, **So You Want to Start a Picture File (117)** by Bruce Miller and Merton Osborn contains some realistic advice.

The Practical Audio-Visual Handbook for Teachers (161) by Herbert E. Scuorzo offers an excellent survey of techniques such as mounting and lamination.

An easy, step-by-step introduction to processes such as dry mounting, wet mounting, and lamination is provided in **Practical Storage and Use of Maps and Posters (175)** by Della Thomas and Helen Lloyd. Plans for an oversized storage case are also included. Unfortunately, this manual is out of print, but you may be able to obtain a copy through inter-library loan.

CHAPTER 10

SPECIAL INDEXES AND FILES

In every trade there are treasured tools which spell the difference between adequate and superior performance. In the library world these tools can take the form of special reference indexes and folders.

One of the most helpful of these devices is a card file of elusive or repeatedly used information.

FUGITIVES FILE

When you've finally come up with the answer to a devilish reference question and suspect it may be asked again someday, this card file is the place to make a notation of the answer and the sources used to find it. No wonder some librarians call this type of index a "fugitives file" since it holds the kind of information that is as hard to capture as the most legendary outlaw.

The fugitives file is also a useful place to anchor facts that are asked for repeatedly, such as the highest and lowest altitudes in the city. This handy summary will salvage time otherwise spent in trotting back and forth to the original sources.

The fugitives file may also incorporate references to resource people in the community who have special talents or interests that might be tapped to answer difficult reference problems. A roster of citizens able to translate various foreign languages can form an invaluable part of this list of human resources. One word of caution! As a matter of common courtesy, check with resource people to make sure they are willing to become consultants. A local resident may be a dedicated collector of rare books, but this doesn't necessarily mean that he will agree to evaluate attic treasures for any casual caller.

SPEAKERS FILE

A "speakers file" or "program planners file" can be a great boon to local clubs, schools, and individuals. These names are poor ones since the contents need not be restricted to speakers, nor need they be devoted entirely to formal programs. To help the harried dance chairman or the parent looking for entertainment for a children's party, the file can be expanded to include magicians, orchestras, puppeteers, square dance callers, barbershop quartets, folk dance groups, etc.

Leads for this file can be obtained from newspaper articles, especially those appearing on the social page. Word-of-mouth clues can also be productive. Occasionally, a local performer will place an ad in the paper asking for engagements.

It is essential to obtain clearance before adding any individual or group to the roster. A form can be developed to speed this process. As soon as the staff becomes aware of a new talent in the community, the form can be sent, explaining the file and requesting permission to add the recipient to the list. He should be asked to specify—

1. The topics on which he will speak, in the case of speakers— or the nature of his performance, in the case of entertainers.

2. The details of his availability.

3. His fee, if any.

LOCAL ORGANIZATIONS DIRECTORY

One of the most popular resources in our reference department is our local organizations directory in which we record the hundreds of groups active in our community. This card file is of inestimable value to citizens planning fund-raising drives, political campaigns, or millage votes. It is also important to the patron who wants to know if there is a chess club in town that he can join or to the widow who is looking for the local chapter of Parents Without Partners. We try to obtain the names of club officers as well as the time and place of meeting. The entries in the organizations file must always be dated so that the currency of the information can be judged. In many instances, elections of group officers are reported in the local newspaper but we've discovered to our sorrow that the coverage is not universal. At regular and frequent intervals the directory must be screened for outdated cards. A form letter or postcard can be used to request the names of new officers.

INFORMATION ON COMING EVENTS

Crucial to good reference work in public libraries is the gathering of information on coming events which are of interest to the library's clientele. The heaviest concentration should, of course, be on events taking place in the local community or in neighboring regions. Scour the area newspapers for announcements and ads. Collect any flyers which are distributed to publicize area affairs. Persuade the local schools, amateur theatrical groups, musical organizations, service clubs, churches, and civic officials to alert the library to any public events they are sponsoring.

This accumulation of information can be the jumping-off point for publishing a regular calendar of events to be distributed to groups and institutions throughout the city. Such an undertaking is both an important public service and a good publicity move for the library. In one small library where funds were not available for preparing multiple copies of a calendar of events, the librarian posted a huge homemade calendar in the library each month on which she recorded coming events in the community.

Careful attention should also be given to events scheduled for other parts of the state. In many states there is a government agency which releases a calendar of events covering the entire state. Regional tourist associations may also publish chronologies of activities in their areas. Summaries of events in larger cities are often issued by their tourist and convention bureaus, municipal offices of public information, or chambers of commerce. Activities in metropolitan areas may even be covered in commercially produced magazines which are designed to be distributed free of charge in restaurants, hotels, and motels.

As part of your state survey, ask to be put on the mailing list for announcements of events scheduled at the outstanding auditoriums and for releases from the important art museums. If there are "big-time" sports teams in the state, obtain schedules of their games. This applies both to professional groups and to the major university teams.

In venturing beyond the boundaries of your own state, you will have to gauge your acquisitions to the requests you receive from your community. If there are major cities in nearby states that regularly attract your patrons, you will want to make every effort to obtain descriptive literature about their coming events.

Coverage on a nationwide scale should center on items of major interest. Discover America Travel Organizations, Inc. issues a free monthly survey, **News About Travel (136)**, which lists the top 20 U.S. travel events each month. The Bureau of Indian Affairs compiles an interesting publication called the **American Indian Calendar (24)**. These are typical of the guides which might be good additions to your overview of the nation.

On the international level, many foreign tourist agencies issue free literature about coming events. Government and commercial interests have joined hands to produce **Events in the Pacific (141)**, a unique summary which is available without charge from the Pacific Area Travel Association. Airlines represent another source of information. Air France has a free booklet called **International Events (1)** while Pan American World Airways distributes two guides without charge. One is **International Trade Fairs**; the other is **Pan Am's Book of Overseas Events (142)**.

Each year the U.S. Department of Commerce issues a world business calendar listing holiday observances in various countries. The title varies from year to year. The current list is called **1970 World Holidays Listed, A Guide for Business Travel**. It is for sale by the Superintendent of Documents for 20 cents.

In building your files of national and international events, remember that photocopies or clippings of special magazine surveys can be very useful. Typical of such aids are the charts which appear in the **Saturday Review** each year under the headings, "World Travel Calendar," "Guide to European Music Festivals," and "Music Festivals USA."

Chases' Calendar of Annual Events, Special Days, Weeks and Months (36) should be a part of your events file or readily available nearby.

If you receive duplicate copies of brochures about coming events, don't throw them away if they are of more than momentary value. Add them to your travel collection.

Weeding events folders poses a special problem. The first temptation is to ruthlessly eliminate anything that is past, but a little hesitation may prove profitable. We have found that many times patrons contact us for added information *after* they have attended an event. On the local and state level we sometimes keep copies of seasonal lists until the new edition arrives the next year. This enables us to at least approximate the location and customary date of a recurring event.

SPECIALIZED REFERENCE FOLDERS

As kissing cousins to our events file, we also maintain folders devoted to special courses being offered in the community and to fund-raising or service campaigns going on in the area.

A folder should be established for what we call "official changes." These are clippings which will eventually be used to update data in the library's basic reference books. Until the changes are recorded, the folder of clippings can be used to answer questions. The deaths of prominent people, the appointment of important public officials, and the outcome of elections are among the newsworthy items which belong in this folder. So do clippings about new developments in areas covered by such tools as the **Guinness Book of World Records**, Kane's **Famous First Facts**, and the **Encyclopedia of Associations**.

Other specialized reference folders can be added for any topics that need concentrated attention. To help with those exacting questions about what time it is in Tokyo, Japan or Kokomo, Indiana, we maintain a collection of materials relating to time zones and time changes. Luckily, Manufacturers Hanover Trust Company will place libraries on a mailing list to receive their **World Time Chart (111)** which is distributed twice a year to reflect Daylight Saving Time and Standard Time. This chart is blessedly easy to use. To this folder we also add newspaper clippings on deviations in time observance and any articles that deal with our time situation in Michigan.

Because we have frequent requests about the distance from Kalamazoo to other cities, we've compiled some tables for easy consultation which we house in our special reference files. In making a table for your city, official state road maps will be of some assistance in determining distances since they usually contain charts showing mileage between cities within a state. For more comprehensive coverage, consult the long-distance moving companies in your community. These companies have detailed guides which they use in establishing mileage.

A folder of current information on foreign exchange rates will help you answer questions about the value of various currencies. Both the Manufacturers Hanover Trust Company **(111)** and the First National Bank of Chicago **(66)** distribute free tables of foreign exchange quotations.

Sometimes special reference aids will outgrow their folders. The questions we receive on etiquette are so intricate and offbeat that we've started to save some of the advice which appears in etiquette columns in newspapers and magazines. Attempting to house this growing collection of clippings in either the general files or the special reference files was not the ideal solution. Instead, we have pasted them into a looseleaf notebook which is divided by subject. This decision nicely illustrates the fact that all "vertical file" material does not need to be housed in vertical files.

IN CONCLUSION

This paragraph is both an ending and a beginning. The ten chapters just concluded have pictured the exciting role which supplementary sources of information can play in library service. These chapters have also explored the practical aspects of acquiring and managing these resources. My hope is that you've garnered enough enthusiasm and know-how to make these informational aids a vital part of *your* library program. It's your turn now to experience the challenge, the fun, and the rewards offered by the vertical file and its satellites.

LIST OF REFERENCES

1. Air France. **International Events.** Air France, Box 707, N.Y., N.Y. 10011. Free.

2. Alexander, Raphael. **Sources of Medical Information.** 1969. Exceptional Books, 200 W. 57th St., N.Y., N.Y. 10019. $4.50.

3. Alumnae Advisory Center, Inc., 541 Madison Ave., N.Y., N.Y. 10022.

4. American Association for State and Local History. **Directory of Historical Societies and Agencies in the United States and Canada.** Published biennially. The Association, 132 Ninth Ave., Nashville, Tenn. 37203. Price of 1969-70 edition $3.75.

5. American Association of Petroleum Geologists, Box 979, Tulsa, Okla. 74101.

6. American Classical League Service Bureau, Miami University, Oxford, Ohio 45056.

7. American Map Co., Inc., 3 West 61st St., N.Y., N.Y. 10023.

8. American Medical Association, 535 N. Dearborn St., Chicago, Ill. 60610.

9. American Quarter Horse Association, P.O. Box 200, 2736 Plains Blvd., Amarillo, Texas 79105.

10. **American Trade Schools Directory, 1969.** Croner Publications, Inc., Queens Village, N.Y. 11428. $12.00.

11. **Aramco World Magazine.** Bimonthly. Arabian American Oil Co., 1345 Avenue of the Americas, N.Y., N.Y. 10019. Free.

12. Art Institute of Chicago, Chicago, Ill. 60603.

13. Artext Prints, Inc., Box 70, Westport, Conn. 06880.

14. Aubrey, Ruth H. **Selected Free Materials for Classroom Teachers.** 3rd ed., 1969. Fearon Publishers, 2165 Park Blvd., Palo Alto, Calif. 94306. $2.00.

15. Audio-Visual Enterprises, 911 Laguna Road, Pasadena, Calif. 91105.

16. Bacon Pamphlet Service, Inc., East Chatham, N.Y. 12060.

17. Ball, Miriam Ogden. **Subject Headings for the Information File.** 8th ed., 1956. H.W. Wilson Co. Out-of-print.

18. Bennett, Wilma. **Occupations Filing Plan and Bibliography.** 3rd ed., 1968. Interstate Printers & Publishers, Inc., Danville, Ill. 61832. Book $3.95. Book plus labels $14.95.

19. Bicycle Institute of America, Inc., 122 E. 42nd St., N.Y., N.Y. 10017.

20. B'nai B'rith Vocational Service, 1640 Rhode Island Ave., N.W., Washington, D.C. 20036.

   Careers in Jewish Communal Service. 35 cents each.

   Occupational Brief Series. 35 cents each.

   Counselor's Information Service. Quarterly. $7 per year.

21. Boating Industry Association. **Boating: A Statistical Report on America's Top Family Sport.** Issued annually. Boating Industry Association, Marketing Dept., 333 North Michigan Ave., Chicago, Ill. 60601. Free.

22. **Booklist.** Twice a month Sept. through July and once in August. American Library Association, 50 E. Huron St., Chicago, Ill. 60611. $10 per year.

23. Brown, Lloyd A. "The Problem of Maps." In **Readings in Nonbook Librarianship** edited by Jean Spealman Kujoth, Scarecrow Press, Inc., 1968, page 269. This article appeared first in **Library Trends**, October, 1964.

24. Bureau of Indian Affairs, U.S. Dept. of the Interior. **American Indian Calendar.** 1970. For sale by Supt. of Documents. 25 cents.

25. Bureau of Labor Statistics, U.S. Dept. of Labor, Washington, D.C. 20212.

> **Occupational Outlook Handbook.** Published every other year. For sale by Supt. of Documents. Price of 1970-71 edition $6.25.

> Reprints from **Occupational Outlook Handbook.** For sale by Supt. of Documents. Reprints from 1970-71 edition 10 cents to 20 cents each. $16.40 for full set of 128 reprints.

> **Occupational Outlook Quarterly.** For sale by Supt. of Documents. $1.50 per year.

> Reprints from **Occupational Outlook Quarterly.** Available free from Bureau of Labor Statistics.

26. Bureau of Outdoor Recreation, U.S. Dept. of the Interior. **Guides to Outdoor Recreation Areas and Facilities.** 1968. The Bureau, Washington, D.C. 20240. Free.

27. Bureau of Reclamation, U.S. Dept. of the Interior, Office of Chief Engineer, Attention: 841, Denver Federal Center, Denver, Colo. 80225.

28. Bureau of Sport Fisheries and Wildlife, U.S. Dept. of the Interior, Washington, D.C. 20240.

29. Alvah Bushnell Co., 925 Filbert St., Philadelphia, Pa. 19107.

30. **Business Service Checklist**. Weekly. U.S. Dept. of Commerce. For sale by Supt. of Documents. $2.50 per year.

31. Canadian Department of External Affairs. **English-Language Publications Available Outside Canada**. The Department, Ottawa, Canada. Free.

32. Canadian Government Travel Bureau, 150 Kent St., Ottawa, Canada.

33. Careers, Inc., P.O. Box 135, Largo, Fla. 33540.

> **Career Briefs**. Single copies 35 cents. Complete set $32.00. Annual subscription $10.00.

> **Career Summaries**. Single copies 20 cents. Complete set $42.00. Annual subscription $10.00.

> **Job Guides**. Single copies 20 cents. Annual subscription $3.50.

> **Career Guidance Index**. 9 issues a year. $6.00 per year.

34. Cessna Aircraft Co., P.O. Box 1521, Wichita, Kansas 67201.

35. Chamber of Commerce of the United States, 1615 H St., N.W., Washington, D.C. 20006.

> **Guide to Foreign Information Sources**. Prepared by the International Group. New edition due in summer of 1970. Price of old edition 25 cents. Inquire about free copy.

> **Sources of State Information and State Industrial Directories**. Prepared by the State Chamber of Commerce Dept. New edition due early in 1971. Price of old edition 40 cents. Inquire about free copy.

36. Chase, Harrison V. and William D. **Chases' Calendar of Annual Events, Special Days, Weeks and Months**. Published annually. Apple Tree Press, Publishers, Box 1012, Flint, Mich. 48501. $3.00.

37. Chemical Bank New York Trust Company. **International Economic Survey**. Chemical Bank New York Trust Company, Church Street P.O. Station, N.Y., N.Y. 10015. Free.

38. Christianson, Elin B. "Variation of Editorial Material in Periodicals Indexed in *Readers' Guide.*" **ALA Bulletin**, February, 1968, pages 173-182.

39. Chronicle Guidance Publications, Inc., Moravia, N.Y. 13118.

> **Chronicle Occupational Briefs.** Four-page brief 35 cents, eight-page brief 50 cents. Complete set $64.50 plus postage. Annual subscription $20.25.

> **Chronicle Occupational Reprints.** Four-page reprint 35 cents, over four pages 50 cents. Complete set $15.00 plus postage. Annual subscription $7.00.

> **Filing Plan.** 300 labeled folders $35.00.

> **Career Index.** Annual and four supplements. $11.00 per year.

40. Coast and Geodetic Survey, Environmental Science Services Administration, Rockville, Md. 20852.

41. **Congressional Directory.** U.S. Congress. For sale by Supt. of Documents. Price of 1970 edition $4.00.

42. George F. Cram Co., Inc., P.O. Box 426, Indianapolis, Ind. 46206.

43. Crown Publishers, Inc., 419 Park Ave. South, N.Y., N.Y. 10016.

44. Cunha, George. **Conservation of Library Materials**. 1967. Scarecrow Press. Page 91.

45. Dane, William J. **The Picture Collection: Subject Headings**. 6th ed., 1968. Shoe String Press, Inc. $6.00.

46. Demco Educational Corp., P.O. Box 1488, Madison, Wis. 53701.

47. Denoyer-Geppert, 5235 Ravenswood Ave., Chicago, Ill. 60640.

48. Detroit Institute of Arts, 5200 Woodward Ave., Detroit, Mich. 48202.

49. **Deutschland Revue.** Quarterly. German National Tourist Office, 500 Fifth Ave., N.Y., N.Y. 10036. 1.50 DM per copy. Inquire about free subscription.

50. Dever, Esther. **Sources of Free and Inexpensive Educational Materials.** 3rd ed., 1965. The Author, P.O. Box 186, Grafton, West Virginia 26354. $5.30. New edition in preparation.

51. Dolph Map Co., Inc., 430 North Federal Highway, Fort Lauderdale, Fla. 33301.

52. Dow Jones & Company, Inc. **List of Free Materials Available to Secondary School Instructors.** Revised annually. Dow Jones & Company, Inc., Educational Service Bureau, P.O. Box 300, Princeton, N.J. 08540. Free. Distributed to school librarians but *not* to public librarians.

53. **Editorial Research Reports.** Published four times a month. Editorial Research Reports, 1735 K St., N.W., Washington, D.C. 20006. $2.00 each. Annual subscription plus semiannual bound volumes containing additional material $108.

54. Educators Progress Service, Inc., Randolph, Wis. 53956.

Educators Guide to Free Guidance Materials. Revised annually. 1969 edition $7.50.

Educators Guide to Free Health, Physical Education and Recreation Materials. Revised annually. 1969 edition $8.00.

Educators Guide to Free Science Materials. Revised annually. 1969 edition $8.25.

Educators Guide to Free Social Studies Materials. Revised annually. 1969 edition $9.50.

Educators Index of Free Materials. Revised annually. $25.00.

Elementary Teachers Guide to Free Curriculum Materials. Revised annually. 1969 edition $9.75.

55. Eisen, Irving and Goodman, Leonard H. **Starter File of Free Occupational Literature.** 1970. B'nai B'rith Vocational Service, 1640 Rhode Island Ave., N.W., Washington, D.C. 20036. $1.25.

56. Encyclopaedia Britannica Educational Corporation, 425 N. Michigan Ave., Chicago, Ill. 60611.

57. **Encyclopedia of Associations.** (v.I **National Organizations of the United States, v.II Geographic and Executive Index, v.III New Associations**) 5th ed., 1968. Gale Research Co., Book Tower, Detroit, Mich. 48226. v.I $29.50, v.II $17.50, v.III $25.00.

58. **Encyclopedia of Careers and Vocational Guidance.** 1967. New edition due in 1971. J.G. Ferguson Publishing Co., 6 North Michigan Ave., Chicago, Ill. 60602. $21.65.

59. Esso European Travel Aids, Humble Touring Service, P.O. Box 802, Poughkeepsie, N.Y. 12602.

60. European Travel Commission, 630 Fifth Ave., N.Y., N.Y. 10020.

61. Fideler Visual Teaching, 31 Ottawa Ave., N.W., Grand Rapids, Mich. 49502.

62. Fidelity Products Co., 705 Pennsylvania Ave. So., Minneapolis, Minn. 55426.

63. Field Enterprises Educational Corporation, Merchandise Mart Plaza, Chicago, Ill. 60654.

64. Field Museum of Natural History, Roosevelt Road and Lake Shore Drive, Chicago, Ill. 60605.

65. **Finance Facts.** Monthly. Educational Services Division, National Consumer Finance Association, 701 Solar Building, 1000 Sixteenth St., N.W., Washington, D.C. 20036. Free.

66. First National Bank of Chicago, International Section, One First National Plaza, Chicago, Ill. 60670.

    Foreign Exchange Quotations. Free.

    International Economic Review. Monthly. Free.

67. **Focus.** Published monthly except July and August. American Geographical Society, Broadway at 156th St., N.Y., N.Y. 10032. 85 cents each. Annual subscription $3.50.

68. Ford Motor Co., The American Road, Dearborn, Mich. 48121.

69. Forest Service, U.S. Dept. of Agriculture, Washington, D.C. 20250.

70. Forrester, Gertrude. **Occupational Literature: An Annotated Bibliography.** 5th ed., 1964. H.W. Wilson Co. New edition scheduled for late 1970 or early 1971. Price of 1964 edition $8.50.

71. Franklin Publishers, Inc., 4429 West North Ave., Milwaukee, Wis. 53208.

72. **Free and Inexpensive Learning Materials.** 15th ed., 1970. Division of Surveys and Field Services, George Peabody College for Teachers, Nashville, Tenn. 37203. $3.00.

73. W.H. Freeman and Company, 660 Market St., San Francisco, Calif. 94104.

74. Freer Gallery of Art, Smithsonian Institution, Washington, D.C. 20560.

75. Friendship Press, 475 Riverside Dr., N.Y., N.Y. 10027.

76. Gale Research Company, 1400 Book Tower, Detroit, Mich. 48226.

77. Gallup Map & Stationery Co., 1330 Walnut St., Kansas City, Mo. 64106.

78. Gane Brothers & Lane, Inc., 1335 W. Lake St., Chicago, Ill. 60607.

79. **Gebbie House Magazine Directory.** Gebbie Directory, P.O. Box 1111, Sioux City, Iowa 51102. Published triennially. New edition due in 1971. Price of 1968 edition $24.95.

80. Geographia Map Co., Inc., 220 West 42nd St., N.Y., N.Y. 10036.

81. Geological Survey, U.S. Dept. of the Interior, Washington, D.C. 20242.

82. Giganti, Carl J. "Pictures in a Small Library." **Wilson Library Bulletin**, Nov., 1940, page 227.

83. Gould, Geraldine N. and Wolfe, Ithmer C. **How to Organize and Maintain the Library Picture/Pamphlet File**. 1968. Oceana Publications, Inc. $5.00.

84. **Grace Log.** Issued 3 times a year. W.R. Grace & Co., 7 Hanover Square, N.Y., N.Y. 10005. Free.

85. Gysbers, Norman C. **Missouri Filing Plan for Unbound Materials on Occupations**. College of Education, Univ. of Missouri, Columbia, Mo. 65202. Free.

86. Hagstrom Co., Inc., 311 Broadway, N.Y., N.Y. 10007.

87. Hammond, Inc., Maplewood, New Jersey 07040.

88. **Headline Series**. Published five times a year. Foreign Policy Association, Inc., 345 E. 46th St., N.Y., N.Y. 10017. $1.00 each. Annual subscription $5.00.

89. Health Insurance Institute. **Health Education Materials and the Organizations Which Offer Them.** Undated. Health Insurance Institute, 277 Park Ave., N.Y., N.Y. 10017. Free.

90. Hearne Brothers, 25th Floor, First National Building, Detroit, Mich. 48226.

91. Hillsdale Educational Publishers, Inc., P.O. Box 245, Hillsdale, Mich. 49242.

92. Hollinger Corporation, 3810 South Four Mile Run Dr., Arlington, Va. 22206.

93. **In Britain**. Monthly. British Travel Association, 680 Fifth Ave., N.Y., N.Y. 10019. Free.

94. Indian Arts and Crafts Board, U.S. Dept. of the Interior. **Fact Sheet 1, Sources of Indian and Eskimo Arts and Crafts: Organizations** and **Fact Sheet 2, Sources of Indian and Eskimo Arts and Crafts: Individuals.** 1968. The Board, Washington, D.C. 20240. Free.

95. Institute for Research. **Careers Research Monographs**. Institute for Research, 537 South Dearborn St., Chicago, Ill. 60605. Single monograph 95 cents, five for $4.75. Discounts on larger quantities.

96. Institute of Life Insurance and Health Insurance Institute. **A List of Worthwhile Life & Health Insurance Books**. Issued annually.

Institute of Life Insurance and Health Insurance Institute, 277 Park Ave., N.Y., N.Y. 10017. Free.

97. Instructional Aids, Inc., Box 191, Mankato, Minn. 56001.

98. Insurance Institute for Highway Safety. **Highway Safety Pamphlets: What's Available—and Where**. Undated. Insurance Institute for Highway Safety, 711 Watergate Office Building, 2600 Virginia Ave., N.W., Washington, D.C. 20037. Free.

99. Fred F. Johnson Co., P.O. Box 7035, Grand Rapids, Mich. 49510.

100. Katz, Bill. **Magazines for Libraries**. 1969. R.R. Bowker Co. $16.95.

101. Kenworthy, Leonard S. and Birdie, Richard A. **Free and Inexpensive Materials on World Affairs**. 3rd ed., 1969. Teachers College Press, Teachers College, Columbia University, 1234 Amsterdam Ave., N.Y., N.Y. 10027. $1.95.

102. Kenya Shell Limited, Shell & BP House, Harambeo Ave., P.O. Box 3561, Nairobi, Kenya, Africa.

103. Lake Survey District, Corps of Engineers, U.S. Dept. of the Army, 630 Federal Building, Detroit, Mich. 48226.

104. **Lamp**. Quarterly. Standard Oil Company (New Jersey), 30 Rockefeller Plaza, N.Y., N.Y. 10020. Free.

105. League of Women Voters of the United States. **Facts & Issues**. The League, 1200 17th St., N.W., Washington, D.C. 20036. From 15 cents to 25 cents.

106. LeGear, Clara Egli. **Maps: Their Care, Repair, and Preservation in Libraries**. Rev. ed., 1956. Library of Congress. Reprints available from University Microfilms. $3.60. A reprint with a new introduction available from Libraries Unlimited, Inc., P.O. Box 263, Littleton, Colorado 80120.

107. **Localized History Series**. Teachers College Press, Teachers College, Columbia University, 1234 Amsterdam Ave., N.Y., N.Y. 10027. $1.50 each.

108. Lovejoy, Clarence E. **Lovejoy's Career and Vocational School Guide**. 1967. Simon and Schuster. $6.50 cloth, $3.95 paper.

109. H.A. Manning Co., 278 Main St., Greenfield, Mass. 01301.

110. Manpower Administration, U.S. Department of Labor. **Occupational Guides**. The Administration, Washington, D.C. 20210. Free.

111. Manufacturers Hanover Trust Company, International Division, 350 Park Ave., N.Y., N.Y. 10022.

    Foreign Exchange Quotations. Free.

    World Time Chart. Free.

112. **Marketing Information Guide**. Monthly. Business and Defense Services Administration, U.S. Dept. of Commerce. For sale by Supt. of Documents. $4.50 per year.

113. **Meet the Press**. Merkle Press, Inc., Box 2111, Washington, D.C. 20013. 10 cents plus stamped, self-addressed envelope. Yearly subscription $3.00.

114. **Men and Molecules**. American Chemical Society, 1155 Sixteenth St., N.W., Washington, D.C. 20036. Transcripts available free.

115. Metropolitan Museum of Art, Fifth Ave. and 82nd St., N.Y., N.Y. 10028.

116. Michelin Tire Corporation, 2500 Marcus Ave., P.O. Box 467, Lake Success (N.H.P.–P.O.) New York 11040.

117. Bruce Miller Publications, Box 369, Riverside, Calif. 92502.

   So You Want to Start a Picture File: An Aid to Better Teaching.
   1968. 60 cents.

   Sources of Free and Inexpensive Pictures for the Classroom. 1968.
   60 cents.

   Sources of Free and Inexpensive Teaching Aids. 1968. 60 cents.

   Sources of Free Pictures. 1967. 60 cents.

   Sources of Free Travel Posters and Geographic Aids. 1965. 60
   cents.

118. Mobil Cruising Service, Mobil Oil Corp., 150 E. 42nd St., N.Y.,
   N.Y. 10017.

119. **Monthly Catalog of United States Government Publications.** Supt.
   of Documents, U.S. Government Printing Office, Washington,
   D.C. 20402. $7 per year.

120. **Monthly Checklist of State Publications.** Library of Congress. For
   sale by Supt. of Documents. $8 per year.

121. National Aeronautics and Space Administration. **Aerospace Bibliography.** 5th ed., 1970. Supt. of Documents. $1.00.

122. National Archives and Records Service, General Services Administration, Washington, D.C. 20408.

123. National Association of Trade and Technical Schools, 2021 L St.,
   N.W., Washington, D.C. 20036.

124. National Audubon Society, 1130 Fifth Ave., N.Y., N.Y. 10028.

125. National Better Business Bureau, Inc., 230 Park Ave., N.Y., N.Y. 10017.

Consumer Information Series. Free with stamped, self-addressed envelope.

Fact Booklets. 15 cents each, 8 for $1.00.

126. National Council of Teachers of English, 508 South Sixth St., Champaign, Ill. 61820.

127. National Gallery of Art, Washington, D.C. 20565.

128. **National Geographic School Bulletin.** 30 weekly issues a year. School Service, National Geographic Society, Washington, D.C. 20036. Annual subscription $2.25.

129. National Home Study Council, 1601 Eighteenth St., N.W., Washington, D.C. 20009.

130. National Park Service, U.S. Dept. of the Interior, Washington, D.C. 20240.

131. National Safety Council, 425 N. Michigan Ave., Chicago, Ill. 60611.

132. National Vocational Guidance Association.

> **Guidelines for Preparing and Evaluating Occupational Materials.** American Personnel and Guidance Association, 1607 New Hampshire Ave., N.W., Washington, D.C. 20009. 40 cents.

> **NVGA Bibliography of Current Career Information.** 5th ed., 1969. American Personnel and Guidance Assoc., 1607 New Hampshire Ave., N.W., Washington, D.C. 20009. $2.00.

> **Vocational Guidance Quarterly.** American Personnel and Guidance Assoc., 1607 New Hampshire Ave., N.W., Washington, D.C. 20009. $5 per year.

133. National Wildlife Federation, 1412 16th St., N.W., Washington, D.C. 20036.

134. **New Publications.** Monthly. U.S. Dept. of Labor, Washington, D.C. 20212. Free.

135. New York Life Insurance Co., 51 Madison Ave., N.Y., N.Y. 10010.

136. **News About Travel.** Monthly. Discover America Travel Organizations, Inc., 1100 Connecticut Ave., N.W., Washington, D.C. 20036. Free.

137. Nystrom, 3333 Elston Ave., Chicago, Ill. 60618.

138. O'Hara, Frederic J. **Over 2,000 Free Publications: Yours for the Asking.** (Signet Reference Q3691) 1968. New American Library. 95 cents.

139. Ohio State Department of Education. **Sources of Occupational Information.** Rev. ed., 1970. Ohio State Dept. of Education, Division of Guidanee and Testing, 751 Northwest Blvd., Columbus, Ohio 43212. Free.

140. Oxford Filing Supply Co., Inc. Clinton Road, Garden City, N.Y. 11530.

141. Pacific Area Travel Association. **Events in the Pacific.** The Association, 228 Grant Ave., San Francisco, Calif. 94108. Free.

142. Pan American World Airways, Inc., P.O. Box 431, Boston, Mass. 02102.

   International Trade Fairs. Free.

   Pan Am's Book of Overseas Events. Free.

143. Park Publishing House, 516 Viewridge Dr., Angwin, Calif. 94508. Occupational monographs $1.00 each. Discounts for larger purchases.

144. Pepe, Thomas J. **Free and Inexpensive Educational Aids.** 3rd ed., 1966. Dover Publications, Inc., 180 Varick St., N.Y., N.Y. 10014. $1.75. New edition due in late 1970.

145. Perfection Form Co., 214 West Eighth St., Logan, Iowa 51546.

146. Pharmaceutical Manufacturers Association. **The Story of Health.** Undated. Pharmaceutical Manufacturers Association, 1155 Fifteenth St., N.W., Washington, D.C. 20005. Free.

147. Phillips Petroleum Company, Bartlesville, Okla. 74003.

148. R.L. Polk & Co., Arrow Guide Division, 600 Washington St., Boston, Mass. 02111.

149. President's Committee on Consumer Interests. **Consumer Education: Bibliography.** 1969. For sale by the Supt. of Documents. 65 cents.

150. **Price Lists.** Superintendent of Documents, U.S. Government Printing Office, Washington, D.C. 20402. Free.

151. **Public Affairs Information Service Bulletin.** Price and frequency depend upon type of service selected. Public Affairs Information Service, Inc., 11 W. 40th St., N.Y., N.Y. 10018.

152. **Public Affairs Pamphlets.** About 15 pamphlets a year. Public Affairs Pamphlets, 381 Park Ave., South, N.Y., N.Y. 10016. 25 cents each. Subscription to 15 issues $3.50.

153. **Publications Co. Directory of Free Teaching Aids, 1968-69.** 1968. Publications Co., 1220 Maple Ave., Los Angeles, Calif. 90015. $5.00.

154. **RCA Electronic Age.** Quarterly. RCA Electronic Age, 30 Rockefeller Plaza, N.Y., N.Y. 10020. Free.

155. Rand McNally & Co., Rand McNally Map Store, 7 West 48th St., N.Y., N.Y. 10020.

156. Ristow, Walter W. "Emergence of Maps In Libraries." **Special Libraries**, July-Aug., 1967, page 409.

157. **Sabena Revue.** Semiannual. Sabena Belgian World Airlines, 720 Fifth Ave., N.Y., N.Y. 10019. $1.50 per copy. Inquire about free subscription.

158. Salisbury, Gordon. **Catalog of Free Teaching Materials.** 7th ed., 1970. Catalog of Free Teaching Materials, P.O. Box 1075, Ventura, Calif. 93001. $2.68.

159. Schmeckebier, Laurence F. and Eastin, Roy B. **Government Publications and Their Use.** 3rd ed., 1969. The Brookings Institution. $8.95.

160. Science Research Associates, Inc., 259 East Erie St., Chicago, Ill. 60611.

   SRA Occupational Briefs. Single brief 45 cents, discount on 25 or more. Complete set $83.50.

   Junior Occupational Briefs. Single brief 47 cents, discount on 25 or more. Complete set $94.50.

   Occupational filing plan. Set of labeled file folders. $17.50.

161. Scuorzo, Herbert E. **Practical Audio-Visual Handbook for Teachers.** 1967. Prentice-Hall, Inc. $7.95.

162. Seal, Incorporated, Derby, Conn. 06418.

163. **Sears List of Subject Headings.** 9th ed., 1965. H.W. Wilson Co. $8.00.

164. **Selected United States Government Publications.** Biweekly. Supt. of Documents, U.S. Government Printing Office, Washington, D.C. 20402. Free.

165. Small Business Administration, Washington, D.C. 20416.

166. **Small Business Reporter**. Ten issues a year. Small Business Reporter, Dept. 3120, Bank of America National Trust & Savings Association, San Francisco, Cal. 94120. $8.50 per year. Single copies of all reports available free.

167. Society for Visual Education, Inc. 1345 Diversey Parkway, Chicago, Ill. 60614.

168. Special Bates Numbering Machine. American Library Line, P.O. Box 2442, Atlanta, Ga. 30318.

169. Standard Paper Manufacturing Co., P.O. Box 1554, Richmond, Va. 23212.

170. **State Administrative Officials Classified by Functions: Supplement II, The Book of the States**. Published biennially. Council of State Governments, Lexington, Kentucky, 1969 edition $3.00.

171. Steck-Vaughn Company, P.O. Box 2028, Austin, Texas 78767.

172. Steelcase, Inc., 1120 36th St., Grand Rapids, Mich. 49508.

173. Stephenson, Richard W. "Published Sources Of Information about Maps and Atlases." **Special Libraries**, Feb., 1970, pages 87-98 +.

174. Texaco Waterways Service, 135 East 42nd St., N.Y., N.Y. 10017.

175. Thomas, Della and Lloyd, Helen. **Practical Storage and Use of Maps and Posters (Practical Projects for the School Library, No. 1)** Rev. ed., 1964. Oklahoma State University Library. Out-of-print.

176. Toronto Public Library. **Subject Headings for Vertical Files**. New edition in preparation. Toronto Public Library, 40 St. Clair Ave. East, Toronto . Price of 1964 edition $3.00.

177. Trans World Airlines, Inc., Air World Education, 605 Third Ave., N.Y., N.Y. 10016.

178. U-File-M Binder Mfg. Co., Inc., P.O. Box 83, Lafayette, N.Y. 13084.

179. United Air Lines, School and College Service, P.O. Box 66141, O'Hare International Airport, Chicago, Ill. 60666.

180. United Business Schools Association, 1730 M St., N.W., Washington, D.C. 20036.

181. United Nations. **Information Services and Embassies in the United States of Members of the United Nations.** United Nations, Office of Public Information, N.Y., N.Y. 10017. Free.

182. U.S. Army Topographic Command, Corps of Engineers, Dept. of the Army, Washington, D.C. 20315.

183. U.S. Civil Service Commission, Washington, D.C. 20415.

184. U.S. Civil Service Commission. **Guide to Federal Career Literature.** 1969. Supt. of Documents. 55 cents.

185. U.S. Dept. of the Navy, Navy Publications and Printing Service Office, Building 4, Section D, 700 Robbins Ave., Philadelphia, Pa. 19111.

186. **United States Government Organization Manual.** Revised annually. Office of the Federal Register, National Archives and Records Service. For sale by Supt. of Documents. 1970-71 edition $3.00.

187. U.S. Naval Oceanographic Office, Department of the Navy, Washington, D.C. 20390.

188. U.S. Training and Employment Service, U.S. Dept. of Labor. **Dictionary of Occupational Titles.** (v.I **Definitions of Titles**, v.II **Occupational Classification and Industry Index**) 3rd ed., 1965. For sale by Supt. of Documents. v.I $5.00, v.II $4.25.

189. University of California, Radio-Television Administration, Los Angeles, Calif. 90024.

   Science Editor. Transcripts 25 cents each.

   University Explorer. Transcripts 25 cents each.

190. University Prints, 15 Brattle St., Harvard Square, Cambridge, Mass. 02138.

191. VF Materials, P.O. Box 481, Lincoln, Nebraska 68501.

192. **Vertical File Index.** Monthly except August. H.W. Wilson Co., 950 University Ave., Bronx, N.Y. 10452. $8 per year.

193. Ward's Natural Science Establishment, Inc., P.O. Box 1712, Rochester, N.Y. 14603 or P.O. Box 1749, Monterey, Calif. 93940.

   Ward's Bulletin. Free.

194. Frederick Warne and Co. Ltd., 101 Fifth Ave., N.Y., N.Y. 10003.

195. Weber Costello, 1900 N. Narragansett, Chicago, Ill. 60639.

196. **What's New in Advertising and Marketing.** 10 issues a year. Advertising and Marketing Division, Special Libraries Association. $5 per year. $3.50 per year to SLA members.

197. William-Frederick Press, 55 E. 86th St., N.Y., N.Y. 10028.

198. Women's Bureau, U.S. Dept. of Labor. **Careers for Women.** The Bureau, Washington, D.C. 20210. Single copies free.

199. **World Business**. Quarterly. Economic Research Division, Chase Manhattan Bank, National Association, 1 Chase Manhattan Plaza, N.Y., N.Y. 10015. Free.

200. **World Wide Chamber of Commerce Directory**. Published annually. Johnson Publishing Co., Inc., Box 455, Loveland, Colo. 80537. $4.00.

201. **Yale Reports,** 75 Howe St., New Haven, Conn. 06511. $2.50 for a set of 26 transcripts.

INDEX

Today's Health, 26, 27
Topographic maps, Geological Survey, 139
Toronto Public Library, 55
Tracings, 62
Trade catalogs, 68-69
Trade school catalogs, 69-70
Trans World Airlines, Inc., 76
Transcripts, 72
Transparent tape, 87, 94-95
Travel literature
  Clipping for pictures, 159, 160
  Covering coming events, 185, 186
  General aspects, 73-76
Trimming
  Clippings, 91
  Pictures, 171
Typewritten labels, 36, 176

U-File-M Binder Strip, 89
Underlining subject headings, 36
United Nations, 76, 143
U.S. Army Corps of Engineers, 140
U.S. Army Topographic Command, 138, 140
U.S. Civil Service Commission, 100-101
United States Government Organization Manual, 25
U.S. government publications
  As pamphlet resources, 67-68
  Free copies, 33
  Guides to, 23-25, 75, 100, 101, 130, 138-140, 162-163
  In state history collections, 130
  Maps, 138-140
  Ordering, 32
  Pictorial material, 162-163
  Reprints, 72, 101-102
  Travel material, 74, 75
  Vocational material, 100-102
University Prints, 163

VF Materials, 34
Variant editions of periodicals, 84-85
Vertical File Index, 17-18, 56, 98
Vertical filing cases
  Deviations in size, 170
  For picture storage, 165-166
  For map storage, 148-149
  General information, 38-39
Vocational Guidance Quarterly, 99
Vocational material
  Currency, 108-109
  Discount and package plans, 107-108
  Evaluation, 108-110
  Guides to, 98-100, 103, 105
  Organization, 110-114
  Ready-made filing systems, 113-114
  Reprints, 101-102, 105, 106
  Series, 101, 102, 104, 105-108, 109-110
  Sources
    Associations, 103-104
    Businesses and industries, 104-105
    Commercial publishers, 105-108
    Educational institutions, 105
    Local governments, 103
    Periodicals, 105
    State governments, 102-103
    U.S. government, 100-102
  Weeding, 108-109
Vocational school catalogs, 69-70
Volunteer assistance, 44, 90, 126, 127

Wall maps, 135-136, 137, 147-148
Weeding
  Coming events information, 186
  General principles and procedures, 42-44
  Maps, 136
  Vocational material, 108-109

219